Rosalie
Leon

¡Viva el español!

Student Edition

¡Adelante!

John De Mado
Linda West Tibensky

Marcela Gerber, Series Consultant

Wright Group

The McGraw·Hill Companies

www.WrightGroup.com

 **Wright Group**

Printed in the United States of America.

Send all inquiries to:
Wright Group/McGraw-Hill
P.O. Box 812960
Chicago, IL 60681

ISBN 0-07-602939-5

5 6 7 8 9 10 QPD 11 10 09 08 07

The **McGraw·Hill** Companies

Contenido

Unidad 5

Unidad 6

Unidad 7

Unidad 8

Unidad 9

¡Viva el español!

Student Edition

¡Adelante!

Un paso más

Objetivos

- To talk about parts of the body and what hurts
- To talk about where things are
- To talk about what someone is wearing and how it looks
- To talk about what people are like and what they are doing
- To compare people and things
- To talk about someone's house and what's inside
- To talk about what fruits someone likes and what time people eat meals
- To talk about time and daily routines
- To talk about activities someone can do, wants to do, and has to do
- To talk about activities someone plans to do or has just finished doing
- To talk about what you know how to do

Colorful buildings in San Juan, Puerto Rico

A fruit stand in
San José, Costa Rica

Two Spanish servers display
large platters of paella.

¿Sabías que...?

- In Spanish-speaking countries, it's customary for friends to give each other a big hello hug (**un abrazo**) if they haven't seen each other in a while.

- More kids study Spanish each year in the United States than there are kids in the whole country of Bolivia.

- Thousands of Latin American and Spanish kids vacation in the United States, then go back to school in their countries!

¡Úsalo!

A Stand in a circle with four classmates. The first person will point to a part of his or her body. The person to the right has to name it. If he or she names it correctly, that person points to a different body part, and the person to the right has to name it. But make sure you don't repeat any! Whoever repeats a body part when pointing or names one incorrectly has to sit down. Start your answers with **Es...** or **Son...**

MODELO —Son los ojos.

B On a slip of paper, describe your location in the classroom. Write down who or what you're in front of and behind. Add something that is near you and something that is far away from you.

MODELO **Estoy delante de Pablo. Estoy detrás de Rosana. Estoy cerca del pizarrón. Estoy lejos de la puerta.**

Then everyone places the slips of paper in a bag. Students take turns picking them out and saying where the person is. The class has to guess who it is! You can't guess when it's your slip of paper.

MODELO —Está delante de Pablo. Está detrás de Rosana...

—¡Es Javier!

C After a full day of activities, the Miraflores family is full of aches and pains. Get together with a partner and tell each other what hurts each member of the family, according to the picture. Then take turns naming an activity from the list below that they have just finished doing and that may have caused the pain.

Partner A: Ask what hurts the person.

Partner B: Answer according to the picture. Then say the person just finished doing an activity that may have caused the pain.

MODELO —¿Qué le duele a la tía?

—A la tía le duelen los ojos. Acaba de usar la computadora.

bailar	usar la computadora	comer mucha comida
patinar	practicar deportes	caminar

D Get together with a partner. Look at the picture above and list as many living room items as you can. Add one descriptive word to each item. The pair who comes up with more correct descriptions in three minutes wins.

MODELO —Hay un sofá verde.

E Look at the picture on page 5 and choose one of the people in it. Then work with a partner and describe yourself as though you were that person. Your partner needs to guess who you are! Switch roles after your partner guesses correctly.

> **MODELO** —Tengo el pelo lacio y largo.
>
> —¿Eres la hija?

F It's laundry day for the Sierra family. Your friend Sergio needs help sorting the clothes. Look at the picture. Work with a classmate and take turns asking and answering the questions.

Papá   Mamá   Pepita   Lucho   Abuelo   Rita   José

1. ¿De quién son los pantalones grandes?

2. ¿De quién es el suéter pequeño?

3. ¿De quién son los calcetines grandes?

4. ¿De quién son los pantalones pequeños?

5. ¿De quién es la camisa mediana?

6. ¿De quién es el vestido?

7. ¿De quién son los calcetines pequeños?

8. ¿De quién es la camisa pequeña?

9. ¿De quién es el impermeable?

G On five cards, write the names of clothing items that some of your classmates are wearing. Specify the color, whether the items are short or long, large or small. Then get together with a partner. Show your partner a card, and ask him or her who the item belongs to. Your partner looks around the room to find out who is wearing the item. Then it's your turn to guess!

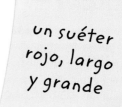

un suéter rojo, largo y grande

> **MODELO** —¿De quién es el suéter rojo, largo y grande?
>
> —Umm... Es de Lina.

H Get together with a partner. Study these pictures and take turns asking and answering questions about them. Using the words below, see who can make up more questions.

> **MODELO** —¿Cómo le queda el abrigo a Clara?
>
> —Le queda muy grande.

grande	corto	pequeño	largo
bien	mal	bonito	feo

I Juan and Isabel Paredes are twins, but they're complete opposites. Take turns with a partner reading these sentences about Juan and answering with a sentence about Isabel.

> **MODELO** —Juan es alto.
>
> —Isabel es baja.

1. Juan es débil.

2. Juan tiene el pelo lacio.

3. Juan siempre tiene frío.

4. Juan tiene el pelo rubio.

5. A Juan le gustan los gatos.

J Get together with a partner. Every time you say something about your house or family, your partner has to say something to top it.

Partner A: Make the statement.

Partner B: Use **más... que** to top your partner's statement.

> **MODELO** —Mi papá es muy fuerte.
>
> —Mi papá es más fuerte que tu papá.

1. Mi hermana es muy inteligente.

2. Mi mamá es muy alta.

3. Mi hermana es muy atlética.

4. Mi casa es muy grande.

5. Mi familia es muy interesante.

6. Mis abuelos son muy divertidos.

Now, write five more statements and switch roles.

Entre amigos

Play a game with three classmates. First make five cards with the word **sí** on them, and five cards with the word **no** on them. Mix them up and place them facedown in a pile.

Now write these words on ten separate cards: **alto / alta, fuerte, generoso / generosa, atlético / atlética, tímido / tímida, popular, impaciente, simpático / simpática, inteligente, cómico / cómica.** Put these cards facedown in a second pile.

One player starts by picking a card from the second pile. This player uses the word on the card to ask the next player to the left if he or she possesses that quality. Remember to use the correct form of the word:

> —**Miguel, ¿eres (tímido)?**

This player then picks a card from the first pile and answers according to the word selected (**sí** or **no**):

> —**No, no soy (tímido).** *or* **Sí, soy (tímido).**

Now this player picks a card from the second pile, and asks a new question of the player to his or her left, and so on. Players receive one point for a correctly formed **"sí"** answer, and one point for a correctly formed **"no"** answer. Play five rounds, then count points to see who is the winner. Reshuffle cards as necessary.

Unidad de repaso

K Get together with a partner. Interview each other to learn something about your homes. Then make a sketch of your partner's home based on his or her answers.

1. ¿Viven tu familia y tú en una casa o en un apartamento?

2. ¿Tienen jardín o patio? ¿Cómo es?

3. ¿Cuántos dormitorios tiene tu casa?

4. ¿Hay un comedor? ¿De qué color es?

5. ¿Comen tu familia y tú en la cocina o en el comedor?

6. ¿Hay un teléfono o un televisor en tu dormitorio?

7. ¿Dónde está el televisor?

8. ¿Hay un despacho?

9. ¿Tiene tu casa sótano o ático?

Entre amigos

Draw a floor plan for a living room on butcher paper. Then draw these household items and cut them out.

un sillón	**un sofá**	**un televisor**	**una lámpara**
un espejo	**una mesa**	**un estéreo**	**una estantería**
un teléfono	**una alfombra**	**un retrato**	**un radio**

Tape the different items that you drew onto your living room. Put things in front of and behind other items, and place items both close to and far away from others.

Then get together with a partner, but don't show your living room! Say where your items are, using **cerca de, lejos de, delante de, detrás de, sobre,** and **debajo de.** Your partner has to place the items in his or her own living room according to what you say. Compare your living rooms and see if they look alike or not! Then switch roles.

L You're moving into this new house today. The movers and members of your family are bringing in the furniture and placing it in the various rooms. Take turns with a partner saying where everything goes, according to the picture.

MODELO **Papá y Alonso / el sillón**

—Papá y Alonso ponen el sillón en la sala de estar.

1. Los hombres / la mesa
2. Mamá y yo / unas lámparas
3. Mi hermana / sus carteles
4. Papá y mi tío Ernesto / nuestro sofá
5. Yo / mis almohadas
6. Mi hermano / el televisor
7. Papá y tú / la alfombra

M These are the things that still need to be brought into the house. Take turns with your partner asking and telling each other where you want to put each of them.

MODELO **—¿Dónde quieres poner la cama?**

—Quiero poner la cama en el dormitorio.

la cama	el tocador	el horno	el lector de DVD	las cortinas
el cuadro	la estantería	el espejo	el tostador	la mesita de noche

N What appliance or kitchen item do you need for these things? Get together with a partner and write sentences about what's needed for each one.

MODELO Necesitamos un horno.

1.

2.

3.

4.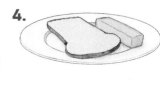

O There was a flood in the Ortega house. What a mess! They made a list of chores that have to be done. With a classmate, take turns choosing a room and saying which family member is doing what. The members of the family are **yo** (for the person who's speaking), Papá, Mamá, Susana, Rodolfo, Pablo, Abuelo, and Abuela. Make sure to assign two or more people to do the big jobs! Distribute chores evenly among everyone. Keep track by writing down the assignments.

MODELO La sala de estar: Mamá y Abuela tienen que quitar el polvo.

La cocina
Barrer el piso
Limpiar el piso
Sacar la basura

Los dormitorios
Recoger las cosas
Pasar la aspiradora
Colgar la ropa

La sala de estar
Quitar el polvo
Pasar la aspiradora
Recoger las cosas

El sótano
Limpiar el piso
Lavar y secar la ropa
Planchar la ropa

Los cuartos de baño
Limpiar el piso
Sacar la basura
Limpiar los espejos

P Get together with a partner and find out which fruits he or she likes. Which ones do you like? Make a list of the fruits that you both like.

Partner A: Ask if your partner likes the fruit in the picture.

Partner B: Answer according to what you like, and ask if your partner likes it.

MODELO —¿Te gustan las peras?

—Sí, me gustan las peras.
  or No, no me gustan las peras. ¿Y a ti?

—A mí también. *or* A mí no me gustan.
  or A mí tampoco. *or* A mí me gustan.

1.

2.

3.

4.

5.

6.

7.

8.

9.

Unidad de repaso

trece ✷ **13**

Q Your mother keeps asking if you want to eat different things. But when she asks, you've always just finished eating something else! Look at the pictures and take turns with a partner asking and answering the questions.

Partner A: You're the mother. Ask the question, choosing one of the foods in the picture.

Partner B: Answer that you've just eaten the other food in the same picture.

MODELO —¿Quieres comer zanahorias?

—No, mamá. Acabo de comer papas.

1.

2.

3.

4.

5.

6.

7.

8.

9.

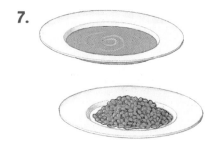 

CONEXIÓN CON LAS MATEMÁTICAS

Averages A friend's father is opening a restaurant for young people. Your friend is doing research to find out people's eating habits. This is the list of questions he prepared. Add two more questions you think could be useful for his research. Then ask and answer the questions with a partner.

MODELO —¿A qué hora tomas el desayuno los fines de semana?

—Tomo el desayuno a las once y media.

1. ¿Qué comes de desayuno de lunes a viernes?
2. ¿Qué comes de desayuno los fines de semana?
3. ¿A qué hora almuerzan tus amigos y tú?
4. ¿Qué les gusta comer de almuerzo?
5. ¿Comes muchas verduras?
6. ¿A qué hora es la cena en tu casa?
7. ¿Tu familia y tú comen mucho o poco de cena?
8. ¿Qué te gusta más, comer dentro de la casa o fuera de la casa?
9. _____
10. _____

Now help your friend's father find out what the most popular answers were. Get together with four classmates. Discuss your answers and decide which ones were the most popular. Find average **(promedio)** times when needed. Write the most popular answers on a chart like this one.

Pregunta	Respuestas	La más popular
1	11:00, 11:30, 11:00, 11:15	(promedio) 11:11

Then a member from each group will go to the board and share his or her group's answers with the rest of the class. How did the results compare?

R You're planning a birthday party, and you've made a list of things you need to do. Get together with three classmates and ask them how they can help. Each one should tell you three things he or she can do.

Take notes of who will do what. Your classmates can't repeat what someone else has offered to do.

MODELO —¿Qué puedes hacer para la fiesta?

—Puedo ir a comprar los vasos.

> comida
> música
> vasos, platos, tenedores, cucharas
> jugos, leche, agua
> limpiar
> piñata

 # CONEXIÓN CON LA SALUD

Nutrition Write five things that you like to eat and five more that you don't like. Then ask several classmates what they like or don't like to eat. Ask **¿Qué te gusta comer?** and **¿Qué no te gusta comer?**

Don't forget to take notes, so you can decide who has more in common with you. Explain your decision to the class.

MODELO —A Juan le gusta la sopa y a mí también. No le gustan las naranjas, y a mí tampoco.

Now get together with two or three classmates who have several preferences in common with you. Together, design a dinner menu for the week. Make sure that every meal has servings from the five food groups. Illustrate your menus, too.

lunes	martes	miércoles	jueves	viernes	sábado	domingo

Unidad de repaso

S Look at the picture below and imagine that it's your room. Your mother is telling you things you have to do. If you've already done what she's asking, tell her so.

Partner A: You're the mother. Tell your partner that he or she has to do these things.

Partner B: Using the picture, say if you'll do them or have already done them.

> **MODELO** —¡Tienes que pasar la aspiradora!
>
> —Acabo de pasar la aspiradora.
>   *or* Voy a pasar la aspiradora ahora.

pasar la aspiradora	**colgar la ropa**	**recoger las cosas del ropero**
sacar la basura	**lavar la ropa**	**recoger las cosas del escritorio**
quitar el polvo	**regar las plantas**	**poner los libros en la estantería**
limpiar las ventanas		

CONEXIÓN CON LAS MATEMÁTICAS

Schedules Your partner is going to make a schedule for your family, so you'll need to say when you do these things during the day. Make sure to mention everyone in your family.

despertarse	ponerse la ropa	quitarse la ropa
cepillarse los dientes	peinarse	bañarse
lavarse	irse de la casa	acostarse
ducharse	levantarse	

MODELO despertarse

> —Mi papá se despierta a las seis y media de la mañana.
> Mi hermana y yo nos despertamos...

Your partner should fill out a chart like this one with the times that you mention.

After you finish filling out schedules for each other, exchange them with another pair. Ask each other questions about the new schedules.

6:30 a. m.	Su papá se despierta.
	Él y su hermana se despiertan.

MODELO —¿A qué hora se despierta el papá de Ricardo?

> —Se despierta a las seis y media.

18 ❀ **dieciocho**   Unidad de repaso

T Get together with a partner. Tell each other seven things you plan to do at these times in the future.

> **MODELO** —¿Qué piensas hacer el fin de semana?
>
> —El fin de semana pienso ir a visitar a mis abuelos.

el fin de semana	**hoy por la tarde**	**hoy por la noche**
hoy por la mañana	**el próximo mes**	**en el verano**
el próximo año		

Switch partners, and tell your new partner what your old partner plans to do.

Entre amigos

Sit in a circle with two classmates. Take turns pretending that you're a server at a restaurant. Ask the person to your right what he or she wants for breakfast. Remember to use the **usted** form, since you're talking to a customer you don't know! Take note of the order. This is a sample order.

> —¿Qué va a comer de desayuno?
>
> —Quiero huevos revueltos, tocino y pan tostado.

The person to your right asks the third person what he or she wants for lunch and takes notes. Then that person asks you what you want for dinner and writes it down.

Now, use your notes to "prepare" a meal for the person to your right. You can draw the meal on a paper plate or paste pictures from magazines or shoppers. "Serve" the meal to the classmate who requested it.

> —Señor (Señorita), los huevos revueltos, el tocino y el pan tostado.

U Marcos has written about his day on Sunday, but he's made some mistakes. With a partner, decide which words need to be changed, and rewrite the paragraph.

> **MODELO** Hoy, yo piensa ir a la casa de María.
>
> Hoy, yo <u>pienso</u> ir a la casa de María.

> Me levanto a las nueve y tengo hambre. Yo comenzamos a comer el desayuno. Mi papá se levanta y también quiero comer. Me voy de la casa y cierran la puerta. Voy a la casa de María. Ella siempre queremos ir al parque. Nosotros no pueden ir a la tienda de ropa los domingos. No abren. Cuando volvemos a la casa de María, almuerza. Yo gusto comer sopa y un sándwich. Los hermanos de María queremos el almuerzo también. Ellos quiero comer espaguetis con uvas. ¡Qué horror!

V Get together with a partner and ask if he or she knows how to do these things. Then your partner gets to ask you. Who knows how to do more things?

> **MODELO** —¿Sabes jugar al béisbol?
>
> —Sí, sé jugar al béisbol. *or* No, no sé jugar al béisbol. ¿Y tú?
>
> —Yo también. *or* Yo no. *or* Sé jugar el béisbol. *or* Yo tampoco.

1. jugar al béisbol
2. nadar muy bien
3. usar la computadora
4. hablar español muy bien
5. poner la mesa
6. lavar la ropa
7. cocinar un pollo con arroz
8. bailar

Then draw your classmate and yourself doing the things you know how to do. Beneath each activity, write sentences that describe what you can do.

W Whom do you know in your school? Claudia Curiosa, the local reporter, wants to find out. Take turns with a partner asking and answering questions.

Partner A: You're Claudia. Ask the questions.

Partner B: Answer Claudia's questions about the people in your school.

MODELO —¿Quién es el director (la directora)?

—El director es (el Sr. Martínez). *or* No sé quién es el director (la directora).

1. ¿Quiénes son los conserjes?

2. ¿Hay un enfermero en la escuela? ¿Dónde trabaja?

3. ¿Sabes quién es la asistente administrativa? ¿Cómo se llama? ¿Dónde trabaja?

4. ¿Quién es la bibliotecaria de tu escuela? ¿Cómo es?

5. De tus maestros, ¿quién es el más alto? ¿Quién es el más cómico?

6. De tus maestras, ¿quién es la más simpática? ¿Quién es la más impaciente?

7. ¿Tus papás saben quiénes son tus maestros?

Entre amigos

Think of someone who works in your school and describe that person. You can describe his or her:

- personality
- habits
- physical appearance
- likes and dislikes

When you have finished writing your description, get together with three or four classmates. Take turns reading your descriptions to each other. See if you can guess who each classmate is writing about.

1

El tiempo libre

Objetivos

- To learn the names of some popular sports
- To learn the names of different games and pastimes
- To talk about things you play
- To learn about pastimes in Spanish-speaking countries

Argentinian fans cheer on their rugby team at a World Cup match.

Spanish race car driver Fernando Alonso with his third place trophy.

Puerto Rican men play dominoes outside San Juan.

¿Sabías que...?

- Soccer is becoming more popular in the United States. But in Spanish-speaking countries—and in the rest of the world, as a matter of fact—it's been the number-one sport for a long time.

- Kids in Spanish-speaking countries play many of the same electronic games you do!

- Many parks in Spain and Latin America have areas with tables for playing chess, checkers, and dominoes.

¿Cómo se dice?

¿Qué quieres hacer?

—Raimundo, ¿quieres jugar al tenis?

—No, no puedo. Voy a jugar al fútbol con los chicos.

la cancha

el tenis

la pelota

el fútbol americano

el baloncesto

el fútbol

el béisbol

el estadio

—¿Es bueno tu equipo de volibol?

—Sí, somos buenos jugadores.

el volibol

el equipo

el jugador   **la jugadora**

¿Sabías que...?

Many sports names in Spanish came from English, which explains why they are so similar in both languages. For example, many Spanish speakers use the word **básquetbol** instead of **baloncesto.** Volleyball is spelled in several different ways, such as **volibol** and **voleibol** (or **vóleibol**). It is also called **balonvolea.**

◎ ◎ ◎ ◎ ◎ Compara ◎ ◎ ◎ ◎ ◎

En inglés	En español
tennis	el tenis
basketball	el baloncesto / el básquetbol
baseball	el béisbol
football	el fútbol americano
volleyball	el volibol

¡Úsalo!

Complete a chart like this one to show how much you like certain sports. Rank each sport from one to six. One is for the sport you like the most, and six is for the one you like the least. Then compare answers with your partner.

MODELO —¿Te gusta el tenis?

         —Sí, me gusta. *or* No, no me gusta.

         —¿Te gusta más el fútbol americano?

Write sentences about the sports both of you like and those both of you dislike.

MODELO Nos gusta el tenis.
         No nos gusta el baloncesto.

	Yo	Ana
	Sí—2	
	No—5	

En resumen

el baloncesto	la cancha
el béisbol	la jugadora
el equipo	la pelota
el estadio	
el fútbol	
el fútbol americano	
el jugador	
el tenis	
el volibol	

CONEXIÓN CON LA CULTURA

Famous Athletes Look at these pictures. They are all famous athletes from Spanish-speaking countries! With a partner, take turns saying what sport each of them plays.

MODELO —Regla Torres es jugadora de volibol.

Pau Gasol   **Sammy Sosa**   **Regla Torres**   **Jorge Campos**

Entre amigos

It's time to "Name That Sport." Get together with three or four classmates.

Cut out as many pictures as you can from old magazines and newspapers. The pictures should show people or things that have to do with the sports that you've learned.

Put the pictures in a bag and trade bags with another group. Pass the bag around your group and take turns picking one picture at a time. Show it to the group and say the name of the sport shown, whether or not you like that sport, how many members are on a team, and the name of a team for that sport, if you know one.

**Es el béisbol. Me gusta. Hay nueve jugadores en un equipo.
Los Yankees son un equipo de béisbol.**

¿Cómo se dice?

¿Cuál es tu pasatiempo favorito?

—¿Quieres jugar a las damas?

—No, quiero probar otro juego.

¿Cuál es tu pasatiempo favorito?

las damas

los juegos electrónicos

el dominó

el ajedrez

—¿Qué te gusta hacer los fines de semana?

—Bueno, mi pasatiempo favorito es ir de pesca.

ir de pesca

montar a caballo

tocar un instrumento

sacar fotos

andar en bicicleta

cultivar plantas

coleccionar estampillas

¿Sabías que...?

In many Spanish-speaking countries in the Caribbean, as well as in Miami, dominoes are a very popular pastime, especially for older adults. Families get together on weekends and the adults play dominoes. On a Sunday afternoon, it's common to hear the shuffle of domino pieces being mixed up for a game. Have you ever played dominoes?

¡Úsalo!

A Well, you've learned about quite a few fun things to do! How would you organize them? One way is to think about how many people it takes to do them.

With a partner, set up a chart like this one:

un jugador o una jugadora	dos o más jugadores	dos equipos
tocar un instrumento	el dominó	el volibol

Now go through the following list of sports, games, and pastimes with your partner. Write each one on your chart under the correct heading.

el tenis	montar a caballo	cultivar plantas
coleccionar estampillas	el ajedrez	las damas
andar en bicicleta	el baloncesto	ir de pesca
el béisbol	sacar fotos	el fútbol

Save your chart. As you learn names for other pastimes, add them to it.

B Work in groups of six. Choose five pastimes each and write their names on separate cards. Everyone puts their cards into a bag. Take turns picking out a card. Ask a classmate if he or she will do that activity with you over the weekend. Your classmate answers according to his or her card. If your cards match, you'll plan to do the activity together. Keep picking out cards until everyone has chosen five.

MODELO —¿Quieres sacar fotos este fin de semana?

—No, no puedo sacar fotos este fin de semana.
or Sí, puedo sacar fotos este fin de semana.

C Look at this picture. Decide what each person's hobby **(el pasatiempo)** is in this family. Take turns with your partner saying what each person does.

 —El pasatiempo favorito del padre es cultivar plantas.

D Prepare a schedule like this one of things you want to do this weekend. Write the names of several activities at different times of the day. Leave some slots blank. Then get together with six or seven classmates and ask if they can do these activities with you.

MODELO —Laura, ¿quieres jugar al tenis el sábado a las diez de la mañana?

—No, no puedo. Voy a jugar al fútbol con Ellen.

HORA	sábado	domingo
10:00 a. m.	fútbol con Ellen	
12:30 p. m.		
3:00 p. m.		
5:00 p. m.		

CONEXIÓN CON LAS MATEMÁTICAS

Circle Graph What do your classmates like to do in their free time?

Get together with two classmates. Do a survey in class to find out everyone's favorite sport, game, and hobby. Each of you chooses one question to ask, such as **¿Cuál es tu deporte favorito?, ¿Cuál es tu juego favorito?, ¿Cuál es tu pasatiempo favorito?**

Note your classmates' answers and get back together with your group. Each of you makes a circle graph to show your results.

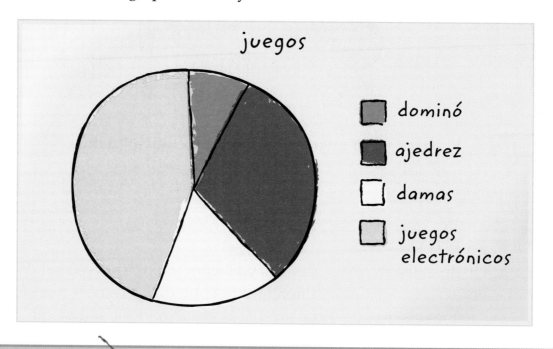

En resumen

el ajedrez	andar en bicicleta
el dominó	coleccionar estampillas
los juegos electrónicos	cultivar plantas
	ir de pesca
las damas	montar a caballo
	sacar fotos
	tocar un instrumento

¿Cómo se dice?

Talking about what you play

Look at these sentences to learn how to talk about playing games and sports.

Singular	**Plural**

Juego al tenis con mi amiga.

Jugamos al béisbol en la primavera.

¿Juegas al fútbol?

¿Ustedes juegan al baloncesto?

Ella **juega** al ajedrez.

Juegan al volibol los sábados.

What do you notice about the way the different forms of **jugar** are spelled?

There is something else you should know about using **jugar.** To talk about what you play, always use **a** after **jugar** (or **al** when the **a** is followed by **el).**

Yo no juego a las damas. Juego al ajedrez.

CONEXIÓN CON LA **CULTURA**

Christmas Traditions In Puerto Rico, it's traditional for people at Christmas time to surprise their friends and relatives with big parties called **parrandas.** First, people meet at one house. Then around midnight, they all gather in front of a friend's or relative's home and burst into song and play music. They do this as loudly as possible, singing to be let into the house right away! The people inside, who're usually asleep, have to wake up and let everyone in. There is always food ready for just such an occasion!

After singing, playing typical instruments, and enjoying some food, the group convinces the hosts to go with them to someone else's house. They keep doing this until five or six in the morning. The hosts of the house they visit at sunrise have to serve breakfast! What are some ways you and your family or friends celebrate special occasions?

¿Sabías que...?

When you talk about playing musical instruments, in English you use the verb "to play." In Spanish, you use **jugar** to talk about playing sports or games. But use **tocar** to talk about playing musical instruments. For example: **Toco la guitarra.** ("I play the guitar.")

¡Úsalo!

A Get together with a partner to find the seven differences between these pictures. Each of you chooses a picture and covers the other one with a piece of paper. Ask each other questions to figure out the differences between the two.

> **MODELO** —¿Dos chicos juegan al fútbol?
>
> —No, dos chicos juegan al fútbol americano.

A

B

B Write down the names of different members of your family. Think about the sports and hobbies they like, and write these, too. Then get together with a partner. Ask each other what the people in your family like to do.

> **MODELO** —¿A qué juega tu papá? *or* ¿Qué le gusta hacer a tu papá?
>
> —Mi papá juega al dominó. *or* A mi papá le gusta jugar al dominó.

C Get together with five or six classmates, and sit across from another team. Each team writes questions about things someone on the other team or team members' family does. Take turns asking the questions. The other team must answer truthfully and in complete sentences. The team with more **"sí"** answers wins!

MODELO —¿Juegas al fútbol? ¿Tu hermana juega al ajedrez?

CONEXIÓN CON LAS MATEMÁTICAS

Multiplication According to legend, a king once owed a reward to an old man. The old man asked the king for this: he would like to get just one grain of rice on the first square of a chess board on the first day. On the second day, he would get double that amount on the second square of the chess board. On the third day, he would get double the previous amount on the third square. How much rice do you think the old man got in the end? Tell a partner whether you think the old man wants more **(más)** or less **(menos)** rice than these amounts.

MODELO El hombre viejo quiere más granos de arroz.
or El hombre viejo quiere menos granos de arroz.

64 granos de arroz
128 granos de arroz
1,500 granos de arroz
9,854 granos de arroz
7,345,018 granos de arroz
18,445,059 granos de arroz
350,766,043,542 granos de arroz

◎ ◎ ◎ **Compara** ◎ ◎ ◎	
En inglés	**En español**
grains	los granos

Entre amigos

How about a game of "Q and A Baseball"?

As a class, think of as many sentences as you can using **jugar** and the sports, games, and pastimes in this unit. Volunteers will write them on the board. Use different names and pronouns, so that all the forms of **jugar** are used—for example:

Papá juega al dominó.   **Tú no juegas al volibol.**

The class will be divided into two teams facing each other. You'll play with a small, soft ball.

A member of one team starts by tossing the ball to someone on the opposite team, and asking a question based on one of the sentences on the board:

¿Juega papá al dominó o al ajedrez?

The person with the ball has ten seconds to correctly answer the question. He or she then throws the ball back to the first team and asks another question. Correct answers score one point. For wrong answers or too much time spent on coming up with an answer, subtract one point.

Set a time limit for the whole game. The team with the highest score wins!

En resumen

	u ➡ ue
	jugar
(Yo)	j**ue**go
(Tú)	j**ue**gas
(Él, Ella, Ud.)	j**ue**ga
(Nosotros, Nosotras)	jug**amos**
(Ellos, Ellas, Uds.)	j**ue**gan

Papá **juega al** dominó.
        toca   la guitarra.

¿Cómo se dice?

Talking about yourself and others

Look at the forms of the verb **ser.** Which form is new to you?

Singular

Soy fuerte.

Plural

Nosotras **somos** fuertes.

¿**Eres** tú la prima de Juan?

¿**Son** ustedes amigos de Lidia?

Él **es** un buen alumno.

Ellos no **son** buenos alumnos.

To talk about yourself and one or more other people ("we"), use **somos.**

¡Úsalo!

A Look at these pictures. Choose one and describe the person in it and what he or she is wearing to a partner, who must guess who the person is. Give one or two clues at a time and answer your partner's questions.

Partner A: Give one or two clues. See how long you can keep you partner guessing!

Partner B: Ask questions about the person and guess who it is.

> **MODELO** —Es una chica. Tiene el pelo castaño.
>
> —¿Juega al baloncesto?

B Get together with a partner. Do you think you really know what he or she is like? Write sentences saying what you think your partner is like. Use the words below.

> **MODELO** Alberto es atlético y popular.

atlético	cómico	generoso	simpático
tímido	impaciente	inteligente	popular

Then share your sentences with your partner, and ask if he or she agrees.

> **MODELO** —¿Piensas que eres atlético y popular?

Now, write some sentences together and say what characteristics you both share.

> **MODELO** Los dos somos simpáticos.

C Think of the qualities players must have in order to practice these sports or pastimes. Then take turns with a partner sharing opinions about what these players are like. Do you agree?

> **MODELO** **jugar al dominó**
>
> **—Son pacientes.**

1. jugar al béisbol

2. jugar al baloncesto

3. jugar al tenis

4. jugar al fútbol

5. jugar al ajedrez

6. jugar al volibol

Then decide whether you and your partner share each quality.

> **MODELO** **—¿Somos pacientes?**

CONEXIÓN CON LAS MATEMÁTICAS

Averages What is the average height of the students in your class?

Get together with three classmates. Find the average height (**el promedio de altura**) of the students in your group in meters and centimeters.

Then convert your measurements to feet (**pies**) and inches (**pulgadas**). Compare your results with those of other groups. Which group was the tallest, on average? The shortest?

> 2.54 centímetros = 1 pulgada
>
> 1 metro = 39.37 pulgadas

> **MODELO** **¿Cuál es el promedio de altura?**

Entre amigos

Get together with five or six classmates and play **Diez Preguntas** ("Ten Questions").

Think of someone in class. Write the person's name on a piece of paper but don't show it to anyone. The rest of your group is allowed ten **sí** or **no** questions to guess who it is. They must use **ser** in every question, and must address you as if you were that person.

> —¿Eres una chica?
> —No, no soy una chica.
> —¿Eres alto?
> —Sí, soy alto.
> —¿Son azules tus ojos?
> —No, no son azules.

When they think they have the answer, they can guess who you are:

> —¿Eres Luis?

But the members of your group must be careful. If their guess is incorrect, you win! You've stumped the group. You've also won if the group uses up all ten questions and still can't guess who you are!

En resumen

	ser
(Yo)	**soy**
(Tú)	**eres**
(Él, Ella, Ud.)	**es**
(Nosotros, Nosotras)	**somos**
(Ellos, Ellas, Uds.)	**son**

¿Dónde se habla español?

España: Los romanos y los árabes

Spain has a rich history. The first inhabitants, as early as 13,000 B.C., lived in caves in the north of Spain. The famous Caves of Altamira are covered with vivid paintings of bison, horses, deer, and wild boar. The pictures were discovered by nine-year-old María de Santuola, who wandered into the caves in 1879 with her dad. She exclaimed, "Look, papa, oxen!"

Much later, Phoenicians and Greeks visited the coasts and islands of Spain. The first two groups to inhabit Spain were the Celts and the Iberians. Later the Romans invaded Spain and stayed from the 1st century B.C. to the 5th century A.D. They were followed by the Visigoths from the north. The Moors, Arabs from the north of Africa, arrived in A.D. 711. **El Cid**, a legendary hero in Spain, led Spaniards to fight the Moors and regain control of Spain. However, the Moors were not expelled from Spain until 1492, when Queen Isabella and King Ferdinand drove them out. Kings and queens have continued to lead Spain until the present, except for the years under dictator Francisco Franco, who ruled from the end of the Spanish Civil War (1936–1939) until his death in 1975. The present King is Juan Carlos, and his wife is Sofía. Although Spain maintains the tradition of the monarchy, it now has a democratically elected government as well.

Each of these people or groups has contributed to the development and culture of Spain, and their influences can be seen in everything from the language to the architecture.

Datos

Capital: Madrid

Ciudades importantes: Barcelona, Bilbao, Sevilla, Valencia

Idiomas oficiales: Español, catalán, vasco, gallego, valenciano

Moneda: El euro

Población: 40.2 millones

¡Léelo en español!

Los romanos En Segovia, una ciudad en el centro de España, se puede ver un acueducto. En el siglo I, los romanos construyeron[1] el acueducto para traer agua de las montañas a la ciudad. Cerca de Segovia, hay un anfiteatro al aire libre[2] de la época de los romanos. Por toda España, todavía[3] hay puentes y caminos de los romanos. Se conoce a los romanos como buenos ingenieros[4] y arquitectos. Séneca es un filósofo romano que vivió en España.

Los romanos también trajeron su idioma y su religión a España. El español viene del latín, el idioma de los romanos. La religión católica es la religión más popular en España.

Los árabes Los árabes del norte de África, o los moros, vivieron en España de 711 d.C. hasta 1492. Hay muchas contribuciones de los moros. Hay palacios elegantes como la Alhambra de Granada y el Alcázar de Sevilla. Hay jardines con muchas flores, árboles y fuentes como los del Generalife. Hay mezquitas[5] para rezar[6] en su religión, el Islam. España tiene muchos productos de los moros porque los moros eran agricultores fantásticos. Hay uvas, y árboles de fruta, como el de naranja. Los moros tienen un papel[7] muy importante en la historia de España.

[1] built   [2] outdoor   [3] still
[4] engineers   [5] mosque   [6] pray   [7] role

Aqueduct in Segovia

¡Comprendo!

Answer in English.

1. Make a timeline showing the different groups that ruled Spain.

2. Draw two circles. Put Romans in one circle and Arabs (Moors) in the other circle. Draw lines from each circle. On each line, write something that group contributed to Spanish culture.

UNIDAD 2

La comunidad

Objetivos

- To talk about important jobs in the community

- To name places in the community

- To talk about what you and others are doing right now

- To talk about people you know

- To learn about communities in Spanish-speaking countries

Central plaza in Mexico City

A Columbian woman makes chairs in Bogotá.

A newsstand on Las Ramblas in Barcelona, Spain

¿Sabías que...?

- People who move to another country often live in communities with others who came from the same place. The United States has many Spanish-speaking communities.

- In smaller towns in Spanish-speaking countries, a favorite place for people to gather to discuss local events is **la municipalidad** (*town hall*).

Lección 1

¿Cómo se dice?

¿Qué hacen las personas?

—¿Qué hace tu tía Amalia?

—Ella es médica. Examina a los pacientes.

el hospital

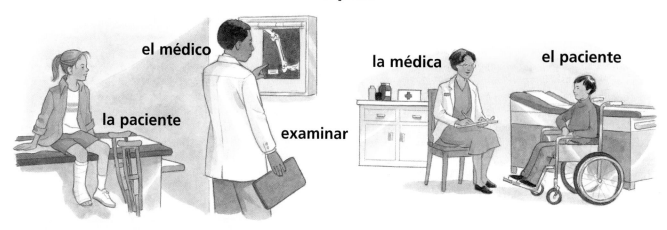

el médico

la paciente

examinar

la médica

el paciente

—¿Quién trabaja en la estación de bomberos?

—Los bomberos. Apagan los incendios.

la estación de bomberos

el bombero

la bombera

46 ❋ cuarenta y seis

Unidad 2

—¿Qué hace tu mamá?

—Es policía. Ayuda a la gente.

la estación de policía

la policía

el policía

ayudar

la gente

¿Sabías que...?

Different languages sometimes describe the same job in different ways. The Spanish word **bombero** comes from **bomba** ("pump"). It gives you the idea of someone who pumps water to put out a fire. What idea do you get from the English word *firefighter*?

CONEXIÓN CON LA CULTURA

Fire Stations In several Spanish-speaking countries, old fire stations have been converted into museums. In Mexico City, the **Museo de Arte Popular** (Folk Art Museum) was built in a remodeled fire station. In Puerto Rico, the historic **Parque de Bombas de Ponce** houses a museum and is a popular tourist attraction.

Parque de Bombas de Ponce

Museo de Arte Popular

¡Úsalo!

Look at the people in the pictures and then read the statements. Get together with a partner and match the people to their statements. There may be more than one correct statement for each person.

Soy bombera.	Soy médica.
Trabajo en un hospital.	Apago incendios.
Trabajamos en una estación de policía.	Ayudamos a la gente.
Trabajo en una estación de bomberos.	Examino a los pacientes.
Soy médico.	Somos policías.
Soy bombero.	

1.

2.

3.

4.

5.

Entre amigos

Time for a game of pantomime! Form small groups and write the names of occupations on different cards.

bombero / bombera
médico / médica
conserje
cocinero / cocinera

policía
maestro / maestra
bibliotecario / bibliotecaria
enfermero / enfermera

Shuffle the cards, then place them in a pile. Take turns drawing one card at a time. Act out the occupation. The group has to guess your occupation:

—¡Eres médica!
—No, no soy médica.
—¡Eres policía!
—Sí, soy policía.

Remember to use feminine words for girls and masculine words for boys.

En resumen

el hospital	el médico	la médica
	el paciente	la paciente
	examinar	
la estación de bomberos	el bombero	la bombera
	apagar	
la estación de policía	el policía	la policía
	la gente	
	ayudar	

¿Cómo se dice?

¿Qué quieres ser?

—¿Qué quieres ser?

—Quiero ser dueña de una compañía. ¿Y tú?

—Quiero ser empleado en una oficina.

la compañía

el dueño

la empleada

el empleado

la dueña

Los dueños son los directores de la compañía. Los empleados trabajan en las oficinas.

la fábrica

la obrera

el obrero

Los obreros trabajan en la fábrica.

—¿Qué hacen tu mamá y tu papá?

—Trabajan mucho. Son vendedores en una tienda por departamentos.

la tienda por departamentos

el vendedor

la vendedora

Los vendedores venden ropa en la tienda por departamentos.

¿Sabías que...?

Many businesses in the United States have **Se habla español** signs in the window. This means that the staff can speak with customers in English or Spanish. People who speak both languages have a valuable skill that can mean extra pay!

CONEXIÓN CON LA CULTURA

Trade In Spanish-speaking countries, vendors sell in a variety of places. Some sell at stands in outdoor markets. Here, you can buy produce, meat, furniture, pottery, herbal remedies, and T-shirts. Others sell in modern malls similar to the ones you may be used to. Centro Sambil in Caracas, Venezuela, is the largest mall in South America.

¡Úsalo!

A All these people have said why they like their jobs. Work with a partner to find out who said what!

Me gusta organizar a la gente para trabajar bien.

Tengo muchos amigos en la fábrica.

Me gusta proteger a la gente.

Me gusta hablar con los clientes.

Mi trabajo es apagar los incendios.

Me gusta ayudar a mis pacientes.

Me gusta trabajar en una oficina.

Me gusta mucho la buena comida.

Me gusta enseñar.

Me gustan mucho los libros.

@ @ @ **Compara** @ @ @

En inglés	En español
clients	los clientes
to protect	proteger
to organize	organizar

B Play a memory game with different colored cards! Get together with a partner. On cards of one color, write different occupations. On cards of another color, write the places where people work. Then spread out all the cards facedown on the table. You're ready to play!

Take turns turning over two cards at a time, one of each color. Say whether or not the person works in this place. If the cards match, keep them and take another turn. If they don't match, put them back and try to remember where they were for next time! Then it is your partner's turn. The winner is the person with the most cards at the end.

MODELO —**El bombero no trabaja en la estación de policía.** *or* **El policía trabaja en la estación de policía.**

Entre amigos

Time to play "Job Talk"! You'll need a ball, plus cards with the names of all the occupations you know in Spanish written on them.

One student draws a card, says the occupation—for example, **el dueño**—and then tosses the ball to someone else.

That student has five seconds to name something related to **el dueño.** It could be the place where **el dueño** works, or something he does, or something he uses, like **el escritorio.** That student then tosses the ball to another player, who must name something else related to **el dueño,** and so on.

If someone says something wrong, repeats what someone else said, or takes more than five seconds to answer, he or she is out, and the previous player selects a new occupation. The winner is the last person left standing!

En resumen

la compañía	el dueño	la dueña
	el empleado	la empleada
la fábrica	el obrero	la obrera
la tienda por departamentos	el vendedor	la vendedora

¿Cómo se dice?

Talking about people you know

Study these examples of how to talk about knowing people.

—**¿Conoces a** la Sra. Velasco?
—Sí, **conozco a** la Sra. Velasco. Es policía.

—**¿Conocen** ustedes **a** alguien de
la fábrica?
—No, no **conocemos a** nadie de
la fábrica.

—¿Quién **conoce al** hombre alto?
—Elena **conoce al** hombre.

A little word comes between **conocer** and the name of a person. What word is it?
That's right—it's **a.** Use **a** when you talk about knowing a specific person. Don't
use **a** before **un** and **una: ¿Conoces un vendedor?**

To talk about "someone," use **alguien.** To talk about "no one," use **nadie.**

Conozco a **alguien** en la tienda.
No conozco a **nadie** en la ciudad.

Notice that when using **nadie** as an object, you also use **no** before the verb.

¡Úsalo!

A You and a partner have to decide how to seat these people for a community dinner. Who will sit next to whom? Why? Think about things people have in common and whom they know. Decide on a seating chart for the three tables.

 Marta:
Es policía y
conoce a Elvira.

 Pedro:
Es hermano de
Andrea.

Cristina:
Es bombera y es
amiga de Laura
y de Silvia.

 Andrea:
Es empleada de
oficina. Conoce a
Julia y a Tomás.

 Luis:
Es cocinero y
es el marido
de Elvira.

Silvia:
Es amiga de
Cristina y de Laura,
y es bombera.

 Tomás:
Conoce a Andrea
y es maestro.

 Roberto:
Es policía y
conoce a Ernesto.

 Laura:
Es amiga de Silvia
y de Cristina, y es
bombera.

 Nuria:
Es cocinera y no
conoce a nadie.

 Elvira:
Es médica y
es la esposa
de Luis.

 Rocío:
Es bombero
y no conoce
a nadie.

 Ernesto:
Es policía y
conoce a Roberto.

 Julia:
Es empleada de
oficina y conoce
a Andrea.

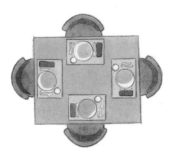 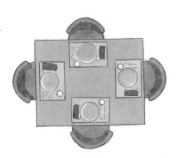 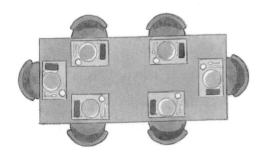

B Look at the names on the list below. Choose three and write them on a card. Then go around the room asking your classmates if they know any of the people. When you have found someone who "knows" a person on your card (meaning they have a matching card), sit down.

MODELO —¿Conoces a los López?

—Sí, conozco a los López. *or* No, no conozco a los López.

Then your teacher will ask who knows each person. Everyone who wrote the same name on his or her card stands up and says that you all (**nosotros** or **nosotras)** know this person.

MODELO —¿Quién conoce a los López?

—Nosotros conocemos a los López.

1. los Rodríguez
2. mi hermana Lupe
3. el agente Cabañillas

4. la doctora Jiménez
5. el Sr. Navarro
6. los cocineros de la escuela

7. mi prima Julia
8. el maestro de deportes

CONEXIÓN CON LOS ESTUDIOS SOCIALES

Historical Figures How well do you know the people you've learned about in social studies? Get together with three classmates. Each of you should think about a historical figure and ask the student on your right if he or she knows the person. If your classmate knows, he or she should make a drawing representing the historical figure.

MODELO ¿Conoces a Cristóbal Colón?

Here are some ideas to get you started. You should brainstorm ideas in your group about other people you have studied in your social studies class.

Cristóbal Colón (*Christopher Columbus*)
Andrew Jackson
Martin Luther King, Jr.

Rosa Parks
George Washington

Entre amigos

Use the occupation cards that you used in the first two **Entre amigos** sections of this unit. Everyone should get one card. Sit in a circle and hold your cards so that everyone can see them.

Take turns asking questions with **conocer:**

—**Marcos, ¿conoces una vendedora?**

Marcos looks for the person holding the **vendedor** card. If it's a girl, he says, **Sí, conozco una vendedora. Se llama** *(the girl's name).* If a boy is holding the **vendedor** card, Marcos says, **No, pero conozco un vendedor. Se llama** *(the boy's name).*

¿Sabías que...?

Did you notice that Spanish speakers use two different words to say "to know"? If you talk about knowing a person, use **conozco** (**Conozco a esa alumna.**). To say that you know how to do something, use **saber (Sé nadar.).**

En resumen

	conocer
(Yo)	cono**zc**o
(Tú)	conoces
(Él, Ella, Ud.)	conoce
(Nosotros, Nosotras)	conocemos
(Ellos, Ellas, Uds.)	conocen

Lección 4

¿Cómo se dice?
Saying what people are doing right now

Look at these sentences. In each sentence, someone is doing something right now. What's the first verb you see in each sentence?

El obrero **está trabajando.**

Rita **está bebiendo** leche.

Graciela **está subiendo** las escaleras.

El vendedor **está vendiendo** frutas.

In each sentence, **estar** is followed by another word that ends in **-ndo.** Here's how to form this word:

For verbs that end in **-ar,** like **caminar** and **trabajar,** take away the **-ar** and add **-ando (caminando, trabajando).**

For verbs that end in **-er** (like **beber**) or **-ir** (like **subir**), take away **-er** or **-ir** and add **-iendo (bebiendo, subiendo).**

¡Úsalo!

A There's a fire in the building! But people don't seem too worried—what are they doing? Talk about it with a partner. Then write a list of all the things the people are doing.

MODELO Los policías están jugando a las damas.

B Play a quick-draw game—in Spanish, of course! The class forms two teams. Each team writes five silly sentences on slips of paper about things an animal is doing. Someone from the other team picks a slip of paper and draws what the sentence says on the board. That person's team has one minute to guess what the animal is doing! Each correct answer gets one point.

> **MODELO** **El gato está tocando la guitarra.**

 **CONEXIÓN** con el **ARTE**

Community Collage Clip pictures from magazines or use your own photos to make a community collage. The pictures should show people involved in different kinds of activities.

Work with two or three classmates and include pictures of people in school, playing games or sports, involved in pastimes, getting ready in the morning or going to bed at night, working around the house . . . It's up to you!

Paste your pictures in an attractive layout on a large piece of butcher paper or posterboard. Next to each picture, write a caption that explains what the people are doing.

> **MODELO** **Las chicas están jugando al fútbol.**
> *or* **Los alumnos están mirando a la maestra.**

Use your community collages to decorate your classroom. What activities did your classmates come up with?

CONEXIÓN CON LOS ESTUDIOS SOCIALES

Jobs What do people do at work? Look at the list of occupations and imagine it's the middle of the afternoon on a workday. Work with a partner and write what each person is doing at work. Then compare your sentences with those of other pairs. See who can come up with the most sentences.

MODELO La médica está examinando a los pacientes.

bombera, médica, director, obrero, asistente administrativo, cocinera, policía, maestra, vendedora, empleado, dueña, enfermero, bibliotecaria, conserje

Entre amigos

Are you a good complainer? With a partner, write six complaints, such as **Tenemos hambre. El piso está sucio. Los platos no están en la mesa.**

Then, join another pair of students. Read them your sentences. They must tell you that they are doing something right now to solve each problem:

—**Tenemos hambre.**
—**Estamos cocinando la cena.**

En resumen

(Yo)	estoy	trabaj**ando**
(Tú)	estás	
(Él, Ella, Ud.)	está	com**iendo**
(Nosotros, Nosotras)	estamos	sub**iendo**
(Ellos, Ellas, Uds.)	están	

¿Dónde se habla español?

GUATEMALA

Guatemala

Guatemala

Of all Latin American countries, Guatemala is the only one in which the native—or indigenous—population is a majority. These people are descendants of the ancient Mayas, whose advanced civilization prospered in southern Mexico and Guatemala during the first ten centuries of our era. Today, more than sixty percent of Guatemalans speak Spanish (which is the country's official language), but the rest of the population speaks one of the twenty-two Mayan dialects. There are many ancient Mayan towns where the native culture is preserved.

Guatemala has a variety of wildlife. The exotic **quetzal**, the country's national bird, is a protected species that lives side-by-side with hummingbirds and parrots, including the macaw. And did you know that there are more jaguars in the rain forests of Guatemala than in any other place in Central America? You can see these big cats in the statues the Mayas sculpted out of stone.

Guatemala is Central America's top producer of coffee. And the next time you eat a banana, it might be one of the two billion that Guatemala exports every year!

> ◎ ◎ ◎ ◎ ◎ **Datos** ◎ ◎ ◎ ◎ ◎
>
> **Capital:** Guatemala
>
> **Ciudades importantes:** Antigua, Chichicastenango, Quezaltenango, Puerto Barrios, San José
>
> **Idiomas:** Español, veintidós dialectos del idioma de los mayas
>
> **Moneda:** El quetzal, el dólar estadounidense
>
> **Población:** 13.9 millones

¡Léelo en español!

Los mayas Los mayas desarrollaron[1] una magnífica civilización en América Central. Hicieron adelantos[2] en matemáticas y astronomía y en la creación de un calendario. Produjeron[3] una maravillosa arquitectura, escultura y pintura. Los indígenas guatemaltecos—que son los descendientes de los mayas—se dedican a[4] la agricultura. Hay un famoso mercado en Chichicastenango. Los jueves y los domingos los indígenas van al mercado para comprar y vender[5] productos. Uno de los productos es la tela[6] que las mujeres hacen a mano.[7] La tela es de muchos colores—roja, azul, verde, amarilla y morada—y tiene diseños[8] de animales, pájaros y formas geométricas como triángulos y cuadrados.

[1] developed   [2] They made advances
[3] They produced   [4] work in   [5] buy and sell
[6] cloth   [7] make by hand   [8] designs

¡Comprendo!

Answer in English.

1. Name three things that distinguish Guatemala from other countries in Central America.

2. What are some of Guatemala's major exports?

3. What were some of the advances of the classical Mayan civilization?

4. What happens in Chichicastenango? Who goes there?

3

En la ciudad

Objetivos

- To learn the names of places in a city
- To discuss ways of getting around in a city and elsewhere
- To find out how to ask for things
- To learn how to give commands, instructions, and directions
- To learn about cities in Spanish-speaking countries

Downtown Bogotá, Colombia

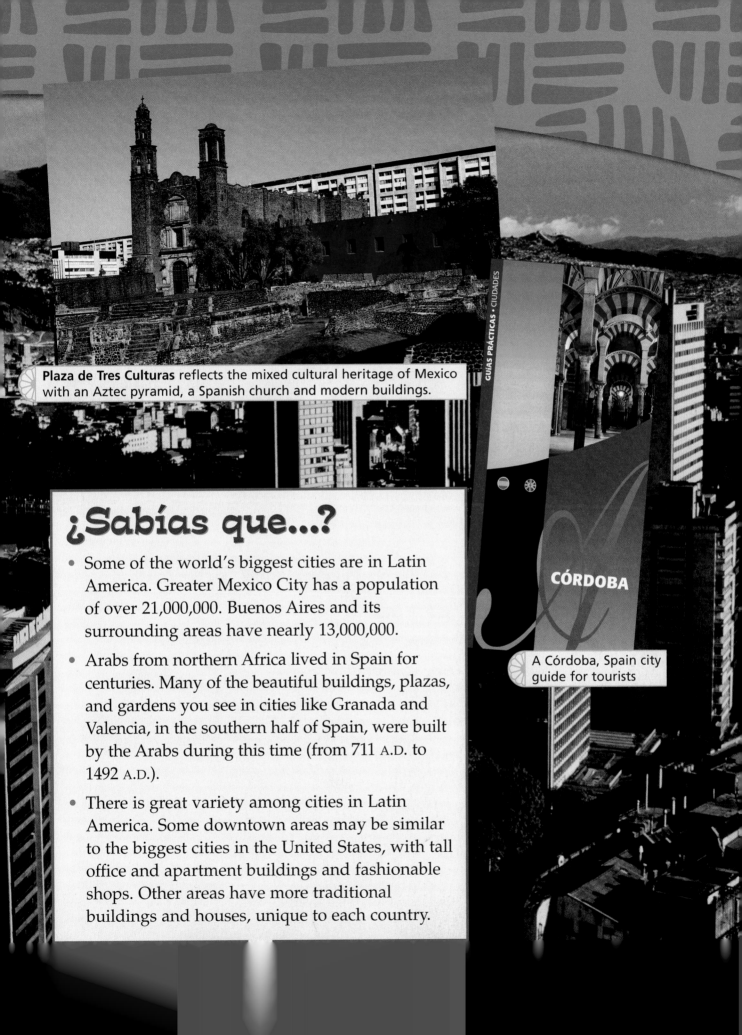

Plaza de Tres Culturas reflects the mixed cultural heritage of Mexico with an Aztec pyramid, a Spanish church and modern buildings.

GUÍAS PRÁCTICAS · CIUDADES

CÓRDOBA

A Córdoba, Spain city guide for tourists

¿Sabías que...?

- Some of the world's biggest cities are in Latin America. Greater Mexico City has a population of over 21,000,000. Buenos Aires and its surrounding areas have nearly 13,000,000.

- Arabs from northern Africa lived in Spain for centuries. Many of the beautiful buildings, plazas, and gardens you see in cities like Granada and Valencia, in the southern half of Spain, were built by the Arabs during this time (from 711 A.D. to 1492 A.D.).

- There is great variety among cities in Latin America. Some downtown areas may be similar to the biggest cities in the United States, with tall office and apartment buildings and fashionable shops. Other areas have more traditional buildings and houses, unique to each country.

¿Cómo se dice?

¿Cómo vamos a ir?

—¿Dónde está la parada de autobús?

—Está en la avenida, cerca del semáforo.

la farmacia

la gasolinera

los semáforos

la calle

la avenida

—¿Cómo vamos a la farmacia? ¿En autobús?

—No, no hay tiempo. Vamos en taxi.

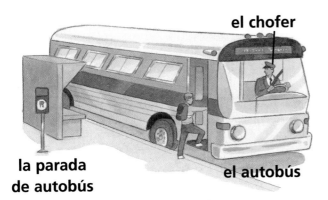

el chofer

la parada de autobús

el autobús

Va **en** autobús.

el taxi

el taxista

Vamos **en** taxi.

abrocharse los cinturones

el coche

Van **en** coche.

Vamos **a** pie.

¿Sabías que...?

Most major cities in Spain and Latin America have extensive subway systems. It's one of the most efficient ways to serve the millions of people who have to get from one place to another in the city each day. The subway has different names in different countries: **el subterráneo, el metro,** and **el subte** are a few of them.

¡Úsalo!

A Look at this picture, choose an item, and write its name on a card. Then get together with a partner and give clues about where the item is located. Your partner has to guess what it is.

> **MODELO** —Está en la calle, delante del autobús.
>
> —¡Es la parada de autobús!

B Take a survey in class to find out how your classmates get from place to place. Interview six people. Ask questions like these:

¿Cómo vas a la escuela por la mañana?
¿Cómo vas a casa por la tarde?
¿Cómo vas a las casas de tus amigos?
¿Cómo vas a las tiendas de la ciudad?

Then report your findings to the class. What forms of transportation do your classmates usually take?

Entre amigos

What would happen if your Spanish-speaking key pal came to visit you?

With a partner, make up a conversation that might take place at the beginning of the visit. Your partner plays the role of the key pal and asks questions about your city or town.

—¿Tu apartamento está en una calle o en una avenida?
—Mi apartamento está en una calle.
—¿Hay una gasolinera en tu calle?
—No, pero no está lejos.
—¿Conoces bien la ciudad?
—Sí, conozco bien la ciudad.

After your partner asks five questions, switch roles and have another conversation. Present your conversations to the class.

En resumen

abrocharse los cinturones

el autobús	la avenida
el chofer	la calle
el coche	la chofer
el taxi	la farmacia
el taxista	la gasolinera
los semáforos	la parada de autobús
	la taxista

Vamos a la farmacia **en** autobús.
coche.
taxi.
a pie.

¿Cómo se dice?

¿Qué hay en el centro?

el centro

—¿Hay muchos rascacielos en el centro?

—Sí, hay muchos. Nuestra ciudad es grande.

el rascacielos

los edificios

la plaza

—¿Está cerca el mercado?

—Sí. Vamos a pie.

el teatro

los automóviles

el estacionamiento

el mercado

CONEXIÓN CON LA CULTURA

Historic Districts Many Latin American countries have centuries-old cities with beautifully preserved historic districts. Many of these colonial cities date from the 1600s and are home today to shops, cafes, and restaurants. Families often go to the old part of the city on weekends to stroll and have lunch.

¿Sabías que...?

In several U.S. cities, there are large Spanish-speaking communities. Do you know where the following Spanish-speaking neighborhoods are located?

La Pequeña Habana   **La Misión**   **El Barrio** *or* **Spanish Harlem**

Lección 2

setenta y uno ✳ **71**

¡Úsalo!

A This class is on a field trip downtown, but everyone's lost. See if you can help the teacher find all of the students. But where's the teacher? Find her first.

Then use these descriptions to figure out who each person is. With a partner, write down where everyone is.

MODELO —Rogelio está en el techo del edificio.

Tomás lleva una gorra roja.	Eva lleva unas botas rojas.
Sandra lleva una blusa roja.	Diego lleva pantalones rojos.
Lisa lleva una falda amarilla.	La maestra lleva un vestido blanco.
Pepe tiene el pelo rojizo.	Saúl lleva una camiseta azul.
Marcos es rubio.	Rogelio lleva una chaqueta roja.

B You have to go to all the places marked with an X on the map. How will you get there? Talk it over with a partner and decide on the route you'll take and the transportation you'll use to get there. Be sure to choose the most direct route.

MODELO —¿Cómo vas a ir al mercado?

—Voy a ir a pie.

—¿Y cómo vas a ir del mercado a la escuela?

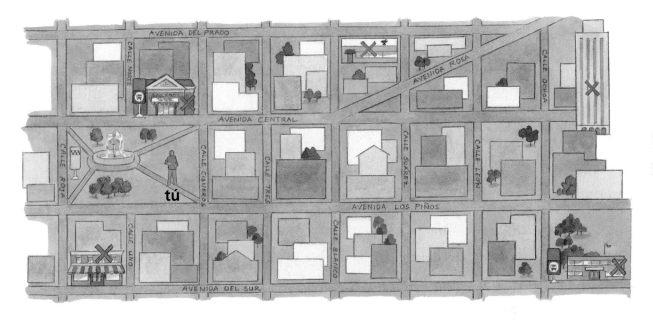

 CONEXIÓN CON LAS **MATEMÁTICAS**

Altitude Many Latin American cities are located at very high altitudes. Look at the graph and put the cities in order, from highest to lowest altitude. Find the altitude of your city or town, as well as of some other important cities in your state and in the country. Work with a partner to make a line graph with these cities and the new ones you find.

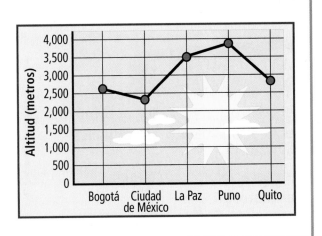

Entre amigos

Where are you going? How are you getting there? What are you going to do there? Form a group with four or five classmates and find out.

On index cards, write the names of all the places in a town or city that you've learned so far. Include places such as **la escuela** or **mi casa.** Put these cards in a bag marked "A."

On other cards, write all the ways you've learned to travel, including **caminar** and **andar en bicicleta.** Put these cards in a bag marked "B."

Sit in a circle. Place both bags in the middle. Take turns drawing a card from each bag and making up a sentence. Say where you're going and how you're getting there.

Voy al parque en taxi.

But that's not all! You must also make up a sentence saying what you're going to do at that place—and it must be something that makes sense.

Voy a jugar al fútbol.

Return the cards to the bags after each draw. If you're able to make one sentence saying where you're going and how you're getting there, you earn one point. If you can also make a complete sentence by saying what you're going to do there, you earn an additional two points.

Play three rounds with your classmates. See who earns the most points.

En resumen

el centro	los automóviles
el estacionamiento	los edificios
el mercado	
el rascacielos	la plaza
el teatro	

¿Cómo se dice?

Giving commands, instructions, and directions

Look at these pictures and sentences. In each example, a person is giving a command or instruction to someone. **Doblar** means "to turn."

doblar	**comer**	**abrir**

¡Dobla aquí!	**¡Come** las verduras!	**¡Abre** la ventana!

Now compare the first sentence in the following pairs below with the second one. Which ones are ordinary statements? Which ones are commands or instructions?

Miguel siempre **pasa** por la farmacia.
¡Pasa por la farmacia, por favor!

Iris siempre **se abrocha** el cinturón en el coche.
¡Abróchate el cinturón, Marcos!

Luis **corre** a la parada de autobús.
¡Corre, Daniela! El autobús está en la parada.

Rosa **escribe** en el pizarrón.
Pancho, **¡escribe** en tu cuaderno!

The second sentence in each pair is a command or instruction to someone else. These commands are called "familiar" commands because you can use them with people whom you address as **tú:** members of your family, friends, and other kids.

Did you notice what form of the verb is used to give a familiar command or instruction?

To make familiar commands with **-ar**, **-er**, and **-ir** verbs, simply use the **él / ella / Ud.** form of the verb.

Look at these words for giving directions. What direction does each one indicate?

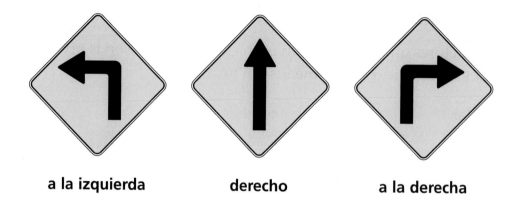

a la izquierda   **derecho**   **a la derecha**

Now look at some commands and instructions that use these words.

¡Dobla a la izquierda!
Sigue derecho por esta calle.
Dobla a la derecha, por favor.

CONEXIÓN CON LOS ESTUDIOS SOCIALES

Traffic Signs Look at these traffic signs. Work with a partner. Choose five and try to say in Spanish what they mean. Your teacher will help you. Use command forms or **Hay...**

MODELO —**Dobla a la izquierda.**

—**Hay una gasolinera.**

¡Úsalo!

A There are so many things to do in this house! With a partner, come up with a list of things you should do to clean it up.

| MODELO | sacar la basura |

Now take turns telling each other to do these tasks. If you give an order correctly, your partner will have to pretend to do it. If you don't, your partner gets to order *you* to do it!

| MODELO | —¡Limpias el piso! |
| | —No, ¡limpia el piso! |

B Imagine that for one day, you could get a parent, a brother, or a sister to do anything you wanted! What would you tell them to do? Be creative and write a "to do" list for the person. Then tell a partner about your list.

| MODELO | —**Compra un coche nuevo, muy bonito.** |
| | **Recoge mis cosas del piso.** |

C Look at this city map. Choose a place in the city where you want your partner to go. Then—without saying the name of the place—give your partner directions to get there. Once you're done giving directions, say **¡Ya estás!** ("You're there!") Your partner has to tell you where he or she is. Switch roles and try again!

> **MODELO** —**Dobla a la derecha por la calle Cisneros, sigue derecho y dobla a la izquierda por la calle Ochoa. Sigue derecho dos calles. ¡Ya estás!**
> —**¡Es la escuela!**

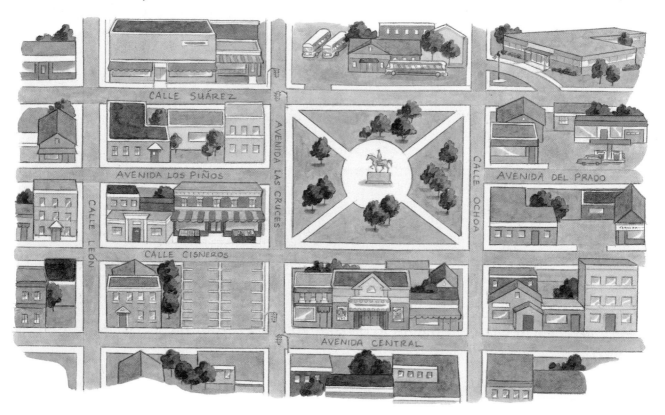

D Get together with two classmates. You're going to blindfold one and have him or her find where you've stationed the other partner. Give the blindfolded partner good directions!

> **MODELO** **Sigue derecho... dobla a la derecha... sigue derecho...**

CONEXIÓN CON LA SALUD

Health and Safety With two classmates, think of topics you have learned about in health class. Prepare a booklet with health and safety tips for your class. Look at these pictures for ideas, and brainstorm new ones!

Entre amigos

Get together with five classmates. Write different activities you can do in class **(leer un libro, escribir en el pizarrón...)** on slips of paper. Each of you should write two activities.

Now place the slips of paper in a bag. Sit in a circle and take turns drawing the slips of paper out. The person who draws a slip has to give an order to the person sitting to the right, for example: **Escribe en el pizarrón.**

The person receiving the order has to do as told, then return to the circle. The group that finishes their twelve activities first wins!

En resumen

-ar	doblar	¡Dobla!	Dobla	a la derecha.
	abrochar	¡Abrocha!		a la izquierda.
-er	comer	¡Come!	Pasa	por la farmacia.
	correr	¡Corre!	Sigue	por la calle.
-ir	abrir	¡Abre!		derecho.
	escribir	¡Escribe!		
		¡Sigue!		

¿Cómo se dice?

Asking for things

Look at these sentences to see how to use the verb **pedir,** which means "to ask for."

Singular	**Plural**

Siempre **pido** sopa para el almuerzo.

Nunca **pedimos** pescado en el mercado.

¿Qué **pides** de desayuno?

¿Ustedes **piden** libros al bibliotecario?

Él **pide** ayuda a la policía.

Ellas **piden** ayuda a la taxista.

Did you notice that only the **nosotros** form uses the **ped-** part of the verb, and all the other forms use **pid-?** This part of the verb is called the "stem." Verbs with different stems for some forms are called "stem-changing verbs." Other verbs that also change their stem from **e** to **i** are **servir,** which means "to serve," and **seguir,** which means "to follow."

Singular			
	pedir	**servir**	**seguir**
Yo	pido	sirvo	sigo
Tú	pides	sirves	sigues
Él, Ella, Ud.	pide	sirve	sigue
Plural			
Nosotros, Nosotras	pedimos	servimos	seguimos
Ellos, Ellas, Uds.	piden	sirven	siguen

¡Úsalo!

A Think of these situations. Work with a partner to answer these questions.

¿**Qué sirven los padres en las fiestas de cumpleaños?**
¿**Qué sirves si alguien está en tu casa a las 12 del mediodía un domingo?**
¿**Qué sirven tus padres de cena en tu casa los domingos?**
¿**Qué sirve tu familia el día de Acción de Gracias** (*Thanksgiving*) **en tu casa?**
¿**Qué sirven los cocineros en tu restaurante favorito?**

B Find out about your classmates' breakfast preferences. Use the words below and **pedir** to ask a partner what he or she usually orders for breakfast when eating out.

MODELO —¿Pides cereal de desayuno?

—Sí, siempre pido cereal. *or* No, no me gusta el cereal.

cereal	huevos fritos	jamón	pan tostado	huevos revueltos
queso	tocino	té	leche	chocolate

Then get together with two other pairs and tell them what your partner likes to order.

MODELO —Sara pide cereal de desayuno. Pide tocino...

CONEXIÓN CON LAS CIENCIAS

Planets Look closely at the names of the planets in Spanish. Did you notice that they're very similar to the English names? Now get together with a partner and close your book. Your partner asks you about the order of the planets, starting from the Sun. Answer using **seguir**.

MODELO —¿Qué planeta sigue a Marte?

—Júpiter sigue a Marte.

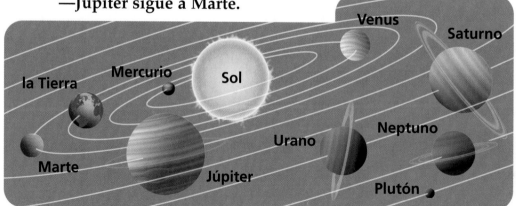

Entre amigos

Sit in a circle with six classmates. The classmate to your left is a customer at a restaurant, and the one to your right is a server.

First, go around the circle asking the person to your left (the "customer") what he or she wants to have. Remember to use the **usted** form. The person whispers a response in your ear.

> —**¿Qué quiere tomar?**
> —**Quiero jugo de naranja.**

Next, ask the person on your right (the "server") what is being served at the restaurant. The person whispers a response in your ear.

> —**¿Qué hay de cena?**
> —**Hay sopa.**

Now it's your turn to speak! Say what the "customer" asked for, and what the "server" is serving.

> —**Susana pide jugo de naranja. Alberto sirve sopa.**

Then switch roles with another classmate.

En resumen

	e → i **pedir**	e → i **seguir**	e → i **servir**
(Yo)	pido	sigo	sirvo
(Tú)	pides	sigues	sirves
(Él, Ella, Ud.)	pide	sigue	sirve
(Nosotros, Nosotras)	pedimos	seguimos	servimos
(Ellos, Ellas, Uds.)	piden	siguen	sirven

¿Dónde se habla español?

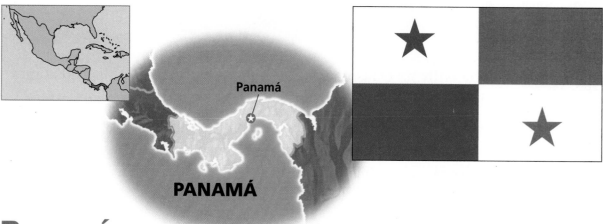

PANAMÁ

Panamá

Panama is an important transportation center because of the Panama Canal. Dozens of ships pass through the canal each day, saving them thousands of miles by cutting across this narrow (forty-mile) strip of land rather than by going around the tip of South America. Panama gained its independence later than the other Central American republics. Although it broke away from Spain in 1821, it was a province of Colombia until 1903. By the following year, plans were made with the United States to complete construction of the canal. The surrounding area, with its commercial, transportation, and trade activities, differs sharply from the rural areas in the rest of the country.

The Cuna, who live on the San Blas Islands, are one of several indigenous groups of Panama. The Cuna women wear elaborately embroidered blouses called **molas** as well as nose rings and numerous bracelets on their arms and legs.

Datos

Capital: Panamá

Ciudades importantes: Colón, San Miguelito, David

Idiomas: Español, inglés

Moneda: El balboa, el dólar estadounidense

Población: 2.9 millones

¡Léelo en español!

El canal de Panamá El canal que une[1] el océano Atlántico y el océano Pacífico es el sitio[2] más famoso de Panamá. La construcción principal canal ocurrió[3] entre 1904 y 1914. En 1913, 43,400 personas trabajaron[4] para construir el canal. Fue muy difícil y muchas personas murieron de enfermedades[5] como la malaria. Pero hoy día, muchos barcos pasan por el canal todos los días. Algunos[6] barcos transportan productos y otros barcos transportan personas. Los barcos que transportan personas se llaman «cruceros». Puedes viajar de Florida a California por el canal. Los Estados Unidos pagó[7] la construcción del canal, pero el 31 de diciembre de 1999 el canal pasó[8] a Panamá.

[1] connects   [2] place   [3] happened   [4] worked
[5] died of diseases   [6] Some   [7] paid for
[8] was turned over to

¡Comprendo!

1. Describe the country of Panama.
2. Which two oceans does the canal connect?
3. Was it easy or difficult to build the canal? What problems might there have been?
4. What types of ships use the canal?
5. Who paid for the canal? Who owns it now?

El transporte de larga distancia

Objetivos

- To talk about long-distance transportation
- To learn the names of countries and continents
- To identify countries where Spanish is spoken
- To talk about your nationality and those of Spanish speakers
- To read about modes of transportation in Spanish-speaking countries

A large ship docks in San Juan, Puerto Rico.

A tour bus in Highlands, Ecuador

An employee checks passengers' tickets on a Spanish train.

¿Sabías que...?

- When traveling by bus or train in Latin America, you often can buy food and drinks from vendors who sell their wares at your window at bus stops and train stations.

- Spain has a fast, modern railroad system. Long-distance trains have TVs, dining cars, game rooms, and even play areas for little kids!

- The world's largest cruise ships make stops at the port of San Juan, in Puerto Rico. Many of these ships are the size of large buildings, housing several pools, restaurants, game rooms, and much more!

¿Cómo se dice?

¿Estás listo para salir?

—¿A qué hora sale el tren?

—A las siete. Tengo que estar en la estación de trenes a las cinco y media.

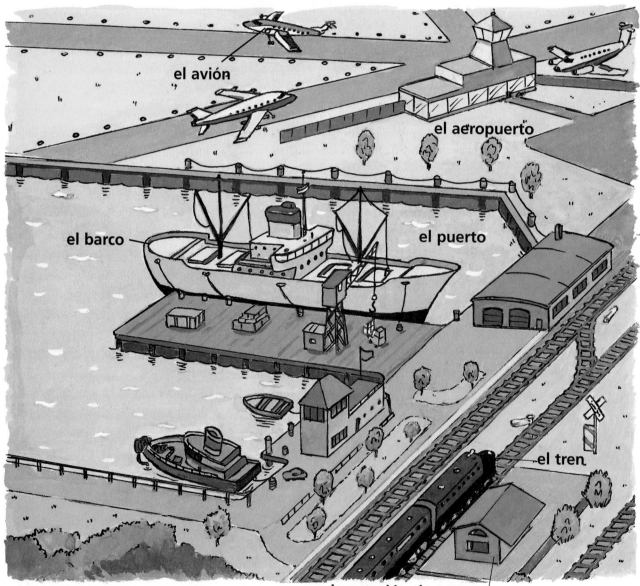

el avión

el aeropuerto

el barco

el puerto

el tren

la estación de trenes

—¿Cuáles son los países de América del Norte?

—Canadá, Estados Unidos y México son los países de América del Norte.

AMÉRICA DEL NORTE

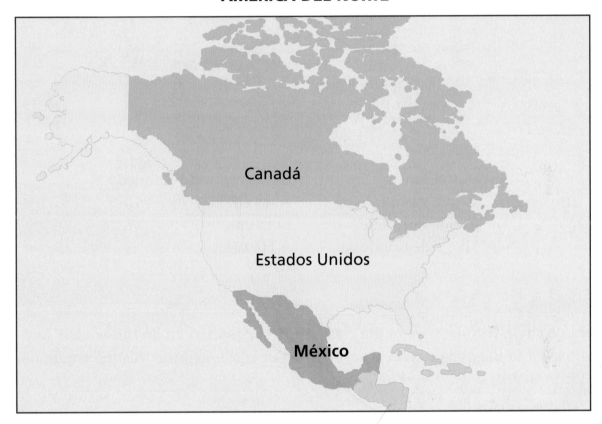

Canadá

Estados Unidos

México

CONEXIÓN CON LOS ESTUDIOS SOCIALES

The Panama Canal The Panama Canal **(el canal de Panamá)** is the busiest and perhaps the most important shortcut in the world. Without it, ships would have to go all the way around the tip of South America in order to travel between the Atlantic and Pacific Oceans. Find **el canal** on the map on page 93.

¡Úsalo!

A You were asking your partner questions and taking notes of the answers, but you forgot to put them in order. You need to repeat the questions and have your partner give you the right answers. Then switch roles and make up new answers!

¿Adónde vas?	Del aeropuerto Kennedy.
¿Y qué vas a tomar?	A las cinco.
¿A qué hora sale?	El avión.
Ah, ¿y de dónde sale?	A Hawai.

B Sit in a circle with the rest of the class. Write a postcard on an index card, and address it to the person who is sitting to your right. Include this information on your postcard:

- where you are
- where you're going
- what you will take to get there
- what time your transportation leaves
- what time you have to be at the place you're leaving from

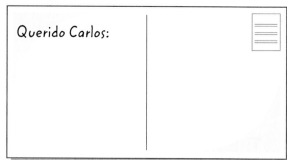

Querido Carlos:

When you finish, "deliver" the mail to your classmate. Read the postcard you receive.

Now your teacher will ask about what some people wrote. If you hear the name of the person who sent you the postcard, explain what you know about the person's plans, according to the message.

Languages You're going to read about languages **(lenguas)** in North America, but first, read these sentences. Decide with a partner whether you think they're true **(verdadero)** or false **(falso).** Then read the paragraph below to find out if you were right!

1. Las lenguas más importantes de América del Norte son el español y el inglés.

2. Hay lugares de América del Norte donde la gente habla francés.

3. El español es la lengua oficial de México.

4. El inglés es la lengua oficial de Estados Unidos.

5. En Estados Unidos la gente habla sólo inglés.

Las lenguas de América del Norte

Hay tres países en América del Norte: Canadá, Estados Unidos y México. Las lenguas más importantes son el español y el inglés. Pero en Quebec (Canadá) el francés es la lengua oficial.

En Estados Unidos el inglés es la lengua más importante. Los indígenas norteamericanos también hablan sus lenguas, como el navajo y el cheroquí. También hay muchas personas de otros países. Hablan inglés y también las lenguas de sus países: español, chino, ruso, árabe... En Estados Unidos no hay lengua oficial.

En México la lengua oficial es el español. También hay muchas personas que hablan lenguas indígenas, como el maya y el chol.

◎ ◎ ◎ Compara ◎ ◎ ◎

En inglés	En español
language	la lengua
official	oficial

En resumen

el aeropuerto	**América del Norte**
el avión	Canadá
el barco	Estados Unidos
la estación de trenes	México
el puerto	
el tren	

¿Cómo se dice?

¿En qué países hablan español?

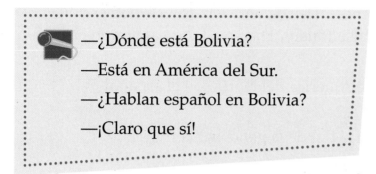

—¿Dónde está Bolivia?

—Está en América del Sur.

—¿Hablan español en Bolivia?

—¡Claro que sí!

AMÉRICA DEL SUR

AMÉRICA CENTRAL

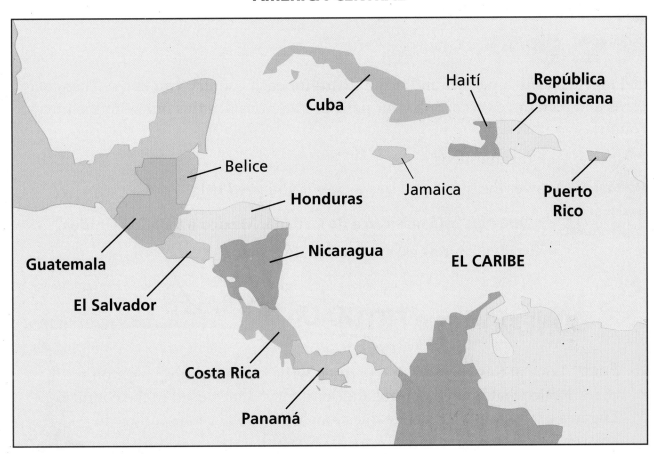

¿Sabías que...?

When you look at a map of the world, you may be used to seeing the United States in the center. World maps made in other countries, however, often show those countries and their continents in the center. If you bought a map in Spain, for example, you might find Spain and Europe in the center, with the United States and the Americas way over to one side.

EUROPA

¡Úsalo!

Get together with a partner and make a card for each country you know. Then take turns and pick three cards. Ask your partner questions like this one with the three countries you have.

Partner A: Ask the questions.

Partner B: Answer the questions. Use a map if you need help.

> **MODELO** —¿Qué país está más cerca de Canadá, México o Estados Unidos?
>
> —Estados Unidos está más cerca de Canadá.

CONEXIÓN CON LOS ESTUDIOS SOCIALES

Facts Look at this chart. With a partner, write five questions based on the chart. Notice that **moneda** means the "currency" that's used in the country. **Lugares** are "places." Exchange questions with another pair and try to answer without looking at the chart.

	Venezuela	**Uruguay**	**Chile**	**España**
Capital	Caracas	Montevideo	Santiago	Madrid
Lengua oficial	español	español	español	español, catalán, vasco, gallego y valenciano
Moneda	el bolívar	el peso	el peso	el euro
Comida típica	las arepas	el chivito	la empanada	la paella
Lugares bonitos	la selva del Amazonas, la isla Margarita	las playas de Punta del Este	los Andes, la Isla de Pascua	Granada, las Islas Baleares, la Costa del Sol

> **MODELO** ¿Cuáles son las lenguas oficiales de España?

◎ ◎ ◎ Compara ◎ ◎ ◎

En inglés	**En español**
capital	la capital
typical	típica

Entre amigos

Play a game with two or three classmates to see how well you know the countries and continents.

Make one set of cards that name these continents or regions: **América del Norte, América del Sur, América Central, Europa,** and **El Caribe.** Make another set of cards with the names of all the countries you learned in this unit. Put both sets facedown in two separate piles.

One player starts by taking a card from both piles. He or she makes a sentence indicating whether the country is or isn't on that continent or in that region:

> **Perú—América del Sur**
> **Perú está en América del Sur.**
> **Honduras—Europa**
> **Honduras no está en Europa.**

The player receives one point for each correct statement. Keep taking turns, discarding the country cards but returning the region and continent cards to the bottom of their pile.

En resumen

América del Sur		América Central	El Caribe	Europa
Argentina	Paraguay	Costa Rica	Cuba	España
Bolivia	Perú	Guatemala	Puerto Rico	
Chile	Uruguay	Honduras	República	
Colombia	Venezuela	Nicaragua	Dominicana	
Ecuador		Panamá		
		El Salvador		

¿Cómo se dice?

Naming countries and nationalities

Look at these pairs of sentences. The names of countries appear in the first sentences. The names of nationalities appear in the second sentences.

Soy de **Canadá.** Soy **canadiense.**
Sebastián es de **Chile.** Es **chileno.**
Tú eres de **Venezuela.** Eres **venezolana.**
Somos de **Estados Unidos.** Somos **estadounidenses.**
Jorge y Felipa son de **Bolivia.** Son **bolivianos.**
Ellos son de **Costa Rica.** Son **costarricenses.**

Did you notice that when you write the name of a country, you use a capital letter, and when you write the name of the nationality, you use a small letter?

Look at the sentences with nationalities again. Most of the words for nationalities are just like many other descriptive words. The ones that end in **-o** are used for males and the ones that end in **-a** are used for females. When you're talking about more than one person, you put an **-s** at the end of the word.

What did you notice about how to talk about where someone is from? What word do you use with a form of the verb **ser** and the name of the country?

Here are some other Spanish-speaking nationalities:

argentino	ecuatoriano	mexicano	peruano
colombiano	español	nicaragüense	puertorriqueño
cubano	guatemalteco	panameño	salvadoreño
dominicano	hondureño	paraguayo	uruguayo

¿Sabías que...?

Some Spanish speakers may use the words **el, la, los** or **las** before the names of countries. For example, they may say **el Perú, la Argentina,** or **los Estados Unidos.** You can say some of the names with or without these words, but you must say **El Salvador,** because **El** is part of the name.

CONEXIÓN CON LAS MATEMÁTICAS

Population Look at these facts about some Spanish-speaking countries. Write the countries in order, from the most populated **(más poblado)** to the least. Then get together with a partner and make comparisons between the countries.

| MODELO | México está más poblado que Argentina. |

Argentina: 38.000.000 habitantes
México: 104.000.000 habitantes
Chile: 15.000.000 habitantes

Uruguay: 3.000.000 habitantes
Venezuela: 24.000.000 habitantes
España: 40.000.000 habitantes

@ @ @ **Compara** @ @ @

En inglés	En español
inhabitants	los habitantes
populated	poblado

¡Úsalo!

A Copy this chart and classify all the nationalities you know in the correct columns, according to the ending of each word.

-ano, -eno, -ino	-eño	-ayo	-ense	-I	-eco

Now take turns with a partner saying a nationality. Your partner answers with the correct country.

Partner A: Say a nationality from your chart.

Partner B: Answer with the country that nationality belongs to.

| MODELO | —Mexicano. |
| | —Es de México. |

B Get together with a partner. Take turns reading each sentence out loud and having your partner complete it with the correct nationality. Use an encyclopedia if you need to. Then, make up your own sentences using nationalities.

> **MODELO** **Una chica de Santo Domingo es dominicana.**

1. Un chico de Buenos Aires es...
2. Un chico de Seattle es...
3. Una chica de La Habana es...
4. Un chico de Oaxaca es...
5. Un chico de Barcelona es...
6. Una chica de San Juan es...

C Look at the map and the children. Take turns with your partner asking about the nationality of each child. Look at a map if you need help with country names.

> **MODELO** —¿De dónde es Ángela?
>
> —Es boliviana.

Elena Margarita

Ricardo

Carlos

Olga

Lucrecia

Oscar

Ángela

Enrique Ernesto

Look at these photos. Discuss with a partner where you think each is from. Write sentences saying what you think and present them to the class.

la paella

las arepas

el mate

la tortilla

el burrito

la hamburguesa

MODELO La paella es de España. Es española.

En resumen

argentino	ecuatoriano	panameño
boliviano	español	paraguayo
chileno	estadounidense	peruano
colombiano	guatemalteco	puertorriqueño
costarricense	hondureño	salvadoreño
cubano	mexicano	uruguayo
dominicano	nicaragüense	venezolano

¿Cómo se dice?
Talking about traveling

Look at these sentences to see how to use the word **en** to talk about how people are traveling.

Vamos a México **en** avión.

Voy al centro **en** tren.

Van a Puerto Rico **en** barco.

The word **en** allows you to connect where people are going with how they are going. You've seen the word **en** before. It has other uses besides talking about how people travel.

El Sr. López está **en** el coche.
La sal está **en** la mesa.
Me voy de la casa **en** dos minutos.
Hace frío **en** el invierno.

¡Úsalo!

A Get together with a partner. Write the names of the countries you have learned on different cards. Then prepare four sets of cards with the modes of transportation you know: **el coche, el tren, el autobús, el avión, el barco, el taxi.**

Put the cards in two piles, one with the country names and the other with the modes of transportation. Take turns picking a card from each pile and making a sentence with them. Your partner can use a map to tell you if your sentence makes sense or not.

> **MODELO** —**Voy a Perú en tren.**
>
> —**Sí, puedes ir en tren.** *or* **No, no puedes ir en tren.**

B You're in Caracas and you need to get to isla Margarita before 11:00 a. m. Read about your choices in the brochure. Then work with a partner to find a possible itinerary. You have $75 for the trip.

> **MODELO** —**Puedo ir en autobús a Cumaná a las…**

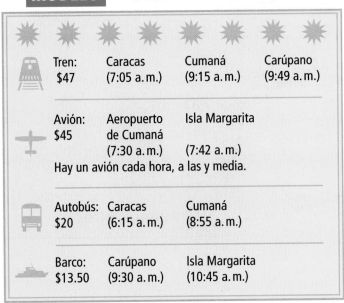

Tren: $47	Caracas (7:05 a.m.)	Cumaná (9:15 a.m.)	Carúpano (9:49 a.m.)
Avión: $45	Aeropuerto de Cumaná (7:30 a.m.)	Isla Margarita (7:42 a.m.)	

Hay un avión cada hora, a las y media.

Autobús: $20	Caracas (6:15 a.m.)	Cumaná (8:55 a.m.)
Barco: $13.50	Carúpano (9:30 a.m.)	Isla Margarita (10:45 a.m.)

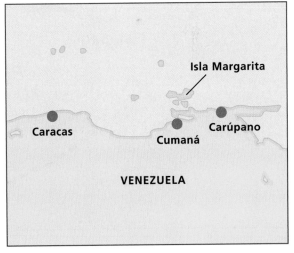

Isla Margarita

Caracas   Carúpano   Cumaná

VENEZUELA

C Miranda is going on a trip. Study her route below. Get together with a partner who closes his or her book while you explain where Miranda is going and how. Your partner draws the route on a map your teacher will give you. Then you close your book while your partner tells you about the return trip. Now, it's your turn to mark her route on the map!

MODELO —Miranda va en avión de Tucson a la Ciudad de México.

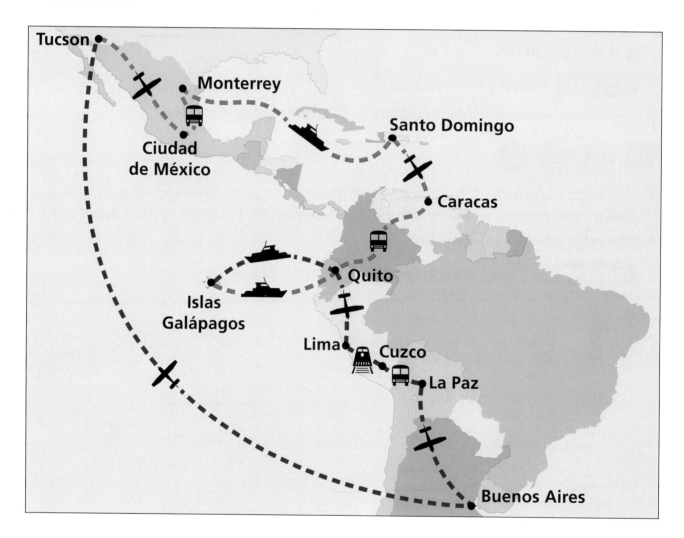

Entre amigos

Read this passage about train travel in Latin America.

Los trenes En muchos países los trenes son un medio de transporte importante. Entre ciudades la gente toma los trenes de una ciudad a otra para visitar a su familia, ir de vacaciones o por razones de trabajo. En las ciudades, la gente puede tomar el metro. El metro es un tren subterráneo. La gente que no vive en la ciudad toma el tren también. Todos los días, el tren lleva a la gente a la ciudad, a las tiendas y a las escuelas.

Now get together in a group with several classmates. Talk about the article, then compare it with train travel in the United States. Look at a map or atlas of the United States.

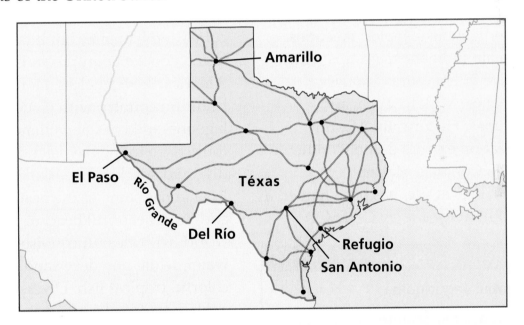

En resumen

Vamos **en** avión.
         barco.
         tren.

¿Dónde se habla español?

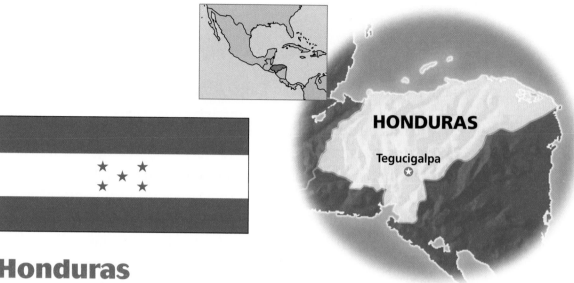

HONDURAS

Tegucigalpa

Honduras

Honduras is the second largest country in Central America. Most of its people are a mixture of Spanish and indigenous peoples: **mestizos.** The main indigenous groups which still live in Honduras are the Tolupanes, Miskito, Pech, and Garifunas. Historically, Mayan civilization extended into Honduras as well. Copán, a Mayan archaeological site, has been named a world heritage site by UNESCO (United Nations Education, Culture, and Science Organization).

Honduras's primary exports are coffee and bananas, but it is still one of the poorest countries in Latin America. Nevertheless, Honduras is a beautiful country with cloud forests, lagoons, and coastal wetlands. Many tourists go to the Bay Islands to scuba dive and snorkel. The island of Roatán has some of the best diving and most beautiful beaches in the world, with clear, turquoise-blue water, white powdery sand, and colorful tropical fish. Divers can explore the coral reef there.

◎◎◎◎◎ Datos ◎◎◎◎◎

Capital: Tegucigalpa

Ciudades importantes: La Ceiba, San Pedro Sula, Trujillo, El Progreso, Choluteca

Idiomas: Español, dialectos indígenas

Moneda: El lempira

Población: 6.6 millones

¡Léelo en español!

Copán: Un centro de los mayas

Primero los olmecas vivieron[1] en Copán, de 900 a.C. hasta 600 a.C. Luego un rey vino[2] con su familia en el año 426. Fundaron[3] la ciudad de Copán y la gobernaron[4] hasta 900 d.C. El centro es grande. Los arqueólogos piensan que 20,000 personas vivían[5] en el valle de Copán en el siglo VIII. Ya los arqueólogos descubrieron más de 3,000 estructuras, y hay más. El centro de las ruinas es la parte principal. Hay sendas[6] con árboles donde se puede caminar para ver las ruinas. La senda va a la gran plaza. En la gran plaza, la Plaza de las Estelas[7], hay muchas estatuas grandes de los gobernadores de Copán. También hay un altar con dibujos del dios de la lluvia, Chac. Otro altar muestra las cabezas de dos serpientes. Hay otra plaza, la Plaza Central. Allí al lado es donde los mayas jugaban su famoso juego de pelota. Al sur está la Escalera de los Jeroglíficos y otro altar que muestra una serpiente con una cabeza humana. También al este están el Templo de las Inscripciones y el Patio de los Jaguares. Hay varios túneles como el Túnel de los Jaguares y las sepulturas.[8] Se puede visitar el Museo de las Esculturas para aprender más sobre las ruinas mayas.

[1] lived   [2] came   [3] They founded
[4] they governed it   [5] lived   [6] trails
[7] monuments   [8] tombs

¡Comprendo!

Answer in English.

Did you visualize Copán as you read the story? Close your eyes for a minute and picture this Mayan town. Now draw the main area as you pictured it. Be sure to include the **Plaza de las Estelas**, the **Plaza Central**, the **Templo de las Inscripciones**, and the **Túnel de los Jaguares.** Draw a compass rose to help you set up the drawing.

5

¡De viaje!

Objetivos

- To talk about travelers
- To talk about planning a trip
- To talk about different travel destinations
- To discuss what you and others do on a typical day
- To discuss what you and others do on vacation
- To learn about tourist attractions in Spanish-speaking countries

Machu Picchu, located in Peru, is a popular tourist spot.

A family checks the departure times of its flight.

Tourists visit La Sagrada Familia in Barcelona, Spain.

¿Sabías que...?

- Latin America offers many sights: snowy mountains, steamy jungles, tropical beaches, and deserts.

- If you travel to Spain, you'll find that they have five languages, not one: **catalán, gallego, valenciano, vasco,** and **castellano** (the one you're learning).

- The highest mountain in the Americas is Mount Aconcagua, on the border between Chile and Argentina. It's about five miles (22,834 feet) high!

- In Central and South America, there are many pyramids and temples left behind by ancient cultures, such as the Mayas, the Aztecs, and the Incas.

Lección 1

¿Cómo se dice?

¿Vas a hacer un viaje?

—¿Adónde quieren viajar ustedes?

—¡Queremos ir a Acapulco porque queremos descansar en la playa!

la agencia de viajes

la playa

descansar

la agente de viajes

el agente de viajes

la viajera

el viajero

EL VIAJE

—Señorita, ¿cuesta mucho un viaje a la playa?

—No, no cuesta mucho. Cuesta seiscientos dólares.

el billete

costar

pagar

 ## CONEXIÓN CON LAS MATEMÁTICAS

Multiplying You're planning a family vacation, and you go to a travel agency. You're still not sure how many people will be able to go, so the travel agent offers you different options. Work with a partner to find the total cost of each trip.

MODELO **El viaje a Miami cuesta…**

✿✿✿✿ Miami ✿✿✿✿	
Billete de avión:	$242 por persona
Hotel:	$75 por noche
Viajeros:	3
Noches:	4

Buenos Aires	
Billete de avión:	$768 por persona
Hotel:	$60 por noche
Viajeros:	5
Noches:	7

Machu Picchu	
Billete de avión: $587 por persona	
Hotel: $20 por noche	
Billete de tren: $35 por persona	
Viajeros: 4	
Noches: 5	

¿Sabías que...?

When traveling by air from Bogotá, Colombia, to Santiago, Chile, passengers on the left side of the plane will see a beautiful view of the snow-capped Andes mountains the whole way.

¡Úsalo!

A The Hernández family wants to go on vacation, so they've decided to visit a travel agency. See how their visit went by completing the dialogue with the correct word in parentheses. Then act out the completed conversation with two classmates.

El Sr. Hernández: Trabajamos mucho todos los días. Queremos (*descansar / pagar*).

La agente: ¿Piensan (*pagar / viajar*) muy lejos?

El Sr. Hernández: Sí. ¿Cuánto va a (*costar / pagar*) un viaje a España?

La agente: ¿Cuántos (*agentes / viajeros*) van a ir?

La Sra. Hernández: Cinco personas van a viajar. Tenemos que comprar cinco (*agencias / billetes*).

La agente: Cinco billetes a España cuestan cuatro mil doscientos cincuenta (*dólares / mapas*).

¿Sabías que...?

Altitude can affect your health. The very high mountains in South America **(los Andes)** frequently cause altitude sickness for travelers. Above 3,000 meters (about 9,800 feet), people who are unaccustomed to high altitudes may develop headaches, nausea, nosebleeds, fatigue, and even an irregular heartbeat or a racing pulse. To avoid this:

- Do not climb more than 2,500 m above sea level in one day.
- After reaching an altitude of 2,500 m, don't climb more than 500 m a day.
- Go to sleep in a place that's lower than the highest altitude reached that day.

B Look at this conversation in a travel agency. It's all mixed up! Work with a partner to rewrite it in the correct order so that it makes sense.

Viajero:	¿Cuánto cuesta el billete de avión?
Viajera:	¿Cómo es México?
La agente de viajes:	Es muy lindo y tiene unas playas muy grandes.
La agente de viajes:	Buenas tardes. ¿Adónde quieren viajar?
Viajera:	El quince de agosto. ¿Cuándo tenemos que pagar?
Viajeros:	Muy bien.
La agente de viajes:	Cuesta 700 dólares. ¿Cuándo quieren ir?
Viajero:	Queremos ir a la playa y descansar.
La agente de viajes:	Pueden ir a México.
La agente de viajes:	El 8 de agosto.

Entre amigos

Ask five people where they want to spend their vacation.

> **—¿Dónde quieres pasar las vacaciones?**
> **—Quiero pasar las vacaciones en Colombia.**

Also ask them how much they think a trip to their destination would cost:

> **—¿Cuánto cuesta un viaje a Colombia?**
> **—Cuesta ochocientos dólares.**

Now get together in a small group and report your findings: **Ana quiere ir a Colombia. El viaje va a costar ochocientos dólares.**

En resumen

el agente de viajes	la agencia de viajes	costar
el billete	la agente de viajes	descansar
el viajero	la viajera	pagar

¿Cómo se dice?

¿Adónde vamos de viaje?

—¿Adónde quieren viajar ellos?

—Ella quiere viajar a la selva. Él quiere viajar a las montañas.

el desierto

el lago

las montañas

la selva

el valle

el volcán

el río

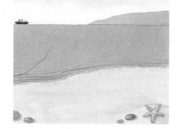

la playa

—¿Cómo son las playas de México?

—México tiene playas muy bonitas, señor.

¡Úsalo!

A Play a quick-draw game with another pair. Get together with a partner and write the new words you have just learned on slips of paper and mix them up. Then get together with another pair and start playing. You pick one word and draw a picture of it for your partner to guess. Then it's your partner's turn. You and your partner have two minutes to guess as many words as you can. The pair that guesses more words wins.

MODELO ¡Es un valle!

B Look at this map and write some questions about it. Then get together with a partner and take turns asking and answering each other's questions.

MODELO —¿Qué es el Tajumulco?

—Es un volcán.

—¿Dónde está el lago Atitlán?

—Está en Guatemala.

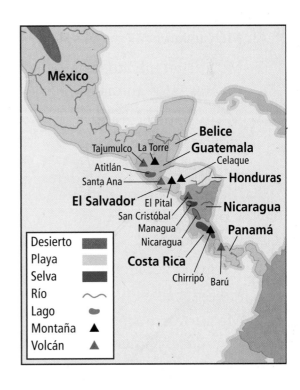

¿Sabías que...?

One of the driest places in the world is the Atacama Desert in northwestern Chile. Some places in the desert go years without rain. Northwestern Mexico also has some very arid regions. This makes the blue waters of the Pacific Ocean that splash against its westernmost shores all the more inviting!

C You are at a travel agency and want to know about vacation options in Latin America. The travel agent makes suggestions. Get together with a partner and take turns playing the vacationer and the travel agent.

Partner A: Explain what you want to do on vacation.

Partner B: Offer a suggestion based on the map.

MODELO —Me gustan descansar y nadar.

—¿Por qué no vas a Puerto Rico?

1. Me gustan los volcanes y los valles.

2. Me gusta el calor y el sol.

3. Me gustan mucho las plantas y los animales.

4. Me gustan las grandes ciudades. Quiero viajar en metro y ver museos.

5. Me gusta mucho nadar y practicar deportes en el agua.

6. Me gusta ver monumentos y lugares históricos.

7. Me gustan mucho el frío y la nieve. ¡Quiero una aventura!

@@@ **Compara** @@@

En inglés	En español
monument	el monumento
historical	histórico

México
Ⓜ

Puerto Rico

Costa Rica

Perú

Argentina

Playa	
Selva	▬
Río	〜
Lago	⬬
Montaña	▲
Volcán	▲
Iceberg	▲
Metro	Ⓜ

Observatories You can travel to a region in Chile with very clear, starry skies perfect for astronomical observation. Many observatories (places with telescopes to watch the sky) have been built there.

Now work with a partner to decide what caption goes with each picture of a space object.

un planeta

una constelación

una estrella

un cometa

◎ ◎ ◎ **Compara** ◎ ◎ ◎

En inglés	En español
observatory	el observatorio
star	la estrella
telescope	el telescopio

Entre amigos

Form a group with two other classmates and choose two destinations that you would like to advertise. Write descriptions of them and illustrate them. Decide what price the tickets should be (you may want to consult prices in a newspaper ad to get an idea).

Then two members of each group go to another group to play the role of the travelers. The group member who stays will play the travel agent. The new groups role-play two would-be travelers talking to the travel agent.

The travel agent will try to interest the travelers in the places on his or her brochure. If you're the travel agent, you might ask questions like these:

¿Adónde quieren ir ustedes?
Señor, usted quiere viajar a Colombia, ¿verdad?

If you're the traveler, you might ask questions like these:

¿Cuánto cuesta el billete?
¿Hay playas cerca de las montañas?

Practice your conversations and present them to the class.

En resumen

el desierto	la playa
el lago	la selva
el río	las montañas
el valle	
el volcán	

¿Cómo se dice?

Talking about things you do and using other common verbs

You've already learned many regular **-ar, -er,** and **-ir** verbs. When you talk about things that you do or about things that are going on now, you say that the verb is in the "present tense."

Visito ciudades.

Descansamos en la playa.

Comemos helados.

Ana **sube** montañas.

Look at this chart to review some regular **-ar, -er,** and **-ir** verbs in the present tense.

	visitar	comer	subir
(Yo)	visit**o**	com**o**	sub**o**
(Tú)	visit**as**	com**es**	sub**es**
(Él, Ella, Ud.)	visit**a**	com**e**	sub**e**
(Nosotros, Nosotras)	visit**amos**	com**emos**	sub**imos**
(Ellos, Ellas, Uds.)	visit**an**	com**en**	sub**en**

You have also learned several common irregular verbs. Look at these sentences. They are also in the present tense.

Soy yo. **Estoy** en Argentina.
Voy a Bariloche en avión.

Es mi hermana Alicia. **Está** en Chile.
Va a Viña del Mar en bicicleta.

Son mis papás. **Están** en Puerto Rico.
Van a la bahía de San Juan en barco.

Somos nosotros. **Estamos** en Perú.
Vamos a Machu Picchu en tren.

Look at this chart to review the present-tense forms of these irregular verbs.

	estar	ser	ir
(Yo)	estoy	soy	voy
(Tú)	estás	eres	vas
(Él, Ella, Ud.)	está	es	va
(Nosotros, Nosotras)	estamos	somos	vamos
(Ellos, Ellas, Uds.)	están	son	van

¡Úsalo!

A Get together with two classmates. Survey them to find out what they do when they're on vacation. Complete a chart like this one.

> **MODELO** —En vacaciones, ¿vas a la playa a nadar?
>
> —Sí. *or* No.

	Yo	Raquel	Tomás
ir a la playa a nadar	✔	✔	✔
leer libros		✔	✔
montar a caballo		✔	
andar en bicicleta			
hablar con los amigos			
pintar			
sacar fotos			

Then report to the class things you all do and things that each person does.

> **MODELO** —Raquel, Tomás y yo vamos a la playa a nadar. Raquel y Tomás leen libros. Raquel monta a caballo.

B Get together with five classmates. Write these places on different cards and mix them up. Each student picks one card. Go around the group saying how you would get to the place on your card. The first person says how he or she would go, the second repeats it and adds his or her own mode of transportation, and so on. If someone can't remember all the preceding sentences, the next person gets to start again.

> **MODELO** —Voy a la playa en coche.
>
> —Tú vas a la playa en coche y yo voy a las montañas en avión.
>
> —Ella va a la playa en coche, tú vas a las montañas en avión y yo voy a la ciudad en autobús.

la playa	las montañas	un lago	visitar a mis abuelos
la ciudad	la escuela	el río	el valle

C Get together with a partner and choose one of these pictures, but don't tell your partner which one. Describe what the person or people are doing and where they are. Your partner has to guess the picture. Then switch roles.

> **MODELO** —Está en un lago. Nada en el lago.
>
> —¿Es Lisa?

1.

Lisa

2.

Sr. y Sra. Vélez

3.

Sr. Alvarado

4.

Tú

5.

Antonio y yo

6.

Rosa y tú

CONEXIÓN CON LOS ESTUDIOS SOCIALES

Geography Look at this map. Take turns with your partner asking and answering the questions.

1. ¿Cómo vas de Estados Unidos a Perú?
2. ¿Qué ciudad es la más importante?
3. ¿Qué ciudades están en la playa?
4. ¿Cuál es el río más importante?
5. ¿Cuál es la carretera más larga?
6. ¿Adónde va el tren?
7. ¿Dónde está el lago Titicaca?

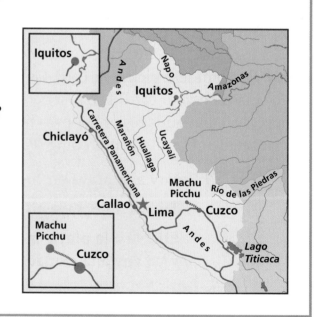

Entre amigos

Get your parents' approval and bring three photos from a vacation to class. You can also draw pictures of a past vacation or of an imaginary one. Include pictures of yourself. Be sure there are different numbers of people in each picture.

Then get together with three partners. Show your photos or drawings. Explain who is in each picture and where you are.

Somos mi hermana y yo. Estamos en el jardín de la casa de mi abuela, en México.

En resumen

	visitar	**comer**	**subir**
(Yo)	visito	como	subo
(Tú)	visitas	comes	subes
(Él, Ella, Ud.)	visita	come	sube
(Nosotros, Nosotras)	visitamos	comemos	subimos
(Ellos, Ellas, Uds.)	visitan	comen	suben

	estar	**ser**	**ir**
(Yo)	estoy	soy	voy
(Tú)	estás	eres	vas
(Él, Ella, Ud.)	está	es	va
(Nosotros, Nosotras)	estamos	somos	vamos
(Ellos, Ellas, Uds.)	están	son	van

¿Cómo se dice?

Using verbs with spelling changes

Do you remember **poder** and **pensar**, two verbs whose stems change when you use them?

—¿**Pue**do viajar a la selva?

—Por supuesto. P**ue**de viajar a Ecuador.

poder (o ➡ ue)

Singular		Plural	
Yo	p**ue**do	Nosotros, Nosotras	podemos
Tú	p**ue**des	Ellos, Ellas, Uds.	p**ue**den
Él, Ella, Ud.	p**ue**de		

Another verb that follows the same pattern as **poder** is **volver,** which means "to return." **Almorzar, probar,** and **costar** also change their stems from **o** to **ue.**

Now look at how to use the verb **pensar.**

—¿P**ie**nsas viajar en el verano?

—No, p**ie**nso estudiar en el verano.

Look at this chart for the forms of the verb **pensar**.

pensar (e ➞ ie)

Singular		Plural	
Yo	p**ie**nso	Nosotros, Nosotras	pensamos
Tú	p**ie**nsas	Ellos, Ellas, Uds.	p**ie**nsan
Él, Ella, Ud.	p**ie**nsa		

Do you remember these two verbs that are the same as **pensar: comenzar** and **cerrar? Querer** is an **-er** verb that follows the same pattern.

¡Úsalo!

A Write down the times when you do these things during a typical day. Then get together with a partner, who will ask you questions and make a schedule of your day. You'll do the same for your partner.

Compare the schedule your partner made with your original one, to see if it's right!

MODELO —¿A qué hora comienzan tus clases?

—Mis clases comienzan a las ocho de la mañana.

> **pensar levantarse**
> **comenzar tus clases**
> **almorzar (tú y tus amigos)**
> **pensar ir a la biblioteca**
> **comenzar a estudiar**
> **cerrar los libros**
> **comenzar tu programa favorito**
> **poder acostarse**

B What's a typical day like for you and your classmates? Take turns asking and answering these questions with a partner.

MODELO —¿Puedes visitar a tus amigos todos los días?

—Sí, puedo. *or* No, no puedo.

1. ¿Puedes mirar la televisión todas las noches?
2. ¿Pueden tus amigos y tú hablar una hora por teléfono?
3. ¿Almuerzan tus amigos y tú en la casa o en la escuela?
4. ¿Cuánto cuesta el almuerzo en la escuela?
5. ¿Vuelves a la casa temprano o tarde?
6. ¿Puedes mirar programas de televisión a las once de la noche?

C These are Paula's notes as she plans her vacation. Get together with a partner. Look at Paula's notes and say what she's planning to do. Write down your sentences. See which pair comes up with more logical sentences based on her notes.

MODELO Paula piensa ir a Argentina. Quiere viajar...

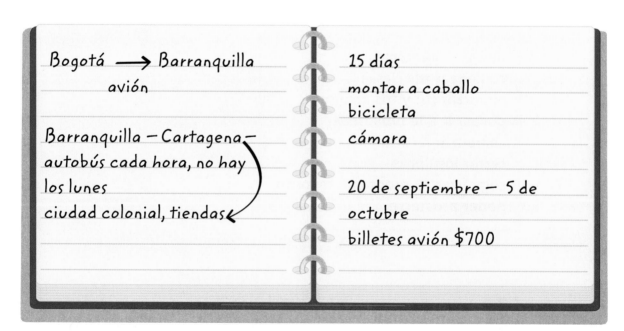

Bogotá ⟶ Barranquilla
avión

Barranquilla – Cartagena –
autobús cada hora, no hay
los lunes
ciudad colonial, tiendas

15 días
montar a caballo
bicicleta
cámara

20 de septiembre – 5 de
octubre
billetes avión $700

Entre amigos

Answer these questions about a vacation you would like to take. Be creative! You may choose places you have seen in this unit or any other place that appeals to you.

Now interview a partner about his or her vacation plans. Take notes (in Spanish!) of his or her answers.

¿Adónde piensas ir en las vacaciones?
¿Cómo piensas viajar?
¿Qué puedes hacer en _____ ?
¿Cuántos días piensas estar en _____ ?
¿Cuándo vuelves?
¿Cuánto cuesta tu viaje?

Turn your notes about your partner's plans into a short written report. Yours might begin like this:

Miguel piensa ir a la playa en California. Piensa ir a California en avión. En la playa puede...

En resumen

	o → ue **poder**	e → ie **pensar**
(Yo)	p**ue**do	p**ie**nso
(Tú)	p**ue**des	p**ie**nsas
(Él, Ella, Ud.)	p**ue**de	p**ie**nsa
(Nosotros, Nosotras)	podemos	pensamos
(Ellos, Ellas, Uds.)	p**ue**den	p**ie**nsan

¿Dónde se habla español?

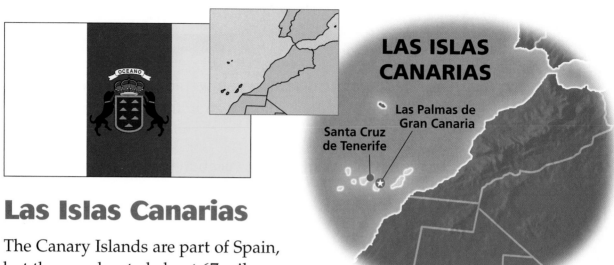

LAS ISLAS CANARIAS

Las Palmas de Gran Canaria

Santa Cruz de Tenerife

Las Islas Canarias

The Canary Islands are part of Spain, but they are located about 67 miles off the western coast of Africa. Only seven of the thirteen islands are inhabited, and these are divided into two provinces. The Canary Islands have rich soil and the perfect year-round climate for vacationers from Spain and many foreign countries. In fact, in some restaurants and cafés, you are more likely to hear English or German spoken than Spanish.

The islands are mountainous, and many are volcanic. The highest peak in Spain, Mt. Teide (12,162 feet), is a dormant volcano in Tenerife. Teide means "snowy mountain" in the language of the Guanches, the first inhabitants of the islands. It is always covered with snow—even in the summer—yet it is not far from the beach, where the water temperature is 72°F. Even though Spaniards on the islands speak Spanish, on La Gomera, some of them can also communicate with each other by whistling!

⊚ ⊚ ⊚ ⊚ Datos ⊚ ⊚ ⊚ ⊚

Santa Cruz de Tenerife

Capital: Santa Cruz de Tenerife

Islas de la provincia de Santa Cruz de Tenerife: La Gomera, Hierro, La Palma, Tenerife

Las Palmas

Capital: Las Palmas de Gran Canaria

Islas de la provincia de Las Palmas: Fuerteventura, Gran Canaria, Lanzarote

Tenerife Beach

¡Léelo en español!

Las Islas Canarias La historia de las Islas Canarias es muy interesante y muchas personas visitan las islas. Los antiguos romanos llamaban[1] las islas "Canaria" por la palabra del latín *canis*, que significa "perro", porque había[2] muchos perros en las islas. También había pequeños pájaros amarillos—los canarios—en las islas. Los guanches, personas altas y rubias[3]—son los indígenas de las islas.

En el siglo[4] XV, las islas formaban[5] parte del reino[6] de Castilla. Cristóbal Colón pasó por[7] la isla de La Gomera antes de su primer viaje[8] a América.

Siempre hace buen tiempo en las islas, y por eso hay mucho turismo. A los turistas les gustan las islas porque brilla el sol y las playas son fantásticas.

View of El Teide volcano from La Gomera Island

[1] called   [2] there were   [3] blond   [4] century
[5] formed   [6] kingdom   [7] passed by   [8] trip

¡Dónde se habla español?

Recognizing Cognates

Before you read the selection, look for cognates. Recognizing cognates will make the reading easier for you. What do you think these words mean: **romanos, turismo?** Use these cognates to help you understand what is being said about the Canary Islands.

¡Comprendo!

Answer the following questions on a sheet of paper.

1. Why are the Canary Islands a popular tourist destination?

2. Who were the original inhabitants of these islands?

3. Why did the Romans call the islands "Canaria"?

4. What famous explorer passed by the islands?

5. Why do you think the Canary Islands have been important to Spain?

6

Un viaje en avión

Passengers board a plane in Santo Domingo, Dominican Republic.

Objetivos

- To name people, places, and things related to air travel

- To learn a few expressions you can use when traveling by air

- To talk about what you and others do and say

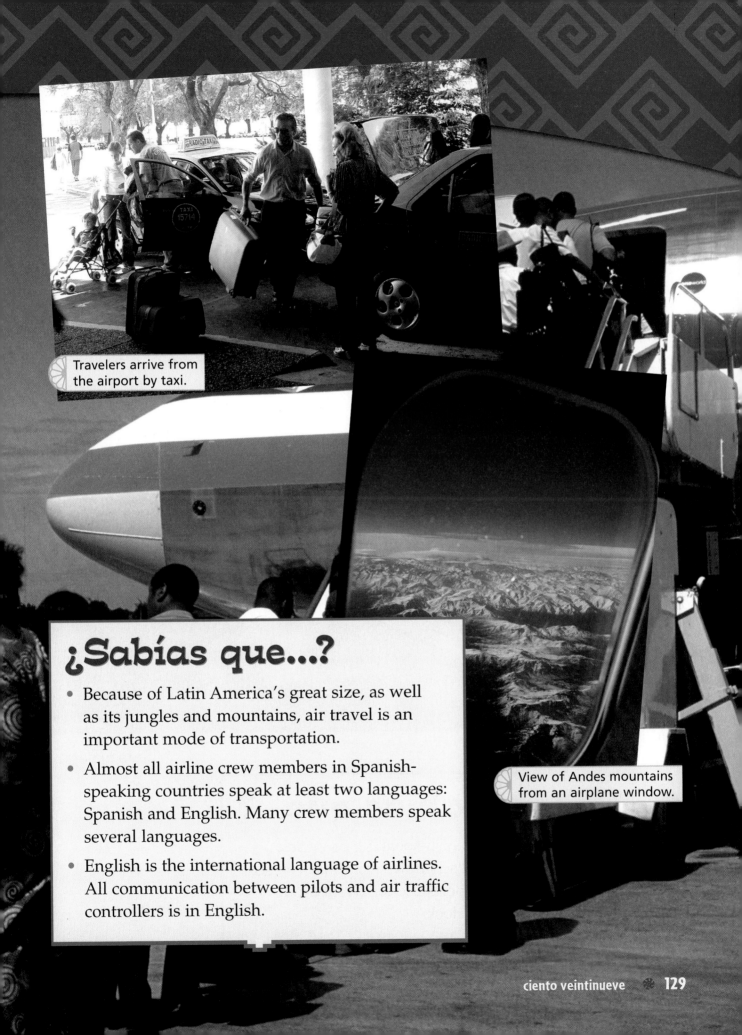

Travelers arrive from the airport by taxi.

¿Sabías que...?

- Because of Latin America's great size, as well as its jungles and mountains, air travel is an important mode of transportation.

- Almost all airline crew members in Spanish-speaking countries speak at least two languages: Spanish and English. Many crew members speak several languages.

- English is the international language of airlines. All communication between pilots and air traffic controllers is in English.

View of Andes mountains from an airplane window.

¿Cómo se dice?

¿Vas con esta línea aérea?

—¿Vas con esta línea aérea?

—Sí. Tenemos que hacer fila con los otros pasajeros.

—¿Tienes tu equipaje?

—Sí, aquí está mi maleta.

el horario

la línea aérea

hacer fila

el equipaje

la maleta

¿Sabías que...?

In Spanish-speaking countries, travel schedules like those you see in airports use the twenty-four-hour clock.

—¿Qué está haciendo la asistente de vuelo?

—Está hablando con un pasajero.

el piloto

la asistente de vuelo

el pasajero

la pasajera

el asistente de vuelo

la piloto

los asientos

 # CONEXIÓN CON LAS MATEMÁTICAS

Weight Limits When you travel, there's a weight limit to your luggage. If your bags are too heavy, you have to pay a fee. According to the fees established by this airline, how much additional money will these passengers have to pay? Work with a partner to find the answer. Then share your findings with the class.

Two suitcases: free up to 50 pounds
Third suitcase: $40
Fourth suitcase: $80
51 pounds to 70 pounds: $25
71 pounds to 100 pounds: $80

80 lb

55 lb

65 lb

40 lb

Sra. Estévez

Sr. Gómez

MODELO La Sra. Estévez tiene una maleta de cuarenta libras y… Tiene que pagar …

¡Úsalo!

You're telling your partner about your plane trip to Chile. But you have jet lag, because the sentences are coming out all wrong! Read these mixed-up sentences to your partner who needs to replace the wrong word with the right one from the list. Take turns saying and correcting the sentences.

asistentes de vuelo	maleta	pasajero	línea	horario
asistente de vuelo	equipaje	pilotos	fila	

MODELO   —En el aeropuerto, voy a la piña aérea chilena.

—En el aeropuerto, vas a la línea aérea chilena.

1. Primero tengo que hacer lista porque hay mucha gente.

2. El número del vuelo está en el gimnasio.

3. Pongo mi manzana pequeña debajo del asiento.

4. En este viaje no llevo mucho horario.

5. Los vuelos ayudan a los pasajeros.

6. Hay dos pizarrones en el avión. Ellos saben volar.

7. El avión lleva una maleta muy grande.

8. Pido un jugo de naranja al piloto.

Entre amigos

Have a "list race." Your teacher will give you and a partner two minutes to list people, places, and things found in an airport. Work together to list as many as you can. Spell the items correctly and use **el** or **la** to show whether each item is masculine or feminine. After two minutes, stop and check your lists. The pair of students with the longest correctly-written list wins.

CONEXIÓN CON LOS ESTUDIOS SOCIALES

Time Zones If you make a phone call at 5 p. m. from the United States to Spain, your Spanish friends may have already gone to sleep. That's because Spain is in a different time zone, so it's much later there! Because of the Earth's rotation, days start earlier the further east you go.

Here are the time differences between some cities.

Caracas: Nueva York + 2 horas　　**Santiago de Chile: Los Ángeles + 4 horas**

La Paz: Chicago + 2 horas　　**Madrid: México, D. F. + 7 horas**

Look at this chart. Based on these passengers' departure time, figure out the arrival time **(la llegada)** for each of these people or groups. Write your answers and share them with a partner. See if the answers match.

		SALIDA	DURACIÓN DEL VUELO	LLEGADA
Aurelio	Madrid—México, D. F.	8:10	10 horas, 45 minutos	
Julia	Nueva York—Caracas	13:30	5 horas	
Los García	Los Ángeles—Santiago de Chile	21:45	4 horas	

MODELO　Aurelio llega a México, D.F. a las…

◎ ◎ ◎ Compara ◎ ◎ ◎

En inglés	En español
duration	la duración

En resumen

el asistente de vuelo	la asistente de vuelo	hacer fila
el equipaje	la línea aérea	
el horario	la maleta	
el pasajero	la pasajera	
el piloto	la piloto	

¿Cómo se dice?

¿Llega a tiempo el vuelo?

—¿El avión está volando ahora?

—No, todavía no vuela. Va a despegar en un minuto.

despegar
El avión despega.

volar
El avión vuela.

aterrizar
El avión aterriza.

El asiento es **cómodo**.

El asiento es **incómodo**.

—¿Llega a tiempo el vuelo?

—En realidad, va a llegar temprano.

—¡No me digas! Siempre llega tarde.

Llegadas		
Vuelo	Hora	Puerta de embarque
516 Madrid	1:45	F6
101 París	3:15	
265 Frankfurt	3:50	

Salidas		
Vuelo	Hora	Puerta de embarque
753 Buenos Aires	2:15	G10
611 Dallas	2:35	G14
302 Miami	3:25	

El vuelo número cinco dieciséis **llega** a las dos menos cuarto.

El vuelo número seis once **sale** a las tres menos veinticinco.

¿Sabías que...?

If you fly to La Paz, Bolivia, be sure to take some deep breaths. The airport there is about 12,000 feet above sea level, making it one of the highest airports in the world!

¡Úsalo!

A The airport is really busy! Choose one of these planes and write down its color, but don't tell your partner which you selected. Your partner asks you questions to guess which one you chose. Then switch roles. Continue until you have talked about all the planes.

> **MODELO** —¿Qué hace el avión?
>
> —El avión está despegando.
>
> —¿Es el avión rojo?
>
> —Sí. *or* No.

B Sara is going to fly from Dallas to Mexico City. Look at her boarding card. Work with a partner and take turns asking and answering the questions.

1. ¿En qué línea aérea vuela Sara?
2. ¿Cuál es su número de vuelo?
3. ¿Cuál es su puerta de embarque? ¿A qué hora es el embarque?
4. ¿A qué hora sale el vuelo?
5. ¿A qué hora va a llegar el vuelo a México, D. F.?

Línea aérea: Fast Airlines

Línea aérea: Fast Airlines

Número de vuelo:	FA 0835
Puerta de embarque:	9
Hora de embarque:	12:40 h
Hora de salida:	13:25 h
Destino:	México, D.F.
Hora de llegada:	16:00 h

Entre amigos

Make your own plane boarding pass. You can go anywhere you want! Look at the boarding pass on page 136 for ideas.

Write the city and the time of departure, as well as your destination and the time of arrival.

Now, imagine that you're at the airport and you run into a classmate who is also traveling. What would you say? Write some questions you'd ask—you can use the ones below as a guide and write some others. Then, get together with a partner and role-play the scene at the airport.

¿Adónde vas?
¿A qué hora sale tu avión?
¿Cuál es tu puerta de embarque?
¿Con qué línea aérea viajas?

¿Sabías que...?

Planes take longer to fly from Europe to the United States than from the United States to Europe. This is due to winds from the west that speed planes up on the way east and slow them down on the way from east to west.

En resumen

El asiento es	cómodo. incómodo.	El avión **sale** a las tres. El avión **llega** a las cinco.	
El avión	despega. vuela. aterriza.	la llegada la puerta de embarque la salida	
El vuelo llega	temprano. a tiempo. tarde.		

¿Cómo se dice?

Talking about things you do

Look at the following scene and read the paragraph that describes it. As you read, pay attention to the various uses of **hacer**.

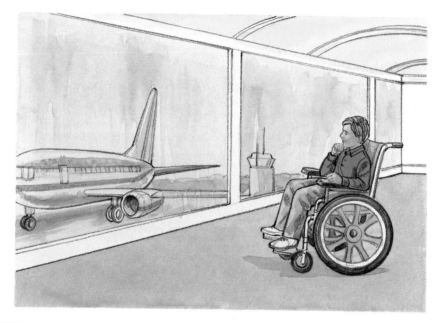

Hace mal tiempo hoy. Los otros pasajeros y yo **hacemos** fila para subir al avión. **Hago** un viaje para ver a mis tíos. Ellos viven en California. Mis tíos siempre **hacen** muchos planes. Pensamos **hacer** un viajecito a Wonderlandia. ¡Qué emoción!

Now look at the chart to see the different forms of **hacer** in the present tense.

hacer

Singular	
Yo	hago
Tú	haces
Él, Ella, Ud.	hace
Plural	
Nosotros, Nosotras	hacemos
Ellos, Ellas, Uds.	hacen

¡Úsalo!

A Make a chart showing which of these activities you do, and where and when you do them. Then ask your partner about each of the things on the list. Switch roles.

hacer fila	hacer los quehaceres	hacer viajes
hacer la cena	hacer huevos revueltos	hacer chocolate caliente

> **MODELO** —¿Haces fila?
>
> —Sí, a veces hago fila en el cine y en la tienda.

Now get together with another pair and tell them what you and your partner do, and when and where you do these things. Remember to use the **nosotros** form to talk about things that you both do.

> **MODELO** —Paula hace fila en el cine y en la tienda. Hacemos los quehaceres los fines de semana en el dormitorio.

CONEXIÓN CON LOS ESTUDIOS SOCIALES

Crafts Look at this map with a partner. Write sentences about who makes which crafts.

> **MODELO** Los guatemaltecos hacen huipiles.

México
los alebrijes

Guatemala
los huipiles

Panamá
las molas

B It's the annual arts and crafts fair at your school and everyone's making something! Work with a partner. Take turns asking what these people are making and answering according to the pictures.

> **MODELO** —¿Qué hace Andrés?
>
> —Hace un pájaro de papel.

Andrés

1.

Amalia

2.

Jorge

3.

Pedro y Teresa

4.

Sr. Rivera

5.

Eva

C What do you do at school? Work with a partner. For three minutes, write as many things as you can that you do in class and at school. The pair who writes more sentences wins! Remember that you don't always need to use the word **hacer**.

> **MODELO** Hacemos dibujos. Vamos a la clase de matemáticas. Jugamos al fútbol.

CONEXIÓN CON EL ARTE

Collage What's the weather like where you live? Get together with three classmates. Create a four-part collage of the seasons where you live. Divide a poster into four parts and assign one part to each group member.

You can paste cutouts from magazines, drawings, and real objects on your poster. Under each season, write what the weather is like.

MODELO **En verano hace calor.**

Entre amigos

Sit in a circle with a group. Each student in turn asks the student to his or her left: **¿Qué haces en tu tiempo libre?** ("What do you do in your free time?") Choose a recorder to take notes of the group's answers.

No answer should be repeated! Everyone must think of an answer.

Remember that many—even most—answers won't contain **hacer.**

> —**¿Qué haces en tu tiempo libre?**
> —**Monto a caballo.** *or* **Juego al fútbol.**

Report your group's answers to the class. Talk about what different students do in their free time.

En resumen

	hacer
(Yo)	ha**go**
(Tú)	haces
(El, Ella, Ud.)	hace
(Nosotros, Nosotras)	hacemos
(Ellos, Ellas, Uds.)	hacen

Lección 4

¿Cómo se dice?

Talking about saying things

The verb for "to say" or "to tell" is **decir.** Look at these pictures and sentences to see how to use it.

Siempre **digo** la verdad.
No me gustan las galletas.

Nunca **decimos** mentiras.
No nos gusta la película.

—¿Qué **dice** la asistente de vuelo?
—**Dice** que vamos a despegar
muy pronto.

—¿Qué **dicen** los chicos?
—**Dicen** que somos inteligentes
y simpáticas.

Decir is an irregular verb. Did you notice that the **yo** form ends in **-go**, and that the **e** changes to **i** in most of the forms?

Did you also notice that in the answers to the two questions, the word **que** follows a form of **decir?** Use **que** whenever a form of **decir** is followed by an explanation of whatever you or someone else is saying.

Now look at the chart to see the different forms of **decir** in the present tense.

decir

Singular	
Yo	digo
Tú	dices
Él, Ella, Ud.	dice
Plural	
Nosotros, Nosotras	decimos
Ellos, Ellas, Uds.	dicen

¿Sabías que...?

Spanish speakers use the verb **decir** for many different things!

- When Spanish speakers say something in error and want to correct it, they often use the word **digo.** For example: **Quiero llegar a las siete, digo, a las ocho.** It's similar to when you say "I mean" to correct something that you just said.

- When Spanish speakers are surprised, they may say **¡No me digas!** ("You don't say!")

- Some Spanish speakers answer the telephone by saying **¿Diga?** Others may say **¿Aló?, ¿Sí?,** or **Oigo** ("I hear you") when answering the telephone.

¡Úsalo!

A Choose any topic and write three sentences that are true and three that are false. Next to each sentence write if it is true (**verdadero**) or false (**falso**).

Then read your sentences to a partner—but don't give yourself away! Your partner has to guess whether you're telling the truth (**la verdad**) or a lie (**una mentira**). Switch roles after you have finished reading your sentences and saying whether your partner is right or not.

> **MODELO** —**Voy a viajar a España en verano.**
>
> —**Dices una mentira.**
>
> —**Sí, digo una mentira.** *or* **No, digo la verdad.**

Entre amigos

Conduct a travel survey among four of your classmates. Ask them ten questions. You may use the ones below and add to them, or make them all up. Make a chart like this one to keep track of their answers.

	Rosa	Javier	Antonio	Cristina
¿Te gusta viajar?	Sí	Sí	Sí	No
¿Te gustan el frío y la nieve?				
¿Te gusta la playa?				
¿Quieres viajar en avión o en tren?				
¿Quieres ir a México o a Argentina?				

Then get together with a different partner and report what everyone says.

> **Rosa, Javier y Antonio dicen que les gusta viajar. Cristina dice que no le gusta viajar.**

B Your partner wants to write a script based on this comic strip **(el cómic)**, but without looking at the book! Your partner will ask you who is in each panel and what each person says, and then try to come up with the correct script. Switch roles for each panel.

> **MODELO** —¿Quién está en el cómic?
>
> —La piloto y la asistente de vuelo.
>
> —¿Qué dice la piloto?
>
> —Dice que van a despegar tarde.

La piloto: Vamos a despegar tarde.

En resumen

	decir
(Yo)	digo
(Tú)	dices
(El, Ella, Ud.)	dice
(Nosotros, Nosotras)	decimos
(Ellos, Ellas, Uds.)	dicen

¿Dónde se habla español?

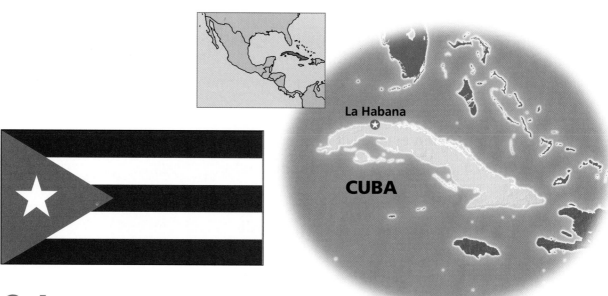

La Habana

CUBA

Cuba

Cuba is located just ninety miles from the coast of Florida. Cuban culture is a mixture of Spanish, African, and indigenous cultures. These influences are seen in many aspects of Cuban life—its religion, music, food, and the arts. In Cuban music, you might hear drums like the **conga,** the **bongo,** or the **bata.** The **maraca,** a type of rattle, comes from pre-Hispanic indigenous groups. The **tres** and **cuatro** are special types of guitars. A very popular Cuban dish is roast pork with **congri** (black beans and rice cooked together) and yucca or **tostones** made out of plantain. Sugar cane was brought to Cuba by the Spanish explorers and continues to be a major crop. Tourism is becoming more and more popular on the island.

◎ ◎ ◎ ◎ Datos ◎ ◎ ◎ ◎

Capital: La Habana

Ciudades importantes: Guantánamo, Pinar del Río, Santiago de Cuba, Cienfuegos

Idiomas: Español

Moneda: El peso cubano

Población: 11.2 millones

¡Léelo en español!

José Martí (1853–1895)

José Martí es el héroe nacional de Cuba. Es un poeta y escritor. Antes de 1898, Cuba pertenecía[1] a España. José Martí quería la independencia de España para la gente de Cuba. Escribió y publicó[2] un periódico para hablar del movimiento de independencia. El gobierno lo echó[3] del país por sus ideas. Vivió y trabajó para la libertad de la gente de Cuba desde otros países, como los Estados Unidos. Era[4] un gran líder y escritor. Todavía es un símbolo de la libertad. Los cubanos lo admiran y lo honran. Cuba finalmente ganó su independencia en 1898.

Fidel Castro (1926–)

Fidel Castro es el líder actual[5] de Cuba. En los años 1950 a muchas personas no les gustaba[6] el dictador Batista, el líder de Cuba. En 1953 Castro y 119 personas más atacaron[7] a los soldados en la ciudad de Santiago de Cuba. Perdieron, pero continuaron luchando[8] por un nuevo gobierno. Por fin, en 1959, Che Guevara, Camilo Cienfuegos y Castro tomaron control del gobierno de Cuba. Castro llegó a ser Presidente. Establecieron un gobierno socialista y comunista. Hasta hoy Castro no permite democracia, sólo comunismo.

[1] belonged   [2] published   [3] kicked him out
[4] He was   [5] present-day   [6] they didn't like
[7] attacked   [8] they kept fighting

¿Dónde se habla español?

Reading Strategy

Focused Reading The readings talk about two famous and important people for Cubans. They both fought for the rights of the Cuban people. As you read, write brief notes about what you learn about each man. Since each reading talks about the past of each man, the verbs you see are in the past tense.

Recognizing Cognates What do you think these words mean: **poeta, movimiento, líder, admiran, socialista, comunista, democracia?** Use these cognates to help you understand what is being said.

Durante estos últimos años hay muchos problemas entre los Estados Unidos y Cuba. Pero para algunas personas de Cuba, Fidel Castro es un líder y héroe.

¡Comprendo!

Answer in English.

Using the notes you took on each person, make a list of what you know about each. Compare the two leaders.

1. What was each fighting for?

2. What tactics did each use?

3. Did each leader succeed?

4. How do Cubans feel about each?

En el hotel

Objetivos

- To name things you find in hotels
- To talk about items you and others need
- To talk about what you and others do
- To discuss different daily routines
- To learn about hotels in Spanish-speaking countries

Hotel Cleopatra in
Tenerife, Spain

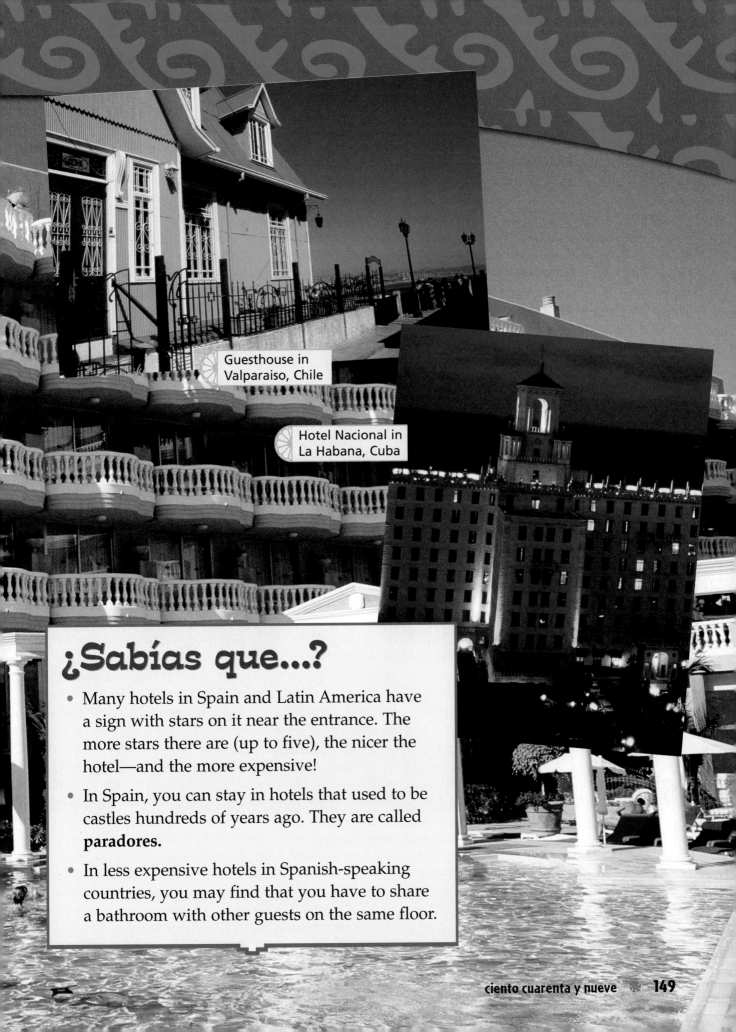

Guesthouse in Valparaiso, Chile

Hotel Nacional in La Habana, Cuba

¿Sabías que...?

- Many hotels in Spain and Latin America have a sign with stars on it near the entrance. The more stars there are (up to five), the nicer the hotel—and the more expensive!

- In Spain, you can stay in hotels that used to be castles hundreds of years ago. They are called **paradores.**

- In less expensive hotels in Spanish-speaking countries, you may find that you have to share a bathroom with other guests on the same floor.

¿Cómo se dice?

¿Necesitan un cuarto?

—¿Necesitan un cuarto, señor?

—Sí, queremos una habitación grande lejos del ascensor.

—¿Es su primera visita a nuestro hotel, señor?

—Sí, somos turistas. Somos estadounidenses.

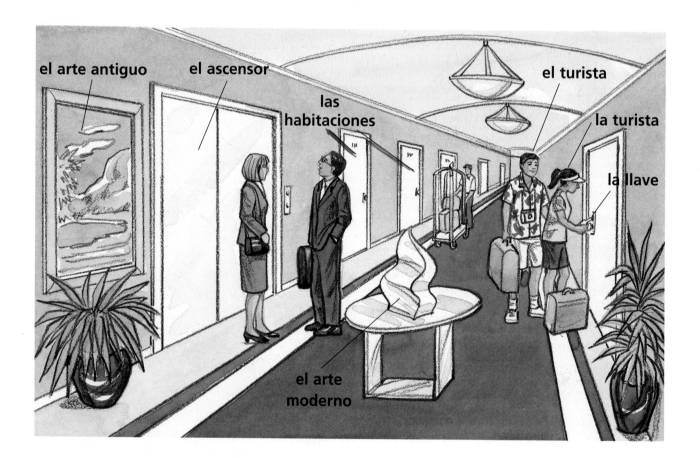

el arte antiguo

el ascensor

las habitaciones

el turista

la turista

la llave

el arte moderno

—Este hotel es muy moderno.

—Sí, pero a mí me gustan más los hoteles antiguos.

CONEXIÓN con el ARTE

Paintings Discuss with a partner which of these paintings you like best. Refer to colors, shapes, objects, or ideas these works make you think of.

> **MODELO** ¿Cuál es el cuadro más moderno y cuál es el más antiguo?
>
> ¿Te gusta más el arte antiguo o el moderno?

"Guernica," Pablo Picasso

"Las Meninas," Diego Rodriguez de Silva y Velazquez

¡Úsalo!

A Read the sentences in the left column to a partner. Your partner has to find a related sentence in the right column and read it to you.

1. El Hotel Plaza tiene muchos años.
2. Juana viaja a Honduras a descansar.
3. ¿Por qué no puedes abrir la puerta?
4. A Carlos le gusta viajar.
5. No quiero subir las escaleras.
6. Nuestro hotel tiene un año, señor.
7. Son turistas.

a. Es muy moderno.
b. ¿Quieres usar el ascensor?
c. Es un turista.
d. Es una turista.
e. No tengo la llave de mi habitación.
f. Es un hotel antiguo.
g. Llegan de Estados Unidos.

B Look at the people in this hotel lobby. Write five sentences they could be saying. Read your sentences to a partner. Your partner has to guess who is saying each one. Then it's your turn to guess who's saying each of your partner's sentences.

MODELO —No me gusta el arte moderno.

—¿Es el hombre del suéter verde?

CONEXIÓN CON LAS MATEMÁTICAS

Adding and Dividing You work for a hotel, and you're in charge of arranging for the hotel buses to pick up some tourists at the airport. There are twenty-three tourists coming from Venezuela, seventeen from Spain, and twelve from Nicaragua. Each hotel bus holds twelve people. How many buses do you need? Tell your partner about the people you will put on each bus.

MODELO —En el autobús uno, van a ir doce turistas venezolanos...

Entre amigos

Imagine how exciting it is to walk into a hotel in a foreign city for the first time!

Prepare a skit with three or four classmates about going to a hotel. You might play the roles of a family of tourists or a group of foreign exchange students. You could also divide your group between arriving tourists and people who work at the hotel.

Begin the skit at the point when you are just getting out of the taxi or bus. Stop when you are just about to enter your hotel room. Your teacher will look at the skit to help with dialogues and make suggestions.

Your group will complete the skit in the next **Entre amigos** activity.

En resumen

el arte antiguo	la habitación
el arte moderno	la llave
el ascensor	la turista
el turista	

Lección 2

¿Cómo se dice?

¿Qué hay en la habitación?

 —¡Mira las sábanas que tienen las camas! ¡Son muy bonitas!

—Sí, pero las camas son muy blandas.

—¿Qué hay en el cajón?

—¡Hay tarjetas postales! Podemos escribir a nuestros amigos.

—¿Cómo está el agua en la ducha?

—¡Bastante caliente! ¿Me puedes dar una toalla?

—Sí, claro.

la ducha

las toallas

el agua caliente

el agua fría

el jabón

la bañera

¿Sabías que...?

In Spanish-speaking cities and towns, you can find small inns called **pensiones** or **fondas,** something like bed-and-breakfast inns in the United States, where the owners also live. These are usually cheaper than large hotels, and they're often more pleasant to stay in.

¡Úsalo!

A Take turns with a partner saying what problems there are in this hotel room and what the person needs.

Partner A: Read the problem.

Partner B: Say what the first person needs.

> **MODELO** —**Quiero dormir pero tengo frío.**
>
> —**Necesitas una manta.**

1. Tengo las manos muy sucias.

2. No hay nada en la cama.

3. Quiero escribir a mis amigos.

4. Tengo mucho sueño.

5. Quiero descansar pero la cama es muy dura.

6. Necesito secarme después de lavarme.

B You have some complaints about your hotel room. Read the complaints in Column A to your partner, who must answer with a solution from Column B.

A	B
En mi habitación no hay toallas.	Ahora traigo una manta.
Necesitamos sábanas.	Puede abrir la ventana.
No hay jabón en el cuarto de baño.	¿Quiere una habitación diferente?
No puedo dormir porque tengo frío.	Claro. Ahora traemos las sábanas.
La cama es muy blanda.	Voy a traer jabón ahora.
Hace calor.	Ahora traen las toallas.

Entre amigos

Continue preparing the skit your group began in the last **Entre amigos.** Now the travelers enter their hotel room or rooms.

What do they have to say? Are they happy with what they've found or not? How does the hotel staff respond?

Besides the hotel itself, the tourists might talk about their clothes, their luggage, the view they can see from their rooms, or their plans for later in the day.

Once you're happy with your script, practice your parts and present your skit to the class. You can make it more interesting by bringing in a few props and costumes from home!

¿Sabías que...?

Hotels are more common than motels in Latin America. Travel between cities and towns is mainly by bus or train, so there is no great need for motels along highways. Are there more motels or hotels near where you live?

En resumen

el jabón

la bañera
la ducha
la manta
la sábana
las tarjetas postales
las toallas

blando   blanda
duro   dura
frío   fría

caliente

¿Cómo se dice?

Talking about daily routines

You've already learned a number of verbs that let you talk about your daily routines, like **bañarse,** "to take a bath," and **ponerse,** "to put on." Here's how to use **dormirse,** which means "to fall asleep." Look at the chart.

Singular			
	ponerse	**bañarse**	**dormirse (o ➡ ue)**
Yo	me pongo	me baño	me duermo
Tú	te pones	te bañas	te duermes
Él, Ella, Ud.	se pone	se baña	se duerme
Plural			
Nosotros, Nosotras	nos ponemos	nos bañamos	nos dormimos
Ellos, Ellas, Uds.	se ponen	se bañan	se duermen

All three of these verbs are reflexive verbs. When you use them, be sure to use the pronouns that correspond to the correct form: **me, te, se,** and **nos.**

Me pongo la ropa.

Te bañas.

Se duerme.

¡Úsalo!

A Get together with a partner. Make one set of cards with the expressions below, shuffle them, and put them in a pile facedown. Draw two cards. Ask your partner which of the two activities he or she does first. Hand your partner the corresponding card. Take turns drawing the cards until they are all gone from the pile.

> **MODELO** —¿Qué haces primero, te secas o te cepillas los dientes?
>
> —Primero me cepillo los dientes.

secarse	lavarse la cara
cepillarse los dientes	bañarse
ducharse	ponerse la ropa
peinarse	quitarse el pijama
despertarse	irse de casa
levantarse	ponerse el pijama
acostarse	quitarse la ropa
dormirse	ponerse los zapatos

B Get together with three classmates and use the cards from the previous activity. Take turns picking a card and acting out the activity. Your classmates have to guess what you're doing! The first one to answer correctly gets the card. The one with the most cards at the end wins.

> **MODELO** —¡Te bañas!
>
> —Sí, me baño. *or* No, no me baño.

C Use these verbs to write the order in which you do these things during the day. Then read your sentences to a partner. Your partner has to find differences between your routine and his or her own.

> **MODELO** Primero, me levanto.

despertarse	quitarse la ropa	peinarse
dormirse	acostarse	secarse
irse de casa	ponerse el pijama	ir a la escuela
desayunar	levantarse	ponerse la ropa
bañarse	volver a casa	ducharse
cenar	quitarse el pijama	

Now come up with things you both do in the same order.

> **MODELO** Primero nos levantamos.

 # CONEXIÓN CON LA SALUD

Fire Safety If you've ever stayed in a hotel, you may have noticed an emergency exit plan on the back of the door. Look at this list and decide which tips are useful during a fire, and which are not. Then prepare a fire safety poster for your classmates with the useful tips.

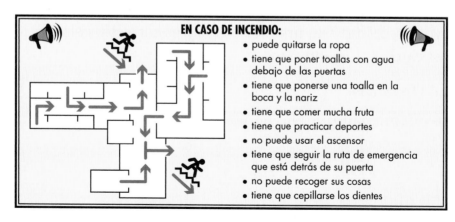

EN CASO DE INCENDIO:
- puede quitarse la ropa
- tiene que poner toallas con agua debajo de las puertas
- tiene que ponerse una toalla en la boca y la nariz
- tiene que comer mucha fruta
- tiene que practicar deportes
- no puede usar el ascensor
- tiene que seguir la ruta de emergencia que está detrás de su puerta
- no puede recoger sus cosas
- tiene que cepillarse los dientes

Entre amigos

What if you went on a group trip and didn't have to stick to a schedule? You'd probably end up doing some things on your own and some things with your friends.

Get together with three or four classmates. Come up with some ideas for an ideal day on a group vacation. Plan your day from morning until evening. Talk about it as if it were happening right then. Include some things that you do on your own and some things you do together. For example:

Me levanto a las seis y media.
Carol se levanta a las siete y cuarto.
A las ocho, Carol y yo tomamos el desayuno en el comedor.
¡Felipe se levanta a las once!

Share your day with other groups. Ask and answer questions about what happens on your imaginary trips.

En resumen

	bañarse	ponerse	dormirse (o → ue)
(Yo)	me baño	me pongo	me duermo
(Tú)	te bañas	te pones	te duermes
(Él, Ella, Ud.)	se baña	se pone	se duerme
(Nosotros, Nosotras)	nos bañamos	nos ponemos	nos dormimos
(Ellos, Ellas, Uds.)	se bañan	se ponen	se duermen

¿Cómo se dice?

Talking about special action verbs

Many of the verbs you've been using are stem-changing verbs. You've studied several whose stems change from **e** to **ie,** and others whose stems change from **o** to **ue.** You've also learned about verbs whose stems change from **e** to **i,** and finally, verbs whose stems change from **u** to **ue.** Look at these sentences to see if you recognize all these different types of verbs.

—¿**Juegas** al fútbol?
—Sí, **juego** todos los días.

—¿No **quieres** cereal?
—No, sólo **quiero** la toronja.

—¿Ustedes **piden** café?
—Nunca **pedimos** café.

—¿A qué hora **almuerza** ella?
—Siempre **almuerza** a las doce.

Can you tell which verb's stem changes from **e** to **i?** Which verb's stem changes to **ue?**

For all these verbs, in which form does the stem not change?

¡Úsalo!

A Look at this crazy hotel. Everyone seems to need something! Get together with two classmates. Write the room numbers on slips of paper and put them in a bag. (Use **la entrada** for the lobby.) Then draw two slips of paper each. Tell your group what the people in your rooms ask for. They have to guess the room number.

> MODELO —**Pide una toalla.**
>
> —**¿Es la habitación 317?**
>
> —**No.**

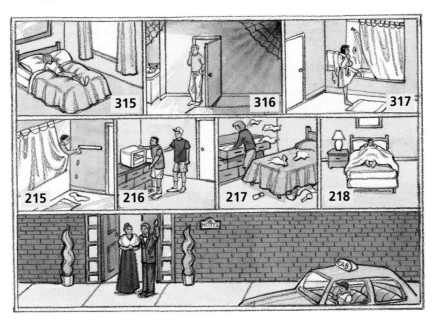

B Get together with three classmates and create a set of ten verb cards. Each of you picks a verb: **querer, jugar, almorzar,** or **pedir** and writes it on one side of the cards. Then you add a person (**yo, tú, él, ella, usted, nosotros, nosotras, ellos, ellas, ustedes**) to each verb. On the other side, write the correct form, such as **quiero** for **querer (yo).**

Take turns showing the first side of the card to the person on your right and having him or her say the correct form. If the person gets it right, he or she gets the card. The person with the most cards at the end wins.

C You're enjoying your vacation at a great hotel on the beach. Below is a schedule of activities. List one activity for each of your relatives, friends, and yourself. Then get together with a partner and explain what each person does.

> **MODELO** **Mi padre juega al golf a las diez de la mañana.**

Actividades	
8:00 a.m. ir de pesca	12:30 p.m. almorzar hamburguesas
10:00 a.m. jugar al golf	2:45 p.m. jugar al dominó
10:00 a.m. montar a caballo	4:15 p.m. jugar al volibol
12:30 p.m. almorzar pescado en la playa	4:15 p.m. ir a clase de salsa

Now compare lists with your partner to see who will do the activities together.

> **MODELO** **Nuestros padres juegan al golf a las diez de la mañana.**

D Get together with a partner. Your teacher will assign one of the lists to you. Cover the other one with a piece of paper. Write an example for each item.

A	B
1. Un libro que quieres leer	**1.** Un programa que quieres ver
2. Una ciudad que quieres visitar	**2.** Una cosa que quieres comprar
3. Una persona que quieres conocer	**3.** Un deporte que quieres practicar
4. Una cosa que quieres hacer	**4.** Una lengua que quieres estudiar
5. Un país al que quieres viajar	**5.** Una comida que quieres comer

Then close your book and exchange the lists of examples with your partner. You have to guess what your partner wants to do with each example.

> **MODELO** *—Moby Dick*
>
> *—¿Es un libro que quieres leer?*
>
> *—Sí, es un libro que quiero leer.*

@ @ @ **Compara** @ @ @	
En inglés	**En español**
program	el programa
language	la lengua

CONEXIÓN CON LA **SALUD**

Balanced Meals Now's your chance to create a lunch menu that an airline will serve on its flights!

Look through magazines and newspapers for different types of food. Make sure to use some foods from each food group. Cut out the pictures and "make" two balanced lunch options by gluing the pictures to a paper plate.

Present your plates with the different foods to the class. Explain what the choices are and what you think passengers will ask for.

| MODELO | Los pasajeros pueden almorzar espaguetis o pollo. Los niños piden los espaguetis con albóndigas. |

Entre amigos

Get together with three classmates and prepare an itinerary for a group of tourists. Decide on the age of your clients and where you're going. Make a five-day itinerary for them. What places will you visit? What modes of transportation will you use? What activities will you do?

Each group will present its trip, and the class will vote for the best one!

En resumen

	u ➡ ue jugar	e ➡ ie querer	e ➡ i pedir	o ➡ ue almorzar
(Yo)	juego	quiero	pido	almuerzo
(Tú)	juegas	quieres	pides	almuerzas
(Él, Ella, Ud.)	juega	quiere	pide	almuerza
(Nosotros, Nosotras)	jugamos	queremos	pedimos	almorzamos
(Ellos, Ellas, Uds.)	juegan	quieren	piden	almuerzan

¿Dónde se habla español?

España y las Américas

Christopher Columbus received money from Queen Isabella of Spain so that he could sail west to India and Asia in search of a better trade route. However, instead of Asia, he found himself in the Caribbean Sea, on a continent until then unknown to Europeans!

After that famous first voyage in 1492, Spain financed Columbus on three more voyages to the Americas. On his four voyages, Columbus explored the Caribbean and claimed Cuba, Hispaniola (the island that is now shared by Haiti and the Dominican Republic), Puerto Rico, and other lands for Spain. He was followed by other Spaniards who led expeditions through most of Central America, South America, and much of the southern half of the United States. Much of their influence can still be seen today in the architecture, language, and customs of the inhabitants of these areas. Did you know that state names like Texas, Nevada, and Florida are originally Spanish words?

Datos

October 12, 1492: Columbus lands in San Salvador, Bahamas.

1493–1496: Columbus's second voyage lands in Hispaniola.

1498: Columbus's third voyage lands in Trinidad.

1502: Columbus's fourth voyage lands in Honduras.

1521: Hernán Cortés establishes Mexico City.

1535: Francisco Pizarro establishes Lima, Peru.

1515–1521: Ponce de León explores Florida.

1539–1542: Hernando de Soto explores the Southeast from the Mississippi to Arkansas.

1540–1542: Francisco Vásquez de Coronado explores the Southwest.

1565: The Spanish establish the city of St. Augustine, Florida.

1609: The Spanish establish the city of Santa Fe, New Mexico.

1706: The Spanish establish the city of Albuquerque, New Mexico.

1700s: Spanish missionaries establish missions throughout California as far north as San Francisco.

¡Léelo en español!

Los conquistadores Después de Cristóbal Colón, muchos españoles llegaron a las Américas. Vinieron por su religión, el oro[1] y la aventura. Hernán Cortés conquistó[2] a los aztecas de México en 1519. Francisco Pizarro conquistó a los incas en 1533 cuando capturó la capital de Cuzco. Juan Ponce de León exploró Florida en 1515. Luego los españoles fundaron[3] la ciudad de San Agustín, Florida, en 1565, muchos años antes de la llegada de los ingleses a Plymouth Rock.

En el sureste de los Estados Unidos, Hernando de Soto exploró la región al oeste del río Misisipí hasta Arkansas. En el suroeste, Francisco Vásquez de Coronado exploró los territorios de Nuevo México, Arizona y parte de Colorado en nombre de España. Los misioneros católicos pusieron muchas misiones en estos territorios y en toda California hasta San Francisco.

[1] gold   [2] conquered   [3] founded

Using What You Know Use your knowledge of American history to help you understand this reading. Tell a partner or your teacher what you already know about Spanish explorers who came to the Americas. Read the chart on page 166 carefully for clues to better understand the reading.

Recognizing Cognates What do you think these words mean: **religión, aventura, capturó, exploró, territorios?** Use these cognates to help you understand what is being said.

¡Comprendo!

The following statements are false. Rewrite them to make them true.

1. The English Pilgrims were the first to establish a city in what is now the United States.

2. Most Spanish explorers came to the Americas in search of fertile farmland.

3. Catholic missionaries conquered the Incas in 1533.

4. Christopher Columbus established Spanish settlements all along the coast of California.

8

Nuestro dinero

Objetivos

- To name people and things found in banks and restaurants
- To learn how to talk about giving things to other people
- To learn to talk about things that happened in the past
- To learn about money used in Spanish-speaking countries
- To learn about currency exchange rates

Bolivianos, the currency of Bolivia

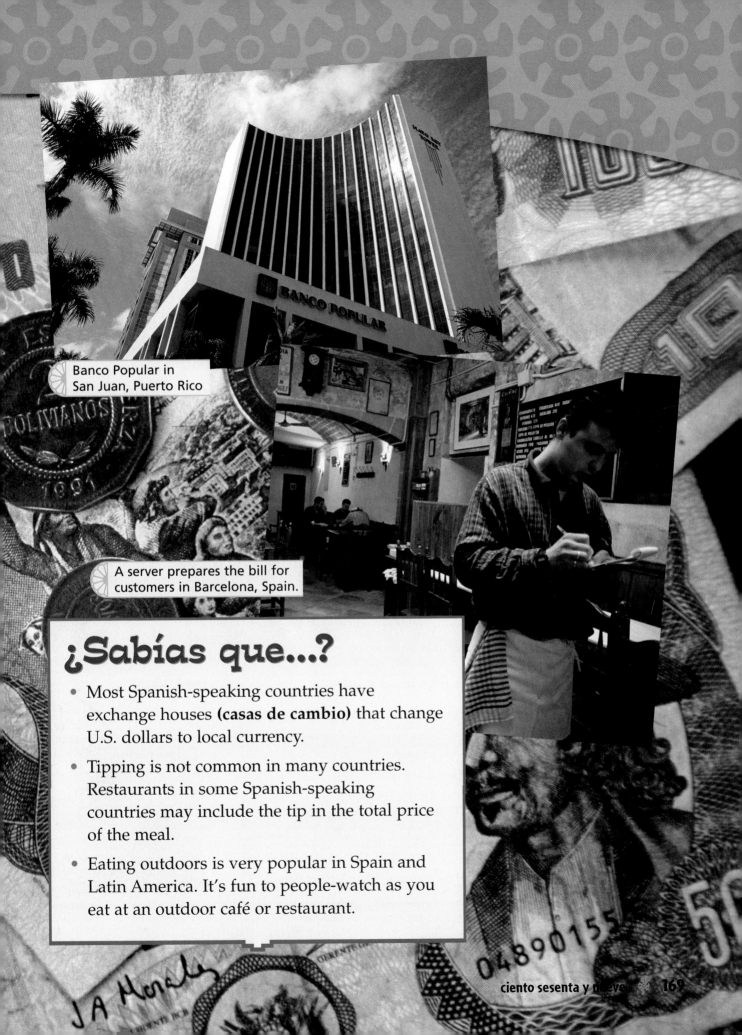

Banco Popular in
San Juan, Puerto Rico

A server prepares the bill for
customers in Barcelona, Spain.

¿Sabías que...?

- Most Spanish-speaking countries have exchange houses **(casas de cambio)** that change U.S. dollars to local currency.

- Tipping is not common in many countries. Restaurants in some Spanish-speaking countries may include the tip in the total price of the meal.

- Eating outdoors is very popular in Spain and Latin America. It's fun to people-watch as you eat at an outdoor café or restaurant.

¿Cómo se dice?

¿Vas a cambiar dinero?

—¿Puedes cambiar dinero en este banco?

—¡Claro! Vamos, hay una ventanilla abierta a la izquierda.

—¿Qué vas a pedir a la cajera?

—Billetes de cien pesos y algunas monedas.

el banco

la cajera

la ventanilla

el cajero

abierta

cerrada

el cajero automático

las monedas

la tarjeta de crédito

el cheque

los billetes

¿Sabías que...?

Since the year 2000, many countries in Europe use the same kind of currency: the euro. Now you can travel to Spain, France, Italy, Germany, and other countries without having to exchange money! The euro symbol looks like this: €

—¿Qué vas a hacer con el dinero?

—Voy a gastarlo, por supuesto.

—Yo prefiero ahorrar mi dinero.

¿Me puede **cambiar** el billete, por favor?

Quiero **ahorrar** mi dinero para comprar una bicicleta.

No quiero **gastar** mucho dinero en la chaqueta.

¡Úsalo!

A Do you prefer spending your money or saving it? Get together with a partner and look at these prices. Take turns saying either that you want the item and prefer spending your money, or that you don't want it and prefer saving.

> **MODELO**   Botas negras: $85.00
> —¿Unas botas negras por ochenta y cinco dólares?
> —Sí, quiero las botas. Prefiero gastar el dinero.
> *or* No quiero las botas. Prefiero ahorrar el dinero.

1. Un avión: $1,000,000.00

2. Una camiseta: $20.00

3. Un libro: $12.00

4. Una bicicleta moderna: $655.00

5. Un radio: $40.00

6. Un televisor viejo: $15.00

7. Un viaje a la selva: $5,000.00

8. Una semana en un hotel nuevo: $1,100.00

B Get together with a partner. One of you will read out loud the problems in Column A. The other will look for a solution in Column B.

A.

1. Tengo que hablar con la cajera.
2. Tengo dinero en el banco.
3. Tengo que traer billetes para comprar el libro.
4. Quiero jugar a los juegos electrónicos en la tienda.
5. La ventanilla del banco está cerrada.

B.

a. Necesitas monedas.
b. Puedes pagar con un cheque.
c. Puedes ir al cajero automático.
d. Tienes que volver mañana.
e. Vas al banco.

C Get together with a partner. Take turns saying what form of payment (**monedas, billetes, cheque** or **tarjeta de crédito**) you would use for these.

MODELO —Pago con monedas.

1.

2.

3.

4.

5.

6.

CONEXIÓN CON LAS MATEMÁTICAS

Multiplying With a partner, study this chart of currencies in some Spanish-speaking countries:

País	Nombre	Subdivisión
España	euro	100 céntimos
Guatemala	quetzal	100 centavos
México	peso mexicano	100 centavos
Panamá	balboa	100 centésimos
Paraguay	guaraní	100 céntimos
Perú	nuevo sol	100 centavos
Venezuela	bolívar	100 céntimos

Bring in the foreign exchange table from a newspaper. Now practice buying some of the foreign currency at the current rate. To buy the foreign currency, multiply the number of dollars by the rate given for the other currency. You'll probably need a calculator. One of you can play the banker, the other the customer.

MODELO —**Tengo cien dólares. ¿Cuántos pesos mexicanos puedo comprar?**

—**Usted puede comprar (cien mil) pesos mexicanos, señora (señor).**

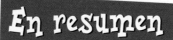 ## En resumen

el banco	la cajera
el cajero	las monedas
el cajero automático	la tarjeta de crédito
el cheque	
los billetes	la ventanilla abierta
	cerrada
ahorrar ⎫	
cambiar ⎬ dinero	
gastar ⎭	

¿Cómo se dice?

¿Te gusta el restaurante?

 —¿Te gusta el restaurante?

—¡Sí! Tiene un menú interesante y la camarera es muy simpática.

el restaurante

el camarero

la cuenta

la camarera

el menú

la propina

 —¿Vas a pedir la cuenta?

—Sí, y voy a darle a la camarera una buena propina.

¿Sabías que...?

On the 29th day of each month, restaurants in Argentina serve **ñoquis** (an Italian dish). People often place a bill under the plate, hoping that this traditional gesture will bring them more money!

¡Úsalo!

A Look at these conversations and pictures. Which ones go together? Take turns with a partner and match each picture with the correct conversation.

A

—Tengo mucha hambre.

—Yo también.

—¿Qué vas a comer?

—Me gusta todo. Este menú tiene platos buenos.

B

—¿Cuánto es?

—Veinte euros. Voy a dejar un euro de propina.
  El camarero es muy simpático.

C

—Por favor, ¿nos puede traer un vaso de agua
  y la cuenta?

—Claro que sí.

D

—¿Qué van a almorzar?

—Quiero sopa y luego pollo.

—Yo, ensalada, luego espaguetis con albóndigas.

—Y de beber, queremos agua.

B Test your memory! Look closely at this picture of a restaurant. Work with a partner and list all the names of items and people that you know in the picture. Then your partner closes the book and you ask questions about where the items are. After five questions, switch roles. See who can get more questions right.

MODELO —¿Dónde está la sal?

—Detrás del pollo.

 CONEXIÓN CON EL **ARTE**

Design Now is your chance to set up your own restaurant! Think about what kind of restaurant you'd like to have. Discuss these questions with four classmates and then design a menu with descriptions and pictures of some of the dishes you will serve. Present your menus to the class and be prepared to answer the questions below.

¿Cómo va a ser el restaurante?
¿Cómo van a ser los camareros?
¿Cómo van a ser los menús?
¿Cuántas mesas va a tener el restaurante?

Entre amigos

Get together with several classmates and put on a skit, either about a scene in a bank or a scene in a restaurant.

If you decide on the bank, one person can play the teller, and the others can be customers. Or one of you can be the bank manager, who comes to talk with the teller. Props are easy. Use play money, pieces of paper for bank forms, and so on.

If you decide on the restaurant, you could be a group sitting down for a meal and ordering from the servers, then asking for the bill, and paying. You can use the menu that you made for the last **Conexión** activity. For props, use table settings, trays, aprons, and pictures of food.

Write a good script! Rehearse! On with the show!

¿Sabías que...?

In the United States, we're used to ordering each course of a meal separately. Restaurants in Spanish-speaking countries often offer a **menú del día.** This includes everything from soup to dessert, and it gives you two or three choices for some courses. Ordering this way is usually less expensive than ordering individual items.

En resumen

el camarero
el menú
el restaurante

la camarera
la cuenta
la propina

¿Cómo se dice?

Talking about giving things to others

The verb "to give" is **dar.** Look at these sentences to see how to use it.

Siempre les **doy** la mano a mis amigos.

¡A mamá siempre le **damos** un dolor de cabeza!

¡Sólo nos **da** unas monedas!

Ustedes me **dan** dos libros.

Did you notice that, in these examples, **dar** is used with **me, le, nos,** and **les?**

Use **me** if the gift is for you, **te** if it is for a friend you are speaking to, and **le** if it is for another person. Use **nos** if you and someone else are receiving it, and **les** if two people you are talking to are receiving it or if several other people are.

Now study the chart of the verb **dar.**

dar

Singular	
Yo	doy
Tú	das
Él, Ella, Ud.	da
Plural	
Nosotros, Nosotras	damos
Ellos, Ellas, Uds.	dan

What other verb do the forms of **dar** resemble: **estar, ir,** or **ser?**

Dar is used in many expressions. **Dar la mano** means "to shake hands." **Dar un paseo** means "to go for a walk." What do you think **dar las gracias** means?

¡Úsalo!

A Make cards with six restaurant items that you know. Then get together with a partner. Ask your partner to give you a certain item. If your partner has it written on a card, he or she has to give it to you. Take turns and continue until one of you has no cards left! The winner is the one holding all the cards.

Partner A: Ask for something that you find in a restaurant.

Partner B: Say whether you'll give it to your partner or not.

MODELO —¿Me das un vaso?

—Sí, te doy un vaso.
or No, no te doy un vaso.

¿Sabías que...?

Some other common expressions with **dar** are:

darse prisa *to hurry up*
dar miedo *to be scary*
darse la vuelta *to turn around*
dar un abrazo *to give someone a hug*

B Courtesy makes life a little nicer. In what ways could you be courteous in these situations? Take turns asking and answering these questions with a partner.

> **MODELO** —La asistente de vuelo te trae un vaso de agua. ¿Qué haces?
>
> —Le doy las gracias.

1. El cajero les da los billetes a ustedes. ¿Qué hacen?
2. La camarera te sirve la cena. ¿Qué haces?
3. El dueño del hotel me trae toallas limpias. ¿Qué hago?
4. Tú le das una propina al taxista. ¿Qué hace él?

C Think of situations in which people do what's listed below. Fill out a chart like this one for yourself. Then interview two classmates and add their answers.

> **MODELO** —¿Quién le da dolores de cabeza a tu mamá?
>
> —Mis hermanos y yo, a veces.

¿Quién... ?	yo	Raúl	Sandra
dar dolores de cabeza (a tu mamá)	mis hermanos y yo	el perro	
dar las gracias (a ti)			
dar la mano (a tu papá)			

Now, get together with a different group and talk to them about the answers on your chart.

> **MODELO** Mis hermanos y yo le damos dolores de cabeza a mi mamá.
>
> El perro le da dolores de cabeza a la mamá de Raúl.

CONEXIÓN CON LOS ESTUDIOS SOCIALES

Jobs Do you know what people do in their jobs?

Write down three different occupations, such as **la maestra, el taxista, la médica,** or **el cajero.** Write each occupation on a separate slip of paper.

Put everyone's slips of paper into a bag. Divide the class into two teams and stand facing each other. Choose one team to go first. Only one student at a time speaks for each team.

Your teacher will pick a slip of paper from the bag and read it. If it says, for example, **el cajero,** the student whose turn it is has five seconds to say something that **el cajero** would normally give to someone.

> **MODELO**   **El cajero me da billetes de cinco dólares.**

Then it's the other team's turn. Anyone who goes over the time limit or gives a wrong answer must sit down. The team with the last person standing wins.

◎ ◎ ◎ Compara ◎ ◎ ◎

En inglés	En español
medicine	la medicina

En resumen

	dar		
(Yo)	doy	a mí	me da
(Tú)	das	a ti	te da
(Él, Ella, Ud.)	da	a él, ella	le da
(Nosotros, Nosotras)	damos	a nosotros, nosotras	nos da
(Ellos, Ellas, Uds.)	dan	a ustedes, ellos, ellas	les da

¿Cómo se dice?

Talking about actions in the past

Look at these pictures and sentences. Can you tell what these people are talking about?

Gasté un dólar en un bolígrafo.

Gastaste seis dólares en un libro.

Gastó siete dólares en el almuerzo.

Gastamos veinte dólares en pantalones cortos.

Gastaron doce dólares en una camisa.

In all these examples, the people are talking about spending money in the past. You use **gasté** to say that you spent something, **gastaste** to tell a friend that he or she spent something, and **gastamos** to say that you and someone else spent something.

Similarly, you use **gastó** to say that someone else spent something, and **gastaron** to say that more than one person spent something. All these forms of the verb **gastar** are in the past tense.

Here are the forms of **gastar** in the past tense.

Singular		Plural	
Yo	gasté	Nosotros, Nosotras	gastamos
Tú	gastaste	Ellos, Ellas, Uds.	gastaron
Él, Ella, Ud.	gastó		

What ending do you use if you're talking to a friend about what he or she spent yesterday? What ending do you use if you're talking to more than one friend?

Since **gastar** is a regular **-ar** verb, once you learn how to use all the past-tense endings with it, you can use any other regular **-ar** verb in the past tense, like **cambiar** and **ahorrar.**

To make it easier to talk about things you and others did in the past, certain words are very helpful.

Ayer caminé en el parque.
Habló con Ricardo **la semana pasada.**
Ahorramos mucho dinero **el año pasado.**

Ayer means "yesterday," and **la semana pasada** means "last week." What does **el año pasado** mean?

CONEXIÓN CON LAS MATEMÁTICAS

Addition This is Sara's credit card statement. Look at her expenses **(los gastos)** and answer the questions with a partner.

❄ ‖‖‖‖ ‖‖ ‖‖‖‖‖‖‖	‖‖‖‖ ‖‖ ‖‖‖‖‖‖ ‖‖‖‖ ‖‖ ‖‖‖‖‖‖‖
Sara Fernández	Cuenta # XXXX–XXXX–XXXX–0203

Fecha	Gastos
29/09/2004	$65.75 Supermercado Mendoza
28/09/2004	$73.24 Zapatos Muñoz
26/09/2004	$87.54 Restaurante Lila
22/09/2004	$9.64 Libros para ti

¿Cuánto gastó Sara el 29 de septiembre? ¿Cuánto gastó Sara el 22 de septiembre? ¿Cuánto gastó Sara la semana del 22 al 29 de septiembre?

¡Úsalo!

A Did you spend any money last week? Estimate how much money you spent each day and on what. Fill out a chart like this one. Then get together with a partner and take turns asking each other how much you spent and what you bought. If you didn't spend money last week, talk about the last time you went shopping or bought something.

	Yo	Mi compañero/a
lunes	$40 / zapatos	
martes		
miércoles		
jueves		
viernes		

MODELO —¿Cuánto dinero gastaste el lunes?

—Gasté cuarenta dólares.

—¿Qué compraste?

—Unos zapatos nuevos.

When you finish, add up what you and your partner spent each day. Tell the class how much money you both spent each day.

MODELO El lunes gastamos cien dólares.

B What was your schedule like last week? Make up a five-day chart of your week. Then get together with two classmates. Tell what you did.

Use these words or others you know:

estudiar	lavar	nadar	mirar	caminar
gastar	ahorrar	ayudar	cambiar	planchar
descansar	comprar	limpiar	bailar	cocinar

MODELO La semana pasada planché cinco blusas.

Entre amigos

Set up your own "store" in the classroom! Can you beat your competitors' prices?

Get together with three classmates. Look through magazines and newspapers for items that fall into one of these categories and cut them out. After you have items for all five categories, put a price tag on each one!

zapatos   suéteres   libros   camisetas   pantalones

You and your classmates will circulate around the room and compare prices. Note how much each item costs at the different "stores." After looking at all the offerings, pick the three items you prefer, in terms of their price and style.

Then you report to the class what you bought, how much you spent, and how much you saved compared to a different store!

Compré un suéter rojo y unos zapatos de deporte nuevos. Gasté treinta y cinco dólares. Ahorré catorce dólares.

En resumen

	gastar
(Yo)	gast**é**
(Tú)	gast**aste**
(Él, Ella, Ud.)	gast**ó**
(Nosotros, Nosotras)	gast**amos**
(Ellos, Ellas, Uds.)	gast**aron**

ayer
la semana pasada
el año pasado

¿Sabías que...?

When writing dates, Spanish speakers usually write the day first, rather than the month. Watch out so you don't get confused! For example, for October 8, they write 8/10 rather than 10/8, which is more common in the United States.

¿Dónde se habla español?

México: Los mayas y los aztecas

Many different indigenous civilizations flourished in Mexico over the last several thousand years. Each group established a ceremonial center where people worshipped their gods and where their leaders, usually priests, instructed them. Unfortunately, much of the information about these groups was destroyed by the Spaniards, who thought the natives were pagans when they observed their customs.

Some of the best-known civilizations are the Toltecs, whose center was Tula; the Mixtecs and Zapotecs, whose centers were Mitla and Monte Albán, Oaxaca; the Aztecs, whose center was Tenochtitlan; and the Mayas, whose centers were Chichen Itza and Uxmal. The **Museo de Antropología** in Mexico City tells the story of these and other indigenous people.

Datos

300 B.C.: Beginning of Teotihuacan civilization in the Valley of Mexico

A.D. 200–750: Beginning of Classical Mexican civilizations: Teotihuacan in the Valley of Mexico, Monte Alban in Oaxaca

300–900: Classical Mayan civilization

600: Huari and Tiahuanaco peoples in the Andes

950: Beginning of the Toltec civilization in Tula, Mexico; invasion of the Mayan city of Chichen Itza

1325: Aztec capital of Tenochtitlan founded

1428–1519: Aztec conquests

1519–1522: Defeat of Aztec empire by Cortés

1533: Defeat of Inca empire by Pizarro

¡Léelo en español!

Los mayas Los mayas son personas indígenas que viven en América Central, especialmente en Guatemala y en el sur de México. Entre los años 300 y 900 floreció[1] su civilización. Su capital fue Chichén Itzá y su ciudad ceremonial fue Uxmal. Estas ciudades están en la península de Yucatán.

Los mayas eran[2] buenos arquitectos. Construyeron[3] palacios, observatorios y templos magníficos. También eran artistas. Puedes ver su arte en los dibujos de sus edificios. Desarrollaron[4] un sistema de números y un alfabeto. Observaron el cielo y las estrellas[5] y se interesaron en[6] la astrología.

Los aztecas Los aztecas vivieron en el centro de México. Su capital fue Tenochtitlan, ahora la Ciudad de México. Su ciudad ceremonial se llamaba Teotihuacán. Está cerca de la Ciudad de México. Los aztecas eran buenos agricultores.[7] Cultivaban[8] muchos alimentos, como el maíz y el chocolate. Su líder, Moctezuma, fue amigo de Hernán Cortés. Los aztecas pensaron que Cortés era su dios[9] Quetzalcóatl porque era blanco con barba[10] y llegó en un caballo.

La bandera mexicana tiene un águila[11] sentada en un cacto con una serpiente en su pico.[12] Es un símbolo de los aztecas y de la ciudad de Tenochtitlan.

[1] flourished   [2] were   [3] They built
[4] They developed   [5] stars
[6] they were interested in   [7] farmers
[8] They grow   [9] god   [10] beard   [11] eagle
[12] beak

Reading Strategy

Using Prior Knowledge Use a map of Mexico. Find the cities mentioned in the reading. Have you ever heard of the Mayas or the Aztecs? Share anything you know before beginning to read. Checking maps and sharing information before reading helps you understand better.

Recognizing Cognates What do you think these words mean: **especialmente, península, serpiente, símbolo?** Use these cognates to help you understand what is being said about the Mayas and the Aztecs.

¡Comprendo!

Take a sheet of paper and fold it in half. At the top of one half, write **Los aztecas,** and at the top of the other half write **Los mayas.** List what you learned about each indigenous group under their title. Add additional information if you know something more. Share your results with a partner.

9

De paseo en la ciudad

Objetivos

- To learn the names of more places in a city
- To talk about where people and places are
- To describe how people are feeling and where things are
- To talk about things that happened in the past
- To have a telephone conversation
- To learn more about Spanish-speaking communities

The walled city of Ávila, Spain

El Zócalo square in Mexico City

¿Sabías que...?

- At the heart of Mexico City is **El Zócalo.** It is a huge square surrounded by many government buildings, and a cathedral that is several centuries old.

- As in the United States, many Latin American cities and towns have names that come from their indigenous cultures. Some examples are Tegucigalpa, Honduras, and Cuzco, Peru.

- It's not unusual to find towns in Spain surrounded by thick ancient walls or the ruins of a castle on a hill or mountain.

A city street in Sucre, Bolivia

¿Cómo se dice?

¿Dónde te busco?

—Te veo en la plaza a las cuatro.

—Pero, ¿dónde? La plaza es muy grande.

—Me puedes buscar cerca de la fuente, delante de la alcaldía.

—De acuerdo. Hasta las cuatro.

la plaza

el museo

la alcaldía

1873

la escultura

la fuente

el monumento

¿Sabías que...?

Spanish speakers can use any of the following expressions to say that they agree with you: **De acuerdo, está bien, vale.** They are some ways of saying "okay" in Spanish.

¡Úsalo!

A Imagine that you're visiting Madrid. There are so many sights to see! Make up a schedule of everything you'll do: see the sights, eat, rest, shop, or visit museums. Then get together with a partner. Take turns asking questions about where to find each other at different times.

> **MODELO** —¿Dónde te busco a las diez de la mañana?
>
> —Me puedes buscar en el Museo del Prado.
>
> —De acuerdo. Te veo en el Prado.

martes
10:00 Museo del Prado
14:30 Plaza Mayor
16:00

Plaza Mayor

Plaza de Cibeles

Parque de Retiro

Museo del Prado

B Several people in this picture are supposed to meet someone—but they can't find each other! You and a partner should pretend you're two of these people. Say where you are and describe an article of clothing you're wearing. Then role-play two people at a time until everyone in the picture has been identified.

> **MODELO** —Hola. Estoy en la plaza, delante de la fuente. Llevo una falda roja. ¿Dónde estás? No te veo.
>
> —Estoy detrás de la alcaldía.

¿Sabías que...?

The Arabs who ruled Spain for seven centuries were masters of architecture. In the hottest parts of the country, they created buildings with cool, refreshing patios, where they could sit and rest. In fact, the cool water running through these patios was the world's first air conditioning. You'll find many such patios in the city of Córdoba, Spain.

CONEXIÓN CON LOS ESTUDIOS SOCIALES

City Planning Here's your chance to be a master city planner! You're going to work with three or four of your classmates to design a beautiful plaza. Where will you put everything? Decide among yourselves and make a rough sketch. Here are just a few things you might include in your plaza.

jardines	calles	museos	fuentes
esculturas	monumentos	aceras *(sidewalks)*	

Can you think of others? Don't forget about trees **(los árboles)** and bushes **(los arbustos)**! And don't forget about benches **(los bancos)** so people can sit and enjoy the view!

Here's a sample plan for a plaza:

Once your group has worked out a rough sketch, make the final version with paint or markers on butcher paper or posterboard. Label the different parts of the plaza.

Talk about your plaza with the other groups. How are your plazas alike? How are they different? Use your plaza designs to decorate the classroom.

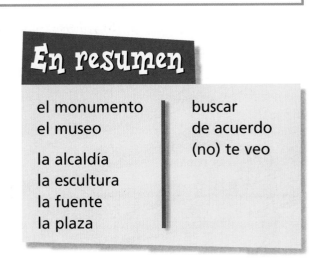

En resumen

el monumento	buscar
el museo	de acuerdo
	(no) te veo
la alcaldía	
la escultura	
la fuente	
la plaza	

¿Cómo se dice?

¿Qué otros lugares hay en la comunidad?

—¿Hay un mercado al aire libre cerca de tu escuela?

—No, pero hay un supermercado muy cerca.

el edificio de apartamentos

el supermercado

el estadio

el zoológico

el mercado al aire libre

el metro

¡Úsalo!

A Where do you go when you want to do or see the following things? Take turns with a partner reading these activities and saying where you do them.

> **MODELO** comprar frutas y verduras
>
> —Voy al mercado al aire libre.

1. comprar cereal
2. ver animales
3. ver jugadores de béisbol
4. vivir en un apartamento
5. llegar a un lugar sin coche
6. aprender
7. ver esculturas y arte
8. ver al médico

CONEXIÓN CON LAS CIENCIAS

Fauna You're working at the zoo, and you have to decide what building each of these animals goes in! The four buildings you're in charge of house mammals, reptiles, amphibians, and birds. Work with a partner to make a chart with these categories, and decide which animals go where. The names for many animals are cognates, so you should be able to figure them out.

Mamíferos	Reptiles	Anfibios	Aves

> **MODELO** El leopardo va en el edificio de los mamíferos.

el conejo	el flamenco	el loro	la salamandra	el cardenal
el oso	el canario	el perro	el ratón	la serpiente
el cocodrilo	el tigre	el gorila	la rana *(frog)*	la tortuga

B Sit in a circle with five classmates and study the picture for a few minutes. One student holds a ball and has to name a place in the picture while throwing the ball to a classmate. The one who catches the ball has to repeat what the first student said, and add another place name.

MODELO —Veo un hospital.

—Veo un hospital y una estación de bomberos.

Keep going around the circle, without repeating place names. Those who can't name a new place are eliminated, until only one student is left!

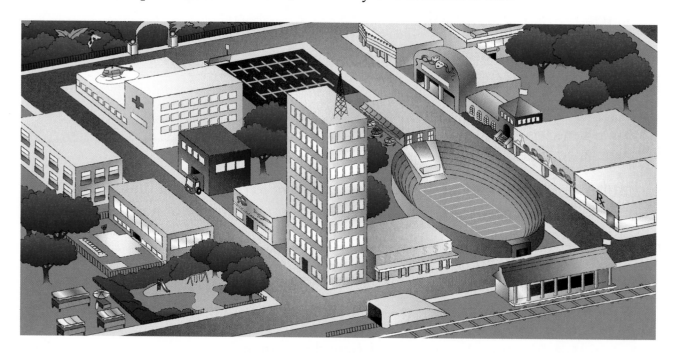

 CONEXIÓN CON LA CULTURA

Shopping Even though malls and large stores are becoming more common in Spanish-speaking countries, many shoppers still prefer going to small specialized stores in their neighborhoods where shopkeepers know their customers by name. Many customers like stopping by almost every day to chat and get individual attention. What are the stores in your community like? Do people like going to several small stores, or do they prefer large stores where they can find everything?

C Ask your partner these questions about his or her neighborhood. To answer, your partner makes a map and shows you the routes. Then switch roles.

MODELO —¿Dónde puedo almorzar?

—En el restaurante. Sigue por mi calle. Dobla a la derecha en…

1. ¿Dónde puedo comprar leche?

2. ¿Qué hago para ir al centro?

3. ¿Cómo llego a la escuela?

4. ¿Dónde puedo ver jugadores de fútbol?

5. ¿Dónde compro frutas?

6. ¿Dónde hay un médico?

7. ¿Dónde puedo jugar al béisbol?

Entre amigos

Get together with a partner. Sit back-to-back so you can't see what the other is writing or drawing.

First sketch an aerial view of a simple neighborhood scene. Include a few different kinds of places in your sketch, such as **un banco,** or **un museo,** and label them. Then take turns describing your sketch as accurately as you can to your partner. He or she must draw it based on what you say. You'll need to use commands and expressions like **a la derecha, a la izquierda, delante de,** and **detrás de.**

When you've finished describing your neighborhood scene, compare your partner's drawing with your own. How close is it to the original?

En resumen

el edificio de apartamentos	el metro
el estadio	el supermercado
el mercado al aire libre	el zoológico

¿Cómo se dice?

Talking about people and places

Study the scene and read the paragraph to see different ways to use the verb **estar**.

Esta tarde mis amigos y yo **estamos** visitando el zoológico. Aurelia y yo **estamos** muy contentos, pero Julio **está** triste. No le gusta ver los animales en las jaulas. A nosotros nos gusta ver el oso polar. La jaula del oso polar **está** cerca de una fuente grande. Después de caminar por todo el zoológico, **estamos** muy cansados. Nos duelen los pies. Todavía tenemos que caminar a la parada de autobús. La parada **está** muy lejos del zoológico. ¡Caramba!

In this paragraph, the verb **estar** is used in three ways:

- to talk about where things are
- to talk about how people are feeling at the moment
- to talk about what someone is doing right now

Now read the paragraph on page 198 again, and see if you can answer these questions:

Can you find an example in which **estar** is used to talk about where things are?

Can you find an example in which **estar** is used to talk about what someone is doing right now? Remember, when you use **estar** in this way, you have to use it together with a verb in the **-ando** or **-iendo** form.

Can you find an example in which **estar** is used to talk about how someone is feeling at the moment?

Here are some examples to help you out. Can you guess what each one means?

Está contenta.   **Está triste.**   **Está cansado.**

Está confundida.   **Está enojado.**   **Está nerviosa.**

Do you remember that you can also use **estar** to talk about things that are only temporary?

¡La sopa **está** muy caliente!

CONEXIÓN CON LA SALUD

Identifying Feelings There can be times when you're not sure how you feel about something, but it's important to find ways of expressing your feelings. How would you say how you feel in these situations?

1. No puedes ir a la fiesta de cumpleaños de una amiga.

2. Tu maestra favorita se va a una escuela que está muy lejos.

3. Tus padres te compran una bicicleta.

4. Estás en un equipo de ajedrez y tienes un juego muy importante el sábado.

5. No duermes mucho y tienes que ir a la escuela.

6. No comprendes la lección de español.

¡Úsalo!

A Get together with two classmates. You have three minutes to write down things that people may be doing in your school right now. Then share the sentences with the class. You get a point for each activity that no other group has written— but the sentences have to make sense! The group with the most points wins.

MODELO **La bibliotecaria está recogiendo los libros de las mesas.**

¿Sabías que...?

English speakers can say "I'm talking to him tomorrow" to talk about something they will do in the future. But remember—Spanish speakers use **estoy hablando** only to talk about something they're doing right now!

B Make a chart like this one and sort these sentences containing forms of **estar**. Work with a partner and take turns reading the sentences. Say whether **estar** is used to ask about where things are (**¿Dónde?**), to say how people are feeling (**¿Cómo se siente?**), or to talk about what someone is doing right now (**¿Qué hace?**). Write the number of each sentence in the correct column.

¿Dónde?	¿Cómo se siente?	¿Qué hace?

1. El camarero está enojado. No tiene propina.

2. Los hermanos están en el parque. Juegan al fútbol.

3. La sal está en la mesa, detrás de la leche.

4. Estoy muy cansada y me voy a dormir.

5. Estamos mirando la televisión ahora.

6. Ustedes están contentos con su nuevo apartamento.

7. Ella está planchando la ropa. Quiere salir luego.

8. La computadora está sobre el escritorio de mi mamá.

C Role-play one of these family members and describe to a partner how you feel and what you're doing. Your partner will guess who you are! Switch roles. Continue until you have played everyone.

Lección 3

Entre amigos

Put your Spanish skills to the test on the phone!

Agree on a time to call your partner on the phone. Decide beforehand who will ask most of the questions and who will answer. Your phone conversation should be only in Spanish. Take notes.

The questioner should ask all of these questions:

¿Cómo estás?
¿Dónde estás ahora?
¿Con quién estás?
¿Cómo está tu familia / amigo / amiga?
(Ask about the person or people your partner is with.)
¿Qué está (están) haciendo?

The next day, tell the class about your phone conversation as though your classmates are listening in while you're talking to the person, and you're telling them what's being said on the phone.

—Jaime dice que está...

En resumen

cansado	cansada
confundido	confundida
contento	contenta
enojado	enojada
nervioso	nerviosa
triste	

¿Cómo se dice?

Talking about more actions in the past

Look at these **-er** and **-ir** verbs you've learned to see how to use them to talk about the past.

Corrimos a la tienda a comprar.

Javier no está. **Salió** al parque.

What endings do you add to the stems of regular **-er** and **-ir** verbs to use them to talk about the past?

To learn other forms of **correr** and **salir** in the past tense, look at these charts.

correr

Singular		Plural	
Yo	corrí	Nosotros, Nosotras	corrimos
Tú	corriste	Ellos, Ellas, Uds.	corrieron
Él, Ella, Ud.	corrió		

salir

Singular		Plural	
Yo	salí	Nosotros, Nosotras	salimos
Tú	saliste	Ellos, Ellas, Uds.	salieron
Él, Ella, Ud.	salió		

Did you notice that the endings for **-er** and **-ir** verbs in the past are the same?

Now look at the past tense of these stem-changing verbs.

volver

Singular	
Yo	volví
Tú	volviste
Él, Ella, Ud.	volvió

Plural	
Nosotros, Nosotras	volvimos
Ellos, Ellas, Uds.	volvieron

Did you notice that the stem doesn't change when you add the endings for the past tense? Other verbs like **volver** in the past tense are **pensar** and **doler.**

pensar

Singular	
Yo	pensé
Tú	pensaste
Él, Ella, Ud.	pensó

Plural	
Nosotros, Nosotras	pensamos
Ellos, Ellas, Uds.	pensaron

doler

Singular	
Yo	dolí
Tú	doliste
Él, Ella, Ud.	dolió

Plural	
Nosotros, Nosotras	dolimos
Ellos, Ellas, Uds.	dolieron

CONEXIÓN CON LA CULTURA

Going Out Spanish speakers often get together with their friends or relatives without planning ahead too much. It's common to make plans on the spur of the moment or drop by a friend's or relative's house. It's also usually considered okay and even polite to arrive a little late to parties, dinners, and other social events. How are these habits similar to or different from the ones you observe in the United States?

¡Úsalo!

A Several things happened to Ana yesterday and they appear in Column A. What happened as a result? Get together with a partner and read the situations to him or her. Your partner finds a result in Column B, and tells you what it is in the past tense.

MODELO —No tiene leche en casa.

—Salió al supermercado.

A.

1. No trae un suéter y hace frío.
2. Se despierta tarde un domingo.
3. Tiene mucha prisa.
4. Tiene un mapa de Madrid.
5. Tiene un accidente en bicicleta.

B.

a. correr a la escuela
b. dolerle la mano
c. salir tarde de casa
d. volver a casa a recoger un abrigo
e. conocer la ciudad

CONEXIÓN CON LAS MATEMÁTICAS

Multiplying This track is 3 miles (**millas**) long. Get together with a partner and make a set of number cards from 1 to 5 and mix them up. These numbers will represent laps around the track. Now one of you draws a card, and the other asks how many miles you ran last week. Answer according to the number of laps on your card. Don't forget there are 3 miles per lap!

MODELO —¿Cuántas millas corriste la semana pasada?

—Corrí nueve millas.

3

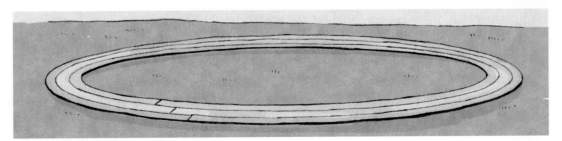

B Your teacher will hand out cards with different times on them. Pretend that you left your house at that time this morning. You need to find the classmates who left at the same time as you did! Go around the classroom and ask people when they left.

MODELO —¿A qué hora saliste?

—Salí a las ocho y cuarto de la mañana. ¿Y tú?

Get together in groups with people who left at the same time. Then your teacher will ask each group the time they left. A member of the group answers for everyone.

MODELO —¿A qué hora salieron?

—Salimos a las ocho y cuarto de la mañana.

C Make a chart like this one. Interview your classmates to find out when they returned home yesterday or the last school day. They should answer truthfully. Include yourself on the chart.

volver a casa

Yo	seis de la tarde
Raúl	seis de la tarde
Sonia	
Alberto	

MODELO —¿A qué hora volviste a casa ayer (el viernes pasado)?

—Volví a las seis de la tarde.

Now get together with a partner and write as many sentences as you can about the time that people returned home. Write first about students individually, and then combine those who returned at the same time.

MODELO Raúl volvió a casa a las seis de la tarde. Yo volví a casa a las seis de la tarde. Nosotros volvimos a las seis de la tarde.

CONEXIÓN CON LOS ESTUDIOS SOCIALES

Biographies Write a biography **(una biografía)** of a person you know—a parent or a friend. Prepare some questions that you'll ask about the most important events in his or her life. Here are some examples and verbs you can use:

¿Cuándo y dónde naciste?
¿Dónde estudiaste?
¿Quiénes son tus padres?
¿Tienes hermanos?
¿Dónde viviste?

vivir	estudiar	aprender	comprar	trabajar
llegar	conocer	nacer *(to be born)*	casarse *(to marry)*	

Then read your biographies to the class.

En resumen

	correr	salir	volver
(Yo)	corrí	salí	volví
(Tú)	corriste	saliste	volviste
(Él, Ella, Ud.)	corrió	salió	volvió
(Nosotros, Nosotras)	corrimos	salimos	volvimos
(Ellos, Ellas, Uds.)	corrieron	salieron	volvieron

¿Dónde se habla español?

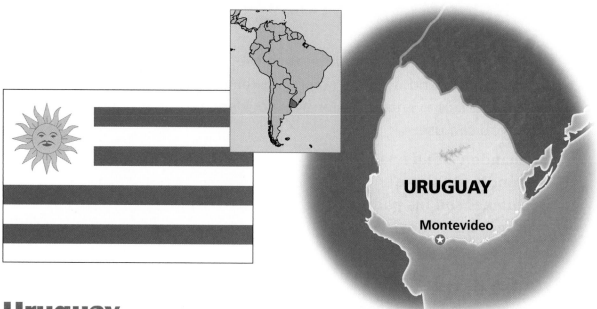

URUGUAY

Montevideo

Uruguay

Uruguay is South America's second smallest country, but it is rich in the arts, history, and beaches. The narrow streets of its capital, Montevideo, are reminiscent of the colonial era. Montevideo also has a European feel to it because of the variety of people who have settled there.

The Río de la Plata separates Uruguay from Argentina. In its estuary is the historical town of Colonia, which once served as a smuggling center.

Most visitors come to Uruguay for its beautiful beaches. Punta del Este is an elegant resort where wealthy people come to relax, eat, and shop. Uruguayans love beef, as do their Argentine neighbors. Many types of beef are grilled **a la parrilla.** You can also find steak sandwiches called **chivitos** and beef stews called **pucheros.** Seafood is plentiful. Drinking a type of tea called **mate** is a daily custom.

Like Argentines, Uruguayans love to dance the **tango.** Uruguay is also rich in the arts. Uruguayans have excelled in poetry, novels, essays, short stories, and plays. The theater is a popular form of entertainment.

◎ ◎ ◎ ◎ ◎ **Datos** ◎ ◎ ◎ ◎ ◎

Capital: Montevideo

Ciudades importantes: Colonia, Maldonado, Fray Bentos, Salto

Idiomas: Español, portugués

Moneda: El peso uruguayo

Población: 3.4 millones

¡Léelo en español!

La literatura latinoamericana: Benedetti

La literatura latinoamericana es rica, interesante y divertida. Muchos autores son famosos en todo el mundo. Por ejemplo, en Argentina, se conoce a Borges, en Colombia se conoce a García Márquez, y en Chile se conoce a Neruda, Mistral y Allende. Mario Benedetti es uno de los escritores uruguayos más famosos. Aquí hay una pequeña selección de sus textos.

Los pocillos*

(*pocillo = taza pequeña)

Los pocillos eran seis: dos rojos, dos negros, dos verdes, y además importados, irrompibles[1], modernos. Habían llegado[2] como regalo de Enriqueta en el último cumpleaños de Mariana, y desde ese día el comentario de cajón había sido que podía combinarse la taza de un color con el platillo de otro. "Negro con rojo queda fenomenal" había sido el consejo estético de Enriqueta. Pero Mariana, en un discreto rasgo de independencia, había decidido[3] que cada pocillo sería usado con su plato del mismo color.

[1] unbreakable   [2] They had arrived

[3] had decided

Reading Strategy

Reading Authentic Texts

When reading authentic literature, first read through the selection and try to get a general idea of what it is about. Read the title carefully. Then find cognates and list their meanings. As you begin reading, when a vocabulary word blocks your understanding take time to look it up in a dictionary, in the back of your book or in a Spanish-English dictionary.

¡Comprendo!

Answer in English.

1. What are the names and nationalities of some famous Latin American writers?

2. Who is one of Uruguay's well-known writers?

3. In the introduction to the story, "Los pocillos," how many cups were there? What colors? How many of each color were there?

4. From whom were the cups a gift?

De un lugar a otro

Objetivos

- To learn useful words for getting around in the city
- To talk about finding (and losing) your way
- To practice telling others politely what to do and what not to do
- To learn more about towns and cities in Spanish-speaking countries

Atocha train station in Madrid, Spain

MONTEVIDEO

A map of Montevideo,
Uruguay

Another form of public
transportation is the moto-taxi.

¿Sabías que...?

- In most Spanish-speaking cities,
  you can find good city maps
  (planos) in newsstands right on
  the sidewalk.

- In Mexico City's **Zona Rosa**
  ("Pink Zone"), you'll find special
  tourist police who will be happy
  to help you out with directions.

¿Cómo se dice?

¿Dónde está tu casa?

—¿Dónde está tu casa?

—Está cerca de la esquina. Hay un farol delante de la casa.

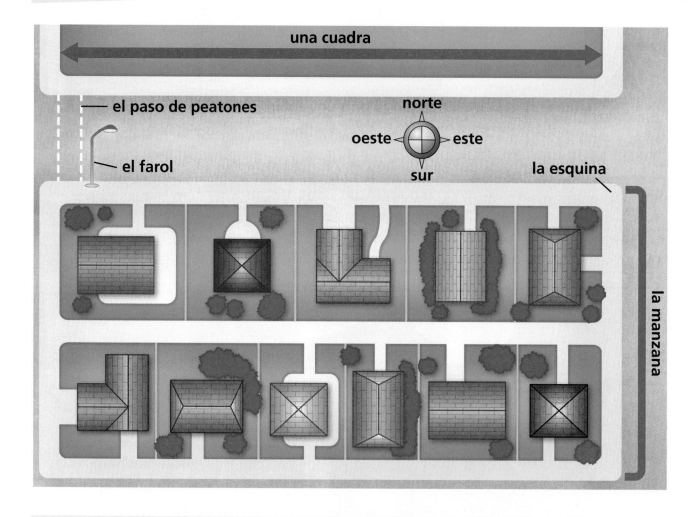

una cuadra

el paso de peatones

el farol

norte

oeste — este

sur

la esquina

la manzana

—Perdón, señor. ¿A cuántas cuadras está el parque de aquí?

—No está lejos. Tienes que caminar dos cuadras más al norte. Allí está.

CONEXIÓN CON LOS ESTUDIOS SOCIALES

Maps Look at this map. Is it a physical map or a political map? What's the difference between the two?

Work with a partner and choose a place on the map (for example, a city, a river, a mountain), but don't tell your partner. Your partner has to ask yes / no questions to guess the place you chose. Then switch roles.

✪ capital	——— río
• ciudad	✛ aeropuerto
▲ volcán	⛰ montaña

MODELO —¿Es un río?

—Sí.

—¿Está al oeste de Medellín?

—No.

◎ ◎ ◎ Compara ◎ ◎ ◎

En inglés	En español
political	político
physical	físico

¿Sabías que...?

Most cities in Spain and other parts of Europe, as well as old colonial towns in Latin America, were built long before cars were invented. The streets in the oldest areas are sometimes only wide enough for one small car at a time to get through. Parking can be a real problem. In some places, it's legal to park with one side of the car (left or right wheels) on the sidewalk.

¡Úsalo!

A You're good at finding your way around. How good are you at reading **un plano de la ciudad?** Take turns with a partner asking and answering these questions. Then compare your answers with those of other pairs.

> **MODELO** —¿Cuántas casas hay en la manzana?
>
> —Hay once casas en la manzana.

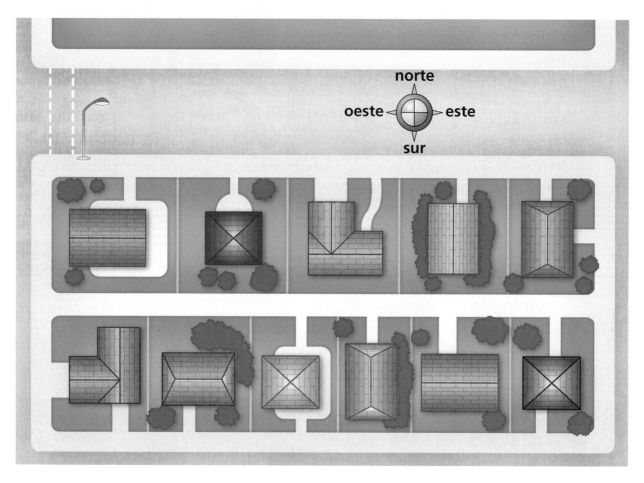

1. ¿Dónde está el farol?
2. ¿La cuadra va de oeste a este o de norte a sur?
3. ¿El farol está al sur o al norte de las casas?
4. ¿El paso de peatones está en la esquina?
5. ¿Es la manzana un cuadrado o un rectángulo?

B Draw a city grid like this one on graph paper. Get together with a partner and choose one list of places each. Draw the places on your map, wherever you want. Then tell your partner how to get there, so that your partner can draw it on his or her map. Start in the lower left corner. Use cardinal points and city blocks to direct your partner. When you finish, compare maps. Do they match?

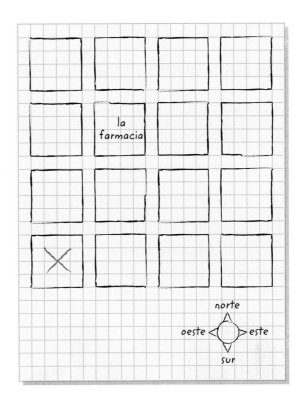

MODELO —¿Dónde está la farmacia?

—Está cerca. Tienes que caminar dos cuadras al norte y luego...

A	B
una farmacia	un hospital
una escuela	una parada de autobús
un teatro	una gasolinera
un mercado	un estacionamiento

En resumen

Ciudad de México está al	norte	de	Acapulco.		el farol
	sur		Monterrey.		el paso de peatones
	este		Morelia.		la cuadra
	oeste		Xalapa.		la esquina
					la manzana

¿Cómo se dice?

¿Queda más adelante o más atrás?

—Perdón, señora. ¿Queda más adelante o más atrás la tienda por departamentos?

— Queda unos veinte metros más atrás.

— Gracias, señora. Tengo que encontrarme con mi papá. No quiero perderme.

Queda más adelante.	**Queda más atrás.**	**perderse**	**encontrarse**

—¿Cómo es el tráfico aquí?

—Bueno, ahora va rápido, pero por las mañanas va despacio.

Va rápido.   **Va despacio.**

¡Úsalo!

A Look at this street. Pretend that you're Andrés. You're not sure where these places are, so you need to ask for directions. Take turns with your partner playing Andrés and asking about each place.

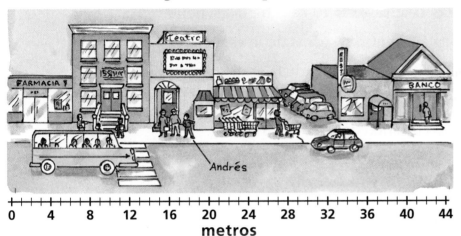

| la escuela |
| el mercado |
| el banco |
| el restaurante |
| el estacionamiento |
| la farmacia |
| el teatro |

MODELO —¿Dónde queda el mercado?

—Queda unos ocho metros más atrás.

B Get together with a partner and ask these questions. Write down his or her answers. Then switch roles.

MODELO —¿Cómo es el tráfico en nuestra ciudad los domingos por la mañana?

—Va muy rápido.

¿Cómo es el tráfico en nuestra ciudad...
   los domingos por la mañana?
   los domingos a las seis de la tarde?
   los lunes a las ocho de la mañana?
   los martes a las cinco de la tarde?
   los miércoles a las diez de la noche?
   los sábados a las siete de la tarde?

C José Zamora lives in Bolivia and he's never visited your city. Answer your partner José's questions.

Partner A: You're José. Ask the questions.

Partner B: Answer José's questions.

> **MODELO** —¿A cuántas cuadras está tu casa de la escuela?
>
> —Mi casa está a cuatro cuadras de la escuela.

1. ¿Vives al norte, al sur, al oeste o al este de la escuela?
2. ¿A cuántas cuadras está tu casa del supermercado?
3. ¿Va rápido o despacio el tráfico delante de tu casa?
4. ¿A cuántas cuadras está tu casa de la casa de un amigo?
5. ¿Puedes perderte en tu ciudad?
6. ¿A cuántos kilómetros estás del aeropuerto?

D Look at these speedometers. Take turns with a partner saying the speed at which people in each car are going, and whether they're going fast or slow.

> **MODELO** Los Jiménez van a setenta millas por hora. Van rápido.

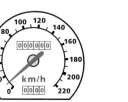

los Jiménez

Alberto

Rogelio y tú

Ramón y Sara

Ana y yo

CONEXIÓN CON LOS ESTUDIOS SOCIALES

Reading Maps Work with a map of your neighborhood or town. You often can get these local maps from the Chamber of Commerce or from real estate offices.

Choose a starting point. It might be your school. Then choose a destination. Write down step-by-step directions in Spanish telling how to get from one point to the other. You don't have to choose the easiest or straightest route!

Give the directions to a partner while he or she traces the route on the map. Can you get your partner to the destination the way you planned? What problems come up?

¿Sabías que...?

In some cities in Latin America, such as Lima and Mexico City, traffic is very heavy all the time, and there are often traffic jams and delays.

En resumen

Queda más adelante.
　　　　　　　 atrás.

encontrarse
perderse

kilómetros
metros
millas

Va　　　despacio.
　　　　　rápido.

Lección 3

¿Cómo se dice?

Giving positive and negative commands and instructions

You've already had some practice giving commands and instructions to people you address as **tú.**

—¡Ay! Estoy cansado.
—**Camina** un poco más. El parque queda más adelante.

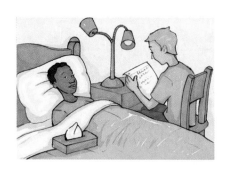

—¿Qué tengo que hacer para la clase de español?
—**Lee** la lección y **escribe** los números en español.

Do you remember what verb form to use when you give a **tú** command using regular **-ar, -er,** and **-ir** verbs? This chart will help.

Verb Type	Infinitive Form	**Él / Ella** Form	Familiar Command
-ar	mirar	mira	**¡Mira!**
-er	correr	corre	**¡Corre!**
-ir	abrir	abre	**¡Abre!**

If you want to give a familiar command with a reflexive verb, you simply add **-te** to the **él / ella** ending:

¡Levántate ahora mismo! Es tarde.

¡Cepíllate los dientes y **lávate** la cara! Luego, puedes salir.

Did you notice that you add an accent mark to these commands? The accent shows which syllable to stress when you say the command.

Look at these pictures and sentences to see how to tell people *not* to do something.

—Estoy enojada con
  Ramón.
—Pues, **no hables** con él.

—Todavía tengo mucha
  hambre.
—**¡No comas** mi
  sándwich!

—José, ¿puedo entrar?
—¡No! Por favor, **¡no
  abras** la puerta!

Did you notice that the verb forms for the negative commands used were like the **tú** form, with one change? Instead of saying **no hablas,** you say **no hables.** Instead of saying **no comes,** you say **no comas.** And instead of saying **no abres,** you say **no abras.**

Look at this chart of negative commands:

Negative Commands

Verb Type	Infinitive Form	Tú Form	Familiar Command
-ar	mirar	miras	**¡No mires!**
-er	correr	corres	**¡No corras!**
-ir	abrir	abres	**¡No abras!**

When you form negative **tú** commands with regular verbs, you use these endings:

For **-ar** verbs, add **-es** to the stem.
For **-er** verbs, add **-as** to the stem.
For **-ir** verbs, add **-as** to the stem.

¡Úsalo!

A What advice would you give a friend in these situations? Use the verbs below and form sentences. When you finish, compare your sentences with a partner's. Are some of them the same?

| escribir | buscar | correr | caminar | leer | abrir | llamar |

1.

Me duelen las piernas.

2.

Quiero aprender más español.

3.

Voy a llegar tarde a clase.

4.

Llaman a la puerta.

5.

Mi amigo no me llama por teléfono.

6.

No encuentro mi abrigo.

B Think of rules that you have to follow at school and at home. Get together with a partner and make a list of things you're *not* supposed to do.

MODELO **No corras en los pasillos.**

C Look at these pictures. Write what you would tell these children to do if you were babysitting for them. Then get together with a partner and take turns reading your sentences to one another. Pretend you're doing what your partner tells you to do.

| levantarse | acostarse | lavarse | bañarse | cepillarse los dientes |

1.

2.

3.

4.

 ## CONEXIÓN CON LA SALUD

Well-being Create a guide to well-being—in Spanish, of course!

Get together with three classmates. Write some tips about the things you should and should not do for each topic below. Everyone needs to contribute something to each category.

Then choose the best tips in your group and write them on separate sheets of paper. Add drawings or pictures from magazines to illustrate your advice. Put your pages together with the rest of the class to create your guide!

| nutrición | ejercicio | salud e higiene personal | medio ambiente* |

* Environment

@@@ **Compara** @@@

En inglés	En español
nutrition	la nutrición
exercise	el ejercicio
hygiene	la higiene

Entre amigos

Are you a considerate person? How many rules for good behavior can you come up with?

Write down as many rules or pieces of advice as you can. You should write at least four.

Think of different situations where these rules are important: with your family, in school, on the street, and so on, but don't write the names of these places. Here are some examples:

en la escuela / dormirse en clase / ¡No te duermas en clase!
durante la cena / hablar con comida en la boca / ¡No hables con comida en la boca!
en la calle / mirar si hay coches / Mira si hay coches.

Exchange your rules with a partner. Read each other's rules and say where they'd be helpful.

¿Sabías que...?

The ideas behind some sayings in English are the same as in Spanish. Sometimes these ideas are even said with similar words. Sometimes different words are used.

¡No pierdas la cabeza! *Take it easy!* or *Don't have a cow!*

No pidas peras al olmo. *You can't get blood from a stone.* (Literally: "Don't expect pears from an elm tree.")

En resumen

caminar	Camina.	¡No camines!
correr	Corre.	¡No corras!
abrir	Abre.	¡No abras!

¿Cómo se dice?

Talking about actions in the past

You already know how to talk about the past with regular **-ar** verbs. Some verbs have spelling changes when you use them to talk about the past.

—¿Cuánto **pagaste** por este libro?

—**Pagué** diez dólares.

—¿A qué hora **sacaste** el perro a pasear?

—**Saqué** el perro a pasear a las seis de la tarde.

—¿Dónde **almorzaste** ayer?

—**Almorcé** en casa.

To learn other forms of **sacar, pagar,** and **almorzar** in the past tense, look at these charts.

sacar

Singular		Plural	
Yo	saqué	Nosotros, Nosotras	sacamos
Tú	sacaste	Ellos, Ellas, Uds.	sacaron
Él, Ella, Ud.	sacó		

pagar

Singular		Plural	
Yo	pagué	Nosotros, Nosotras	pagamos
Tú	pagaste	Ellos, Ellas, Uds.	pagaron
Él, Ella, Ud.	pagó		

almorzar

Singular		Plural	
Yo	almorcé	Nosotros, Nosotras	almorzamos
Tú	almorzaste	Ellos, Ellas, Uds.	almorzaron
Él, Ella, Ud.	almorzó		

Did you notice that there is a spelling change only in the **yo** form of these three verbs? The other past-tense endings are exactly the same as for other regular **-ar** verbs.

Other verbs that end in **-gar, -car,** and **-zar** change in the same way for **yo.**

Yo

secar	sequé (c ➡ qu)
buscar	busqué (c ➡ qu)
llegar	llegué (g ➡ gu)
jugar	jugué (g ➡ gu)
comenzar	comencé (z ➡ c)

¡Úsalo!

A These are some things that David did last Thursday. Get together with a partner and pretend that your partner is David. Ask David questions using the verbs below. David will answer using the clock in the pictures.

| llegar | sacar | jugar | almorzar | comenzar | estudiar |

> **MODELO** —¿A qué hora llegaste a la escuela el jueves pasado?
>
> —Llegué a las ocho y veinte.

1.

2.

3.

4.

5.

B Think about what you did yesterday and then fill out a table like this one. First, show if you did the activity. Then answer when, what, and where you did it. Finally, get together with a partner and ask about his or her activities yesterday.

Ayer...	Sí	No	¿Cuándo?	¿Qué?	¿Dónde?
almorzar					
jugar a algo					
pagar algo					

C Think about the last time you went shopping. What did you buy? How much did you spend? Make a list of five things you have bought recently and the approximate price you paid. Then work with a partner and ask each other what you bought. Who has spent more money lately?

> **MODELO** —¿Qué compraste recientemente?
>
> —Compré un suéter.
>
> —¿Cuánto pagaste por el suéter?
>
> —Pagué treinta dólares.

Compara	
En inglés	**En español**
recently	recientemente

CONEXIÓN CON LOS ESTUDIOS SOCIALES

Chronology These famous events in United States history are out of order. Write a paragraph explaining what happened first, next, and last. Then compare your answers with those of a partner. Look up the events in an encyclopedia or online if you need to.

> **MODELO** Primero, Cristóbal Colón llegó a América. Luego...

Comienza la Guerra *(War)* Civil estadounidense.

Estados Unidos paga quince millones de dólares por la Compra de Luisiana.

Los peregrinos *(Pilgrims)* llegan a América.

Cristóbal Colón llega a América.

Comienza la Guerra de la Independencia estadounidense.

Entre amigos

Find out what your classmates did last week. Go around the classroom asking people if they did each of these things last week. Try to find someone who did the first item on the list before asking about the next one.

(pagar) por el desayuno
(almorzar) un sándwich de pollo
(comenzar) a leer un libro nuevo
(sacar) la basura por la noche
(llegar) a casa después de las siete de la tarde
(jugar) con juegos electrónicos
(buscar) un libro en la biblioteca

—**¿Pagaste por el desayuno?**
—**No. Tomé el desayuno en casa.**

En resumen

	sacar	pagar	almorzar
(Yo)	sa**qu**é	pa**gu**é	almor**c**é
(Tú)	sacaste	pagaste	almorzaste
(Él, Ella, Ud.)	sacó	pagó	almorzó
(Nosotros, Nosotras)	sacamos	pagamos	almorzamos
(Ellos, Ellas, Uds.)	sacaron	pagaron	almorzaron

¿Dónde se habla español?

Ceuta y Melilla

Ceuta and Melilla are two cities in the north of Africa, located in the northern part of Morocco. Both cities became Spanish in the fifteenth century, when the Spanish won control and settled there. They were formally annexed to Spain in 1988, because Spain promised to help Morocco sell its products in the European Union. However, both cities already had their own Spanish customs, and people there already spoke Spanish.

Ceuta is an ancient, strategic port. Its people are primarily Roman Catholic. The cathedral, **la Capilla de Nuestra Señora de África,** the fort of **Monte Hacho,** the **Llano Amarillo** and the **Casa Grande** are its most famous monuments.

Melilla has more of a Moroccan

ESPAÑA

Ceuta — Melilla

MARRUECOS

influence. In 1497 Pedro de Estopinan conquered the city for Spain. Inside the walled section of the city, you can find the church of **la Purísima Concepción** with its entrance: **la Puerta de Santiago,** which bears the coat of arms of Charles V. Both cities continue to have a strong connection with Spain. Many people from Ceuta and Melilla travel to mainland Spain to work because they speak the language.

Datos

Capital: Madrid, España (control); Rabat, Marruecos (ubicación)

Ciudades importantes: Ceuta y Melilla

Idiomas: Español, árabe, francés, beréber

Moneda: El euro (España), el dirham (Marruecos)

Población: Ceuta: 76,000; Melilla: 69,000

¡Léelo en español!

España en África Muchas personas no piensan en España cuando piensan en África. Pero España tiene una larga historia en el continente africano. España está a unas nueve millas,[1] o catorce kilómetros, de Marruecos en el Estrecho[2] de Gibraltar. Lógicamente, durante varios siglos España ha tenido mucho contacto con África. Las Islas Canarias son parte de España desde 1479. Los españoles viven en Melilla desde 1496. Ellos ganaron el control de Ceuta en 1580. Sidi Ifni, en la costa de Agadir, fue español a desde 1860, pero ahora es parte de Marruecos. También Tarfaya y el Sahara Español eran[3] parte de España hasta su independencia.

Un grupo de gente española que vive en África son los judíos sefardíes.[4] Muchos judíos vivían en España antes de 1492. En los siglos VII a XV, los judíos vivían con los cristianos y los árabes. Contribuyeron a la economía, las ciencias, las matemáticas, la poesía, la filosofía, las leyes y la medicina. En Toledo ayudaban con las traducciones[5] de obras griegas y hebreas[6]. Todos vivían en paz hasta 1492, cuando los reyes Isabel y Fernando expulsaron[7] a los judíos de España que no se convirtieron[8] en cristianos. Muchos judíos fueron al norte de África. Allí continuaron practicando[9] su religión, siguiendo sus tradiciones y hablando su idioma, el ladino, que es una combinación de hebreo y español. En los años 1950 y 1960 muchos judíos sefardíes fueron a vivir a Israel.

Reading Strategy

Graphic Organizers Use a graphic organizer to summarize the history of Spain in Africa. Draw a center circle with "Spain" written in it. Then draw lines with circles at the end for each connection you find for Spain in Africa and label them. Give a title to your diagram.

Recognizing Cognates What do you think these words mean: **lógicamente, contacto, contribuyeron?** Use these cognates to help you understand what is being said about the history of Spain in Africa.

¡Comprendo!

Answer in English.

1. Using your graphic organizers, make a list of all of Spain's contacts with Africa.

2. What are some of the contributions of the Jewish population in Spain prior to 1492?

3. What happened to the Sephardic Jews who went to live in North Africa? Why did they leave Spain? Did they all stay in North Africa?

De compras

Objetivos

- To learn the names of people and places related to shopping
- To talk about buying gifts
- To learn the names of things you find in music stores, jewelry stores, and shoe stores
- To talk about what someone did or where someone went
- To talk about how or where people were in the past
- To talk about the weather and the temperature in the past

A shopping mall in La Paz, Bolivia

Window shoppers look at a shoe store display.

A shopper checks out CDs at a music store on Calle Florida in Buenos Aires, Argentina.

¿Sabías que...?

- Colombia is one of the world's leading producers of emeralds, beautiful green precious stones.

- You can find leather items of excellent quality in places like Argentina, Spain, and Colombia.

- Indoor shopping malls in Latin America are popular places for kids to meet and have fun, just as in the United States.

Lección 1

¿Cómo se dice?

¿Qué piensas comprar?

—¿Qué piensas comprar?

—Tengo que comprar un regalo para mi mamá.

—¿A ella le gustan los collares?

—¡Buena idea! Vamos a la joyería. Vamos a hablar con el joyero.

La joyería

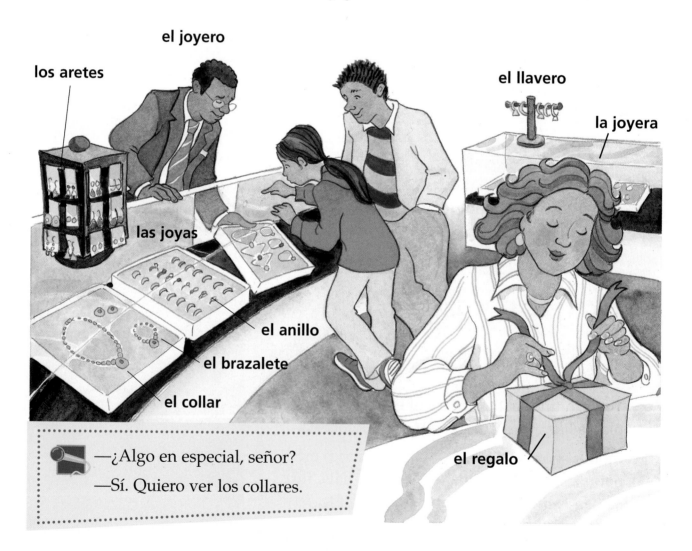

el joyero

los aretes

el llavero

la joyera

las joyas

el anillo

el brazalete

el collar

el regalo

—¿Algo en especial, señor?

—Sí. Quiero ver los collares.

¡Úsalo!

A Choose three items that could be bought at a jewelry store and write them on one card. Imagine that you bought these things. Then walk around the classroom asking classmates what they bought. Try to find someone who bought the same items.

 **MODELO** —¿Qué compraste en la joyería?

—Compré un anillo, ¿y tú?

B With four or five classmates, study these people and what they're wearing for one minute. Try to remember everything you can. (You may want to take notes.)

When the minute is up, turn the page and answer as many questions as you can. The winning group is the one with more correct answers!

1. ¿Lleva un anillo la mujer del vestido azul?

2. ¿Cuántos brazaletes lleva la mujer rubia del vestido rojo? ¿Dónde?

3. ¿Quién lleva un arete?

4. ¿Qué joyas lleva el hombre del sombrero?

5. ¿Lleva aretes la mujer rubia del vestido verde?

6. ¿Qué lleva el hombre que está con la mujer del vestido azul?

7. ¿Quién lleva un collar, un anillo y unos aretes similares?

8. ¿Cuántas mujeres no llevan collar?

C These are the windows of a famous jewelry store. Get together with two classmates and secretly choose one window. Write down its number. Your classmates will ask you questions to try to guess which window you chose.

MODELO —¿Hay tres anillos?

—Sí.

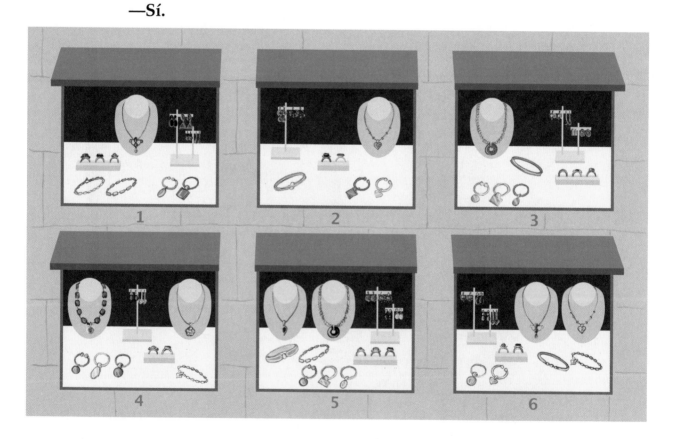

Entre amigos

See how well you know your classmates.

Guess how many of them are wearing or have with them the following items:

un anillo   **un collar**   **un llavero**   **un brazalete**   **unos aretes**

Write your guesses down on a piece of paper.

Now listen as your teacher calls out the names of the different items in sequence. Stand up if you are wearing that item or have it with you at school. Remain seated if you don't.

Be sure to count how many people stand as the different items are named. Make a bar graph like this one with the results.

How close were your guesses to the actual numbers?

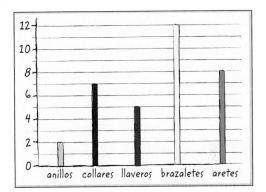

CONEXIÓN CON LA CULTURA

Earrings In Spanish-speaking countries, it's common for baby girls to have their ears pierced soon after they're born. They usually wear small hoop earrings until they're older. It's one way to tell the girls from the boys!

En resumen

el anillo	los aretes
el brazalete	la joyería
el collar	la joyera
el joyero	las joyas
el llavero	
el regalo	

¿Cómo se dice?

¿Son baratos o caros los zapatos?

—¿Son baratos o caros los zapatos?

—¿Qué dice el zapatero?

—Dice que cuestan setenta y cinco dólares.

—Entonces, son caros.

La zapatería

el cinturón

la zapatera

las bolsas

el zapatero

las sandalias

los zapatos

—¿Vas a comprar el audiocasete o el disco compacto?

—Bueno, pienso comprar el disco compacto.

La tienda de música

el videocasete

el disco compacto

el audiocasete

 CONEXIÓN CON LA CULTURA

Music Have you ever heard of **rock en español?** Yes, it's rock —in Spanish! Rock 'n' roll originated in the United States, but soon Spanish speakers (especially in Argentina and Mexico) started playing and singing it too, at first in English. Over time, **rock en español** has evolved, with lyrics in Spanish, and it has become its own distinct musical style. It adds many elements from Latin and African music to create a new kind of sound. **Rock en español** has become so popular in the United States that there are now *Grammys* and other awards in this category. Some famous bands include **Los Fabulosos Cadillacs, La Ley, Soda Stereo,** and **Maná.**

¡Úsalo!

A Think of three relatives and a gift each of them would like. Then make a list and go shopping! Switch roles after you choose your gifts.

Partner A: Look for gifts for three relatives that total less than $50 and ask for prices.

Partner B: Prepare a price list that includes all items and tell your partner the prices.

B Look at the prices of items at the mall. Then take a look at Jorge's receipts. Work with a partner to figure out what he probably bought.

MODELO —¿Qué compró Jorge?

—Compró...

collar, $100	disco compacto, $15	audiocasete, $10
bolsa de mujer, $40	cinturón de mujer, $25	zapatos de mujer, $50
sandalias de mujer, $30	anillo, $80	aretes, $30
zapatos de hombre, $55	bolsa unisex, $45	sandalias de hombre, $35
cinturón de hombre, $15	videocasete, $20	

Joyería Diamante

Total ------ $110

Disco 100

Total....$25

Zapatería Casas

Total......$160

CONEXIÓN CON LOS ESTUDIOS SOCIALES

Making Maps Where are your favorite stores in town? Draw a map of your neighborhood, and label the following:

- Where to get the best pizza
- Where to get the best ice cream
- Where to get the best burger
- Where to buy the best music

Add two more places that you consider to be the best at what they sell. Then get together with a partner. Ask and answer questions about each other's map and the places you labeled.

> **MODELO** —¿Dónde está tu tienda de helados favorita?
>
> —Está en la avenida Alameda. Camina tres cuadras al este de la escuela. Está en la esquina con la calle Rojas.
>
> —¿Es caro o barato el helado?

Think about your relatives' favorite stores as well, and share those with your partner. Say whether your relatives go there often or only sometimes.

> **MODELO** —La tienda de ropa favorita de mi mamá es... Va allí muchas veces.

En resumen

el audiocasete
el cinturón
el disco compacto
el zapatero

la tienda de música
la zapatería
las bolsas
las sandalias

barato(a)
caro (a)

¿Cómo se dice?

Talking about what happened

Can you tell what these people are talking about?

—¿Qué hicieron ustedes ayer?

—Fuimos al zoológico.

—Y tú, ¿qué hiciste ayer?

—Fui al parque con mi familia.

Look at the verb **hacer** to see how to use it to talk about the past:

hacer

Singular		Plural	
Yo	hice	Nosotros, Nosotras	hicimos
Tú	hiciste	Ellos, Ellas, Uds.	hicieron
Él, Ella, Ud.	hizo		

¿Sabías que...?

Spanish speakers use only one verb **(hacer)** to say what English speakers say with two: *to do* and *to make.* **Hacer** is used to talk about many actions for which there are no specific verbs. You already know **hacer frío** and **hacer calor.** Other useful expressions are **hacer deporte, hacer la cama,** and **hacer la tarea** *(to do homework).*

Now look at these irregular verbs you know to see how to use them in the past tense:

ir

Singular		Plural	
Yo	fui	Nosotros, Nosotras	fuimos
Tú	fuiste	Ellos, Ellas, Uds.	fueron
Él, Ella, Ud.	fue		

ser

Singular		Plural	
Yo	fui	Nosotros, Nosotras	fuimos
Tú	fuiste	Ellos, Ella, Uds.	fueron
Él, Ella, Ud.	fue		

Did you notice that the past-tense forms of **ir** and **ser** are exactly the same?

¡Úsalo!

A Get together with a partner and write ten different activities on cards. Use the verbs on the list. Then switch cards with another pair. Take turns asking each other what you did yesterday or at some time in the past. Answer according to the card you draw.

> **MODELO** comer pollo con papas
>
> —¿Qué hiciste ayer?
>
> —Comí pollo con papas.

escribir	hablar	recoger	visitar	usar	sacar
comer	pintar	estudiar	jugar	aprender	caminar
comprar	barrer	abrir	ir	hacer	

B Complete a chart like this one with some things you did this past weekend.

	¿Qué hice?	¿Qué hicieron mis compañeros?
el sábado por la mañana		
el sábado por la tarde		
el sábado por la noche		
el domingo por la mañana		
el domingo por la tarde		
el domingo por la noche		

Now move around the room and ask your classmates what they did over the weekend. If you find people who did something you did, too, write their names on your chart.

MODELO —¿Qué hiciste el sábado por la mañana?

—Jugué al fútbol.

Then tell the class some of the same activities you and others did at the same time.

MODELO —Marcela y yo jugamos al fútbol el sábado por la mañana.

C Get together with a partner and prepare two sets of cards. On one set, write events that have happened (a beach vacation, dinner out with your family, something you bought, a place you visited, a sports event, a class at school). On the other set, write the adjectives in the list below. Then put both piles facedown and take turns picking a card from each pile. Decide together whether the event and the description match. If they do, you get to keep the cards! The one with more cards at the end wins.

fácil	difícil	importante	interesante	aburrido
divertido	terrible	fantástico	caro	barato

D Get together with a partner and talk about where you think Patricia and Laura went over the weekend, based on what's in their bags. Find three differences.

MODELO —¿Patricia y Laura fueron al zoológico este fin de semana?

—Sí, fueron al zoológico.

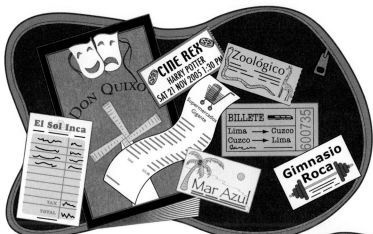

Patricia

Laura

En resumen

	hacer	ir, ser
(Yo)	hice	fui
(Tú)	hiciste	fuiste
(Él, Ella, Ud.)	hizo	fue
(Nosotros, Nosotras)	hicimos	fuimos
(Ellos, Ellas, Uds.)	hicieron	fueron

¿Cómo se dice?

Talking about where or how people were

Look at the way you use the verb **estar** to talk about the past.

—¿Dónde **estuviste** ayer por la tarde?
—**Estuve** en casa de mis amigos.

Ayer por la tarde **estuvo**
en casa de sus amigos.

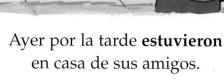

—¿Dónde **estuvieron** ayer por la tarde?
—**Estuvimos** en casa de nuestros amigos.

Ayer por la tarde **estuvieron**
en casa de sus amigos.

Did you notice that the stem **est-** changed to **estuv-?** **Estar** is an irregular verb, like **hacer, ser,** and **ir.**

This is how you use **hacer** in the past:

Ayer **hizo** mucho sol.

Hicimos muchas cosas en el parque.

Look at **hacer** and **estar.** What's the same? What's different?

	hacer	estar
Singular		
Yo	hice	estuve
Tú	hiciste	estuviste
Él, Ella, Ud.	hizo	estuvo
Plural		
Nosotros, Nosotras	hicimos	estuvimos
Ellos, Ellas, Uds.	hicieron	estuvieron

Hacer and **estar** have the same endings when you're talking about the past.

Now compare **estar** with **tener** in the past:

	estar	tener
Singular		
Yo	estuve	tuve
Tú	estuviste	tuviste
Él, Ella, Ud.	estuvo	tuvo
Plural		
Nosotros, Nosotras	estuvimos	tuvimos
Ellos, Ellas, Uds.	estuvieron	tuvieron

You can use what you know about **estar** to use **tener** in the past. Just take off the **es-** at the beginning, and the forms are the same!

¡Úsalo!

A Find someone in your class who has been to these places. You can't go on to the next question until you find someone who has been to the place mentioned in the previous question.

1. Estuvo en la escuela ayer: _____

2. Estuvo en casa de sus tíos la semana pasada: _____

3. Estuvo en casa de unos amigos el fin de semana pasado: _____

4. Estuvo en el parque el domingo pasado: _____

5. Estuvo en una pizzería la semana pasada: _____

6. Estuvo en el cine el mes pasado: _____

7. Estuvo en la oficina del dentista en los seis meses pasados: _____

8. Estuvo en la oficina del médico en el año pasado: _____

> **MODELO** —¿**Estuviste en la escuela ayer?**
>
> —**Sí, estuve en la escuela.** *or* **No, no estuve en la escuela.**

En inglés	En español
pizzeria	la pizzería
dentist	el / la dentista

©©© **Compara** ©©©

B How did you feel in these situations? Take turns with a partner. Read a situation, and your partner tells you how you may have felt as a result, using the words from the list below.

> **MODELO** —**Me levanté tarde.**
>
> —**Luego tuviste prisa.**

tener calor	tener frío	estar cansado(a)	tener miedo	estar triste

1. No llevé mi abrigo.

2. Hizo mucho sol.

3. Hizo 20°F.

4. Un amigo se fue de la ciudad.

5. Trabajé mucho.

6. No dormí ayer.

7. Salí a medianoche.

8. Perdí mi libro favorito.

C Someone stole all the ice cream from the freezer. You have to find the culprits. Interview your classmates and ask them where they were between 5:00 and 7:00 p. m. yesterday. Then decide who is the main suspect.

MODELO —¿Dónde estuviste ayer de las cinco a las siete de la tarde?

—En la clase de piano.

—¿Quién más estuvo allí?

—Mi hermana.

Entre amigos

Work with a partner. Talk about your last shopping trip to one of these places:

una joyería	una zapatería
una tienda de música	una tienda de ropa

Take turns asking and answering questions like these:

¿En qué tienda estuviste? ¿Cuándo estuviste allí? ¿Cuánto tiempo estuviste? ¿Qué compraste?

Be sure to write down what your partner purchased. When you've finished, get together with two other pairs of students. Tell them all the information you have about your partner's shopping trip.

En resumen

	estar	tener
(Yo)	estuve	tuve
(Tú)	estuviste	tuviste
(Él, Ella, Ud.)	estuvo	tuvo
(Nosotros, Nosotras)	estuvimos	tuvimos
(Ellos, Ellas, Uds.)	estuvieron	tuvieron

¿Dónde se habla español?

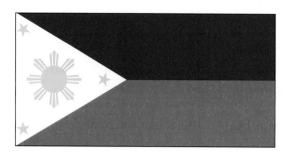

Manila

ISLAS FILIPINAS

Las Islas Filipinas

The Philippines is an island country in the Pacific Ocean. Although there are 7,400 islands, people live on only 400 of them. Ninety-five percent of the population lives on eleven islands.

While looking for a route to the Spice Islands, Ferdinand Magellan, from Portugal, landed in the Philippines in 1521. He converted many of the native people to Christianity, but was killed in a battle.

There is great ethnic diversity in the Philippines. The first inhabitants of the Philippines lived there some

30,000 years ago. In the 1300s Muslim traders arrived. After Magellan, Spanish explorers in 1542 named the islands after King Philip II of Spain. In 1898, the United States took control of the Philippines.

The climate on these islands is hot and humid. There is a wide variety of plants and animals. Banyan and palm trees as well as bamboo flourish. Crocodiles, monkeys, snakes, and tropical birds live there.

Philippine food is a combination of American, Chinese, Malay, and Spanish dishes.

Datos

Capital: Manila

Ciudades importantes: Cagayán de Oro, Davao, Quezon City, Baguio, Cebu

Idiomas: Filipino (un variante del Tagalog), inglés, dialectos indígenas

Moneda: El peso filipino

Población: 84.6 millones

¡Léelo en español!

Las Filipinas y Felipe II Felipe II (1527–1598) fue un rey de España. Durante su época, España fue un país muy poderoso.[1] Era el país más poderoso del mundo. Durante su época, se dice que "el sol nunca se ponía en el Imperio[2] español" porque españa tenía territorios alrededor del[3] mundo. El imperio español fue uno de los imperios más grandes en la historia del mundo. Incluía[4] Bélgica, Holanda, parte de Italia, América Central, América del Sur, México, Cuba, Puerto Rico, la República Dominicana, partes de los Estados Unidos y África y las Islas Filipinas. Felipe invitó al famoso artista El Greco a venir a España y vivir y pintar en Toledo. Felipe II construyó el monasterio del Escorial, donde está enterrado[5] con su familia. Felipe creó la Armada, un grupo de barcos, para luchar contra[6] Inglaterra. Perdió una batalla y así España empezó a perder su poder en el mundo. El fin del Imperio español ocurrió con la guerra de 1898 con los Estados Unidos. Estados Unidos ganó y España perdió Cuba, Puerto Rico y las Islas Filipinas.

[1] powerful   [2] Empire   [3] all around the
[4] included   [5] buried   [6] to fight against

Reading Strategy

Summarizing As you read, summarize the main points in English and write short notes in your own words. Then put your notes together to summarize the reading.

Recognizing Cognates What do you think these words mean: **época, monasterio, batalla?** Use these cognates to help you understand what is being said about the Spanish Empire.

¡Comprendo!

Answer in English.

1. What cultures have contributed to today's culture in the Phillipines?

2. What does the expression **"el sol nunca se ponía en el Imperio español"** mean? Look at a world map or a globe: was this true?

3. What were some of Felipe II's major accomplishments?

4. Now put your notes together to create a summary of the story of Felipe II and the Spanish Empire.

UNIDAD

12

¡A la playa!

Objetivos

- To learn the names of beach and water sports
- To describe beach activities
- To talk about more things you and others did in the past
- To talk about things that are near or far away
- To talk about what things are for
- To learn about vacation times in Spanish-speaking countries

Colorful houses on
a Dominican beach

Galapagos marine iguanas in Ecuador

A mother and son snorkel off Roatan Island, Honduras.

¿Sabías que...?

- La Costa Brava, on Spain's Mediterranean coast, is a world-famous stretch of beach visited every year by tourists from all over the world.

- Acapulco, on the Pacific coast of Mexico, is famous for the professional divers who plunge almost 100 feet from cliffs into the swirling surf below.

- At the bioluminescent bay in Vieques, a small island off the coast of Puerto Rico, you can go kayaking at night and see the water glow where your oar disturbs the water. Tiny microorganisms in the water produce this glow.

¿Cómo se dice?

¿Qué haces en la playa?

—¿Qué cosas llevas a la playa?

—Bueno, llevo una sombrilla.

la sombrilla

la arena

quemado

los caracoles

tomar el sol

el salvavidas

bronceada

el protector solar

las conchas

—¿Qué te gusta hacer en la playa?

—Me gusta tomar el sol.

—A mí también. Me gusta estar bronceado.

—¿Qué te gusta hacer en el mar?

—Me gusta bucear.

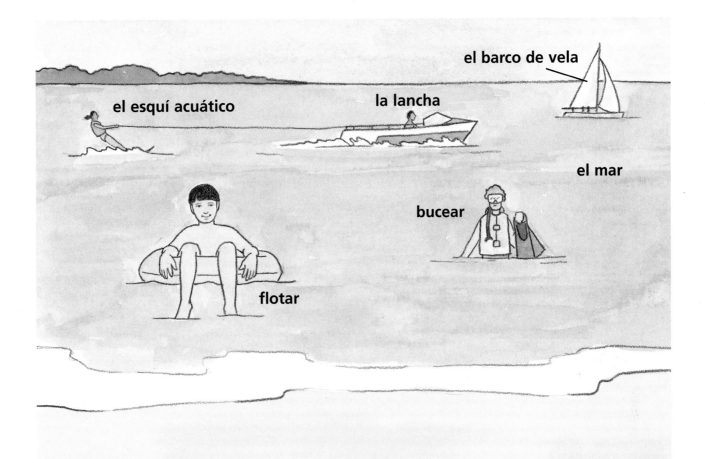

el barco de vela

el esquí acuático

la lancha

el mar

bucear

flotar

 —¡Qué bonita está la arena en esta playa!

—¿Podemos nadar aquí?

—No. Se prohíbe nadar.

—¿Por qué?

—Porque es peligroso.

las olas

¡Se prohíbe nadar!

¡Peligro!

CONEXIÓN CON LA CULTURA

Seafood After a day by the sea, tourists in the coastal cities of Ecuador, Peru, and Chile like to try seafood dishes such as **ceviche,** raw fish served cold in a spicy sauce, and **frutos del mar** (fruits of the sea or seafood). Local restaurants often feature beautifully polished **conchas** (sea shells) as decorations.

¡Úsalo!

A Imagine that you're packing for a weekend at the beach. What will you take? Make a list of the items you'll take and compare lists with a partner. Are you taking the same things? Is there anything else you'd take with you?

B Are these people suntanned, or did they burn? Take turns with a partner describing each one.

MODELO —Los chicos están quemados.

C Use a list like this one to rank your favorite beach activities from 1 (most favorite) to 10 (least favorite). Then get together with a partner and ask questions so you can rank his or her favorites. You can use these questions, plus others of your own.

bucear	
nadar	
flotar	2
tomar el sol	
ir en barco de vela	
hacer esquí acuático	
hacer figuras en la arena	
ir en lancha	1
recoger caracoles y conchas	

¿Te gusta… ?
¿Qué te gusta más… ?
¿Cuál es tu cosa favorita?
¿Qué no te gusta hacer?

When you're done, compare the list you made for your partner with the one he or she wrote. Do they match? Do you share any favorite activities?

CONEXIÓN CON LA SALUD

Beach Safety Make a beach health and safety poster with a partner. List important things to keep in mind when you go to the beach. Look at these pictures for ideas. Then prepare your poster and decorate it with pictures from magazines, drawings, and real objects. Display your finished posters at the library.

MODELO Siempre usa protector solar en la playa.

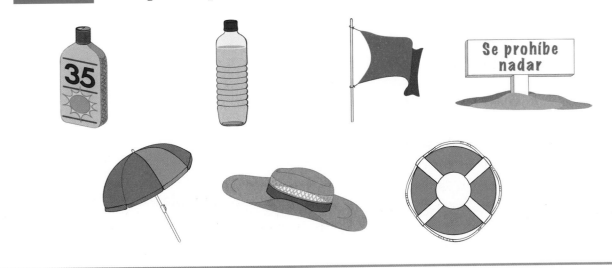

D Think of rules at school and in your classroom. Get together with a partner and create a poster listing things that you can't do there. Start every sentence with **Se prohíbe...** Be creative! The pair with the most sentences wins.

MODELO **Se prohíbe caminar en las mesas.**

Entre amigos

Get together with three other classmates and make a tourist poster for a beach area you know.

Think of a headline for your poster: **¡Arena, sol, mar y olas!** or **¡Toma una lancha o barco de vela y toca el sol!** You get the idea. Be sure to include:

- the name and location of the beach
- how to get there
- where you can stay
- the things you can do there

Present your poster to the class. When all the posters have been presented, your classmates will vote for the best ones!

En resumen

el barco de vela	la arena	bucear
el esquí acuático	la lancha	flotar
el mar	la sombrilla	tomar el sol
el protector solar	las conchas	
el salvavidas	las olas	estar bronceado(a)
los caracoles		quemado(a)
		¡Peligro!
		¡Se prohíbe nadar!

¿Cómo se dice?

Talking about other actions in the past

Look at the stem-changing verb **pedir** to see how to use it in the past.

Yo **pedí** un sándwich de pollo.

Silvia **pidió** una hamburguesa.

Mis papás **pidieron** espaguetis.

Look at this chart to learn the other forms of **pedir** in the past.

pedir (e ➞ i)

Singular		Plural	
Yo	pedí	Nosotros, Nosotras	pedimos
Tú	pediste	Ellos, Ellas, Uds.	pidieron
Él, Ella, Ud.	pidió		

Did you notice that the stem of **pedir** only changes in the third-person form (**Él, Ella, Ud.** and **Ellos, Ellas, Uds.**)? The other past-tense forms are exactly the same as for regular **-ir** verbs.

Another verb that works like **pedir** is **servir.**

Yo **serví** unos sándwiches de pollo.
El camarero **sirvió** el almuerzo.

Now look at the way you use the verb **dormirse** in the past.

Yo **me dormí.** Silvia también **se durmió.** Mis papás no **se durmieron.**

dormirse (o ➔ u)

Singular		Plural	
Yo	me dormí	Nosotros, Nosotras	nos dormimos
Tú	te dormiste	Ellos, Ellas, Uds.	se durmieron
Él, Ella, Ud.	se durmió		

Like **pedir,** the stem of **dormirse** only changes in the third-person form.

Now, look at how you use the verb **poder** to talk about the past.

poder (o ➔ u)

Singular		Plural	
Yo	pude	Nosotros, Nosotras	pudimos
Tú	pudiste	Ellos, Ellas, Uds.	pudieron
Él, Ella, Ud.	pudo		

Did you notice that the stem of **poder** changes for every subject? Another verb that works like **poder** is **poner(se).**

Puse la mesa a las seis.
Mis padres **se pusieron** los abrigos.

poner (o ➔ u)

Singular		Plural	
Yo	puse	Nosotros, Nosotras	pusimos
Tú	pusiste	Ellos, Ellas, Uds.	pusieron
Él, Ella, Ud.	puso		

¡Úsalo!

A Pablo went to the beach for a day but he has a cast on his leg. Look at this picture and take turns with a partner saying what you think Pablo could and could not do. Write these things down. You can use these activities and others you come up with. The pair who comes up with more sentences wins!

MODELO Pablo pudo leer. No pudo nadar.

leer	nadar	tomar el sol	hacer figuras en la arena
recoger conchas	bucear	jugar al fútbol	

B Get together with a partner. Find out if he or she asked for the following things yesterday. Then your partner gets to find out about you!

> **MODELO** —¿Pediste un vaso de agua ayer?
>
> —Sí, pedí un vaso de agua.

pedir un vaso de agua	pedir permiso para ir al cuarto de baño
pedir leche con la cena	pedir un libro en la biblioteca
pedir una hamburguesa	pedir el almuerzo en la cafetería
pedir la hora	pedir la cena en un restaurante

Now switch partners and tell your new one what your first partner asked for yesterday.

> **MODELO** —José pidió un vaso de agua con la cena ayer...

@ @ @ **Compara** @ @ @

En inglés	**En español**
permission	el permiso

C What did Claudia put on to go to the beach? Get together with a partner. Each of you chooses one of the drawings of Claudia. Cover the other one with a piece of paper. Then take turns asking your partner what Claudia wore in his or her picture to discover the three differences between them!

> **MODELO** —¿Se puso el protector solar?
>
> —Sí. Se puso el protector solar.

A.

B.

Averages Find the average time when you and your classmates fall asleep. Get together with three classmates and fill out a chart like this one. Take turns asking the others what time they fell asleep yesterday and the two days prior to that. **Anteayer** means "the day before yesterday."

	Ayer	Anteayer	El día antes de anteayer
Yo	10:00		
Compañero 1	10:05		
Compañero 2	8:45		
Compañero 3	10:30		

MODELO —Yo me dormí a las diez ayer. ¿A qué hora se durmieron ustedes ayer?

—Yo me dormí a las diez y cinco.

—Yo me dormí a las nueve menos cuarto.

—Yo me dormí a las diez y media.

When you have filled out the table, find the time that on average (en promedio) you all went to bed. Report it to the class.

MODELO —En promedio, nos dormimos a las nueve y veinticinco.

En resumen

	pedir	dormirse	poder
(Yo)	pedí	me dormí	pude
(Tú)	pediste	te dormiste	pudiste
(Él, Ella, Ud.)	pidió	se durmió	pudo
(Nosotros, Nosotras)	pedimos	nos dormimos	pudimos
(Ellos, Ellas, Uds.)	pidieron	se durmieron	pudieron

Lección 3

¿Cómo se dice?

Pointing out what's near and far

In English, you use different words to talk about the people or things that are near you and those that are farther away—such as *this* boy or *that* boy *over there.* It's the same in Spanish.

Este chico está bronceado.

Ese chico está un poco quemado.

Aquel chico está muy quemado.

Esta chica no sabe nadar.

Esa chica sabe flotar.

Aquella chica sabe nadar muy bien.

Which words help you talk about *this* boy or *this* girl? Which words help you talk about *that* boy or *that* girl? Which words help you talk about *that* boy *over there* or *that* girl *over there?*

Singular		Plural	
Masculine	**Feminine**	**Masculine**	**Feminine**
este	esta	estos	estas
ese	esa	esos	esas
aquel	aquella	aquellos	aquellas

¡Úsalo!

A Get together with a partner and pretend you're at the beach. You're sitting on a towel and looking at all these people. Talk with your partner about what you see them doing as you point to them in the picture. Use the correct forms of **este, ese,** and **aquel,** depending on how far away from you they are.

MODELO —**Esa señora está muy quemada.**

B Get together with a partner. Choose one item from each of these pictures to take to the beach. Notice that some are closer and some are farther away. Take turns asking, answering, and pointing to the object that you'll take.

MODELO —¿Qué traje de baño te gusta más?

—Quiero llevar aquel traje de baño.

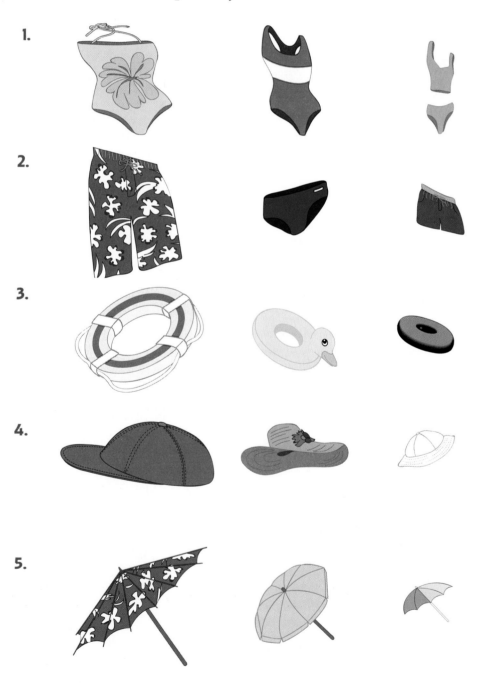

Entre amigos

Get together with two other classmates. Each of you will draw pictures of three things you want to buy and take to the beach. Place the pictures in different positions in the room, some of them close to you and others farther away.

Then pretend you're shopping. Talk about the things you want to buy.

—¿Te gusta aquella camisa roja?
—Sí. Pero me gusta más esa camisa azul.

Ask your classmates why they prefer that item.

—¿Por qué prefieres esa camisa azul?
—Prefiero esa camisa porque…

Find classmates who agree with you on an item and tell the class why you picked it.

Nosotros escogimos una camisa azul porque. . .

¿Sabías que...?

The Pacific coastline of Costa Rica boasts great surfing conditions. Every year professional and amateur surfers come from around the world to participate in competitions at Costa Rican beaches like Playa Hermosa.

En resumen

este	esta
ese	esa
aquel	aquella
estos	estas
esos	esas
aquellos	aquellas

¿Cómo se dice?

Talking about what things are for

Look at these sentences. Notice the three different uses of the word **para.**

Hoy es jueves.
Tengo que lavar el coche **para** el sábado.
El sábado va a llegar mi abuelita.

Compré el regalo ayer. Es un traje de baño **para** mi papá.

Uso el protector solar **para** tomar el sol.
No quiero quemarme.

In the first example, **para** is used to indicate when something is supposed to be done. In which example is **para** used to show what something is used for? In which example is **para** used to indicate who will receive something?

CONEXIÓN CON LA CULTURA

Holidays In Spain and other Spanish-speaking countries, workers have more vacation days than in the United States. Many cities can become very hot in the summer, and people like to get away to the beach or to the mountains. A four-week vacation is not unusual, and kids may get to spend the whole summer away from home!

¡Úsalo!

A Take turns with a partner asking each other what you use these items for. See if you can come up with more than one use for some of them.

> **MODELO** **el protector solar**
>
> —¿Para qué usas el protector solar?
>
> —Uso el protector solar para tomar el sol.

1. la plancha   **2.** las llaves   **3.** el bolígrafo

4. el horno   **5.** el salvavidas   **6.** las sandalias

B This is a page from Jorge's assignment notebook. He wrote down everything he needs to do on the day it's due. Take turns telling a partner what Jorge has to do this week.

> **MODELO** —**Tiene que acabar de leer un libro de español para el lunes.**

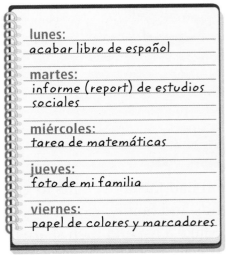

lunes:
acabar libro de español

martes:
informe (report) de estudios sociales

miércoles:
tarea de matemáticas

jueves:
foto de mi familia

viernes:
papel de colores y marcadores

C Look at Luisa's family and the gifts that she wants to give them for the holidays. Work with a partner and decide what gifts you think she will give to whom.

> **MODELO** —¿Para quién es la gorra roja?
>
> —Para su hermano.
>
> —Pienso que es para su papá.

1.

2.

3.

4.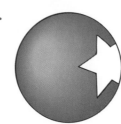

5.

6.

7.

8.

D If you had the above gifts to give away to your friends and family, whom would you give them to? Make a list and then share it with a partner.

> **MODELO** La gorra roja es para mi hermana.

gorra roja — mi hermana

CONEXIÓN CON LA SALUD

Skin Protection What do you usually do to protect your skin from the sun when you're on vacation? Get together with a partner and ask if he or she usually does these things. Then, if necessary, give your partner some advice as to what he or she should be doing better.

> ponerse una camiseta blanca
>
> usar protector solar
>
> ponerse debajo de una sombrilla
>
> no salir al sol
>
> ir a la playa por la mañana temprano o tarde por la tarde
>
> ponerse una gorra

MODELO —¿Usas protector solar para protegerte del sol?

—No.

—Tienes que usar protector solar.

¿Sabías que...?

In Spanish speaking countries, some gift-giving traditions are different from those in the United States. For example, in many countries children don't receive gifts from Santa Claus on Christmas Day, but they get them from the Three Wise Men or Three Kings, who arrive on the night of January 5. What different gift-giving traditions do you know about in the United States?

En resumen

¿Para cuándo? **para** el sábado

¿Para quién? **para** mi papá

¿Para qué? **para** tomar el sol

¿Dónde se habla español?

Los cubanoamericanos

When Fidel Castro took control of Cuba in 1959, many Cubans left their homeland to settle in the United States. They did not want to live under communist rule. The largest group settled in Miami and in southern Florida, but many also went to other cities, like Chicago. Most of the Cubans who came here at that time were professionals—doctors, lawyers, teachers, and businessmen.

They learned English and became citizens of the United States while maintaining their Cuban culture. Many have made significant contributions to the United States. Through the years, other Cubans have tried to leave Cuba and enter the United States by sailing the ninety miles between Cuba and Florida in all types of homemade boats. Today there are many Cuban baseball players, musicians, and singers that have become popular throughout the United States.

Cuban American population (percentage)

■	9.0 – 28.9	■	0.2 – 1.4
■	1.4 – 9.0	□	Less than 0.2

◎ ◎ ◎ ◎ ◎ Datos ◎ ◎ ◎ ◎ ◎

Hispanohablantes en EE.UU.: 30 millones

Cubanoamericanos: 1.3 millones

Ciudades principales: Miami, Chicago

¡Léelo en español!

Gloria Estefan y Celia Cruz: Dos cantantes de ascendencia cubana

Celia Cruz, "la Reina de la Salsa" nació en Cuba. Empezó a cantar en La Habana en los años cincuenta. Salió de Cuba en 1960. Cantó hasta su muerte[1] en 2003. Hoy tiene unos ochenta discos. Se conoce[2] en muchos países del mundo. Es una de las latinas más famosas de todos los tiempos. Su música es popular entre muchas personas de muchas generaciones, aún los roqueros y los raperos. Su última canción, "La negra tiene tumbao", es una mezcla de salsa y rap latino. Sus canciones "Guantanamera" y

"Carnaval" son populares hoy día también. Ella siempre llevaba una peluca[3] y tacones[4] muy altos. Es una estrella internacional y una leyenda en el mundo de la música.

Gloria Estefan es otra cantante que nació en la Habana, Cuba. Nació el primero de septiembre de 1957 y su familia salió a Miami en 1959. Su familia era pobre, pero Gloria aprendió a tocar la guitarra de joven y cantó las canciones populares del día. En 1975, durante una boda,[5] Gloria cantó una canción con el conjunto,[6] Miami Latin Boys. Al líder del conjunto, Emilio Estefan, le gustó Gloria y ella se hizo[7] parte de su conjunto. Luego se casaron[8]. El nombre del conjunto cambió a Miami Sound Machine. En 1990, hubo[9] un accidente con el autobús del conjunto y Gloria casi muere. Pasó mucho tiempo en el hospital y en menos de un año empezó a cantar de nuevo. Unas de sus canciones populares son "La Conga", "1–2–3", "Rhythm is Gonna Get You", "Don't Wanna Lose You" y "Get on Your Feet". Hoy día ella es una de las latinas más famosas en el mundo de la música.

[1] death [2] She is known [3] wig
[4] high heels [5] wedding [6] band
[7] became [8] they got married [9] there was

¡Comprendo!

Answer in English.

1. What is Celia Cruz's nickname?
2. When did Celia leave Cuba? When did Gloria leave?
3. How many albums did Celia make?
4. What is Celia known for wearing?
5. Describe Gloria's childhood.
6. How did Gloria join a band?

Appendix

Pronouns

Subject

Singular	Plural
Yo	Nosotros / Nosotras
Tú	Vosotros / Vosotras
Él	Ellos
Ella	Ellas
Ud.	Uds.

Reflexive

Singular	Plural
me	nos
te	os
se	se

Adjectives

Demonstrative Adjectives

Singular / Plural Masculine	Singular / Plural Feminine
este / estos	esta / estas
ese / esos	esa / esas
aquel / aquellos	aquella / aquellas

Verbs

Regular Verbs

-ar Verbs: Model hablar

	Present	Preterite
Yo	hablo	hablé
Tú	hablas	hablaste
Él / Ella / Ud.	habla	habló
Nosotros / Nosotras	hablamos	hablamos
Vosotros / Vosotras	habláis	hablasteis
Ellos / Ellas / Uds.	hablan	hablaron

Gerund: hablando
Familiar commands: ¡Habla! ¡No hables!

-er Verbs: Model comer

	Present	Preterite
Yo	como	comí
Tú	comes	comiste
Él / Ella / Ud.	come	comió
Nosotros / Nosotras	comemos	comimos
Vosotros / Vosotras	coméis	comisteis
Ellos / Ellas / Uds.	comen	comieron

Gerund: comiendo
Familiar commands: ¡Come! ¡No comas!

-ir Verbs: Model abrir

	Present	Preterite
Yo	abro	abrí
Tú	abres	abriste
Él / Ella / Ud.	abre	abrió
Nosotros / Nosotras	abrimos	abrimos
Vosotros / Vosotras	abrís	abristeis
Ellos / Ellas / Uds.	abren	abrieron

Gerund: abriendo
Familiar commands: ¡Abre! ¡No abras!

Stem-Changing Verbs

o to ue: Model probar

	Present	Preterite
Yo	pruebo	probé
Tú	pruebas	probaste
Él / Ella / Ud.	prueba	probó
Nosotros / Nosotras	probamos	probamos
Vosotros / Vosotras	probáis	probasteis
Ellos / Ellas / Uds.	prueban	probaron

e to ie: Model pensar

	Present	Preterite
Yo	pienso	pensé
Tú	piensas	pensaste
Él / Ella / Ud.	piensa	pensó
Nosotros / Nosotras	pensamos	pensamos
Vosotros / Vosotras	pensáis	pensasteis
Ellos / Ellas / Uds.	piensan	pensaron

u to ue: Model jugar

	Present	Preterite
Yo	juego	jugué
Tú	juegas	jugaste
Él / Ella / Ud.	juega	jugó
Nosotros / Nosotras	jugamos	jugamos
Vosotros / Vosotras	jugáis	jugasteis
Ellos / Ellas / Uds.	juegan	jugaron

e to i: Model servir

	Present	Preterite
Yo	sirvo	serví
Tú	sirves	serviste
Él / Ella / Ud.	sirve	sirvió
Nosotros / Nosotras	servimos	servimos
Vosotros / Vosotras	servís	servisteis
Ellos / Ellas / Uds.	sirven	sirvieron

Spelling Changes

-car: **Model** sacar

	Present	Preterite
Yo	saco	saqué
Tú	sacas	sacaste
Él / Ella / Ud.	saca	sacó
Nosotros / Nosotras	sacamos	sacamos
Vosotros / Vosotras	sacáis	sacasteis
Ellos / Ellas / Uds.	sacan	sacaron

Familiar commands: ¡Saca! ¡No saques!
Present participle: sacando

-gar: **Model** pagar

	Present	Preterite
Yo	pago	pagué
Tú	pagas	pagaste
Él / Ella / Ud.	paga	pagó
Nosotros / Nosotras	pagamos	pagamos
Vosotros / Vosotras	pagáis	pagasteis
Ellos / Ellas / Uds.	pagan	pagaron

Familiar commands: ¡Paga! ¡No pagues!
Present participle: pagando

-zar: **Model** almorzar

	Present	Preterite
Yo	almuerzo	almorcé
Tú	almuerzas	almorzaste
Él / Ella / Ud.	almuerza	almorzó
Nosotros / Nosotras	almorzamos	almorzamos
Vosotros / Vosotras	almorzáis	almorzasteis
Ellos / Ellas / Uds.	almuerzan	almorzaron

Familiar commands: ¡Almuerza! ¡No almuerces!
Present participle: almorzando

Irregular Verbs

dar

	Present	Preterite
Yo	doy	di
Tú	das	diste
Él / Ella / Ud.	da	dio
Nosotros / Nosotras	damos	dimos
Vosotros / Vosotras	dais	disteis
Ellos / Ellas / Uds.	dan	dieron

Present participle: dando
Familiar commands: ¡Da! ¡No des!

decir

	Present	Preterite
Yo	digo	dije
Tú	dices	dijiste
Él / Ella / Ud.	dice	dijo
Nosotros / Nosotras	decimos	dijimos
Vosotros / Vosotras	decís	dijisteis
Ellos / Ellas / Uds.	dicen	dijeron

Present participle: diciendo
Familiar commands: ¡Di! ¡No digas!

estar

	Present	Preterite
Yo	estoy	estuve
Tú	estás	estuviste
Él / Ella / Ud.	está	estuvo
Nosotros / Nosotras	estamos	estuvimos
Vosotros / Vosotras	estáis	estuvisteis
Ellos / Ellas / Uds.	están	estuvieron

Present participle: estando
Familiar commands: ¡Está! ¡No estés!

hacer

	Present	Preterite
Yo	hago	hice
Tú	haces	hiciste
Él / Ella / Ud.	hace	hizo
Nosotros / Nosotras	hacemos	hicimos
Vosotros / Vosotras	hacéis	hicisteis
Ellos / Ellas / Uds.	hacen	hicieron

Present participle: haciendo
Familiar commands: ¡Haz! ¡No hagas!

ir

	Present	Preterite
Yo	voy	fui
Tú	vas	fuiste
Él / Ella / Ud.	va	fue
Nosotros / Nosotras	vamos	fuimos
Vosotros / Vosotras	vais	fuisteis
Ellos / Ellas / Uds.	van	fueron

Present participle: yendo
Familiar commands: ¡Ve! ¡No vayas!

oír

	Present	Preterite
Yo	oigo	oí
Tú	oyes	oíste
Él / Ella / Ud.	oye	oyó
Nosotros / Nosotras	oímos	oímos
Vosotros / Vosotras	oís	oísteis
Ellos / Ellas / Uds.	oyen	oyeron

Present participle: oyendo
Familiar commands: ¡Oye! ¡No oigas!

poder

	Present	Preterite
Yo	puedo	pude
Tú	puedes	pudiste
Él / Ella / Ud.	puede	pudo
Nosotros / Nosotras	podemos	pudimos
Vosotros / Vosotras	podeis	pudisteis
Ellos / Ellas / Uds.	pueden	pudieron

Present participle: pudiendo
Familiar commands: ¡Puede! ¡No puedas!

poner

	Present	Preterite
Yo	pongo	puse
Tú	pones	pusiste
Él / Ella / Ud.	pone	puso
Nosotros / Nosotras	ponemos	pusimos
Vosotros / Vosotras	ponéis	pusisteis
Ellos / Ellas / Uds.	ponen	pusieron

Present participle: poniendo
Familiar commands: ¡Pon! ¡No pongas!

querer

	Present	Preterite
Yo	quiero	quise
Tú	quieres	quisiste
Él / Ella / Ud.	quiere	quiso
Nosotros / Nosotras	queremos	quisimos
Vosotros / Vosotras	queréis	quisisteis
Ellos / Ellas / Uds.	quieren	quisieron

Present participle: queriendo
Familiar commands: ¡Quiere! ¡No quieras!

saber

	Present	Preterite
Yo	sé	supe
Tú	sabes	supiste
Él / Ella / Ud.	sabe	supo
Nosotros / Nosotras	sabemos	supimos
Vosotros / Vosotras	sabéis	supisteis
Ellos / Ellas / Uds.	saben	supieron

Present participle: sabiendo
Familiar commands: ¡Sabe! ¡No sepas!

ser

	Present	Preterite
Yo	soy	fui
Tú	eres	fuiste
Él / Ella / Ud.	es	fue
Nosotros / Nosotras	somos	fuimos
Vosotros / Vosotras	sois	fuisteis
Ellos / Ellas / Uds.	son	fueron

Present participle: siendo
Familiar commands: ¡Sé! ¡No seas!

tener

	Present	Preterite
Yo	tengo	tuve
Tú	tienes	tuviste
Él / Ella / Ud.	tiene	tuvo
Nosotros / Nosotras	tenemos	tuvimos
Vosotros / Vosotras	tenéis	tuvisteis
Ellos / Ellas / Uds.	tienen	tuvieron

Present participle: teniendo
Familiar commands: ¡Ten! ¡No tengas!

traer

	Present	Preterite
Yo	traigo	traje
Tú	traes	trajiste
Él / Ella / Ud.	trae	trajo
Nosotros / Nosotras	traemos	trajimos
Vosotros / Vosotras	traéis	trajisteis
Ellos / Ellas / Uds.	traen	trajeron

Present participle: trayendo
Familiar commands: ¡Trae! ¡No traigas!

venir

	Present	Preterite
Yo	vengo	vine
Tú	vienes	viniste
Él / Ella / Ud.	viene	vino
Nosotros / Nosotras	venimos	vinimos
Vosotros / Vosotras	venís	vinisteis
Ellos / Ellas / Uds.	vienen	vinieron

Present participle: viniendo
Familiar commands: ¡Ven! ¡No vengas!

Reflexive Verbs

Model lavarse

	Present	Preterite
Yo	me lavo	me lavé
Tú	te lavas	te lavaste
Él / Ella / Ud.	se lava	se lavó
Nosotros / Nosotras	nos lavamos	nos lavamos
Vosotros / Vosotras	os laváis	os lavasteis
Ellos / Ellas / Uds.	se lavan	se lavaron

Present participle: lavándome, lavándote, lavándose; lavándonos, lavándoos, lavándose
Familiar commands: ¡Lávate! ¡No te laves!

Numbers

0 cero	**26** veintiséis	**51** cincuenta y uno	**76** setenta y seis
1 uno	**27** veintisiete	**52** cincuenta y dos	**77** setenta y siete
2 dos	**28** veintiocho	**53** cincuenta y tres	**78** setenta y ocho
3 tres	**29** veintinueve	**54** cincuenta y cuatro	**79** setenta y nueve
4 cuatro	**30** treinta	**55** cincuenta y cinco	**80** ochenta
5 cinco	**31** treinta y uno	**56** cincuenta y seis	**81** ochenta y uno
6 seis	**32** treinta y dos	**57** cincuenta y siete	**82** ochenta y dos
7 siete	**33** treinta y tres	**58** cincuenta y ocho	**83** ochenta y tres
8 ocho	**34** treinta y cuatro	**59** cincuenta y nueve	**84** ochenta y cuatro
9 nueve	**35** treinta y cinco	**60** sesenta	**85** ochenta y cinco
10 diez	**36** treinta y seis	**61** sesenta y uno	**86** ochenta y seis
11 once	**37** treinta y siete	**62** sesenta y dos	**87** ochenta y siete
12 doce	**38** treinta y ocho	**63** sesenta y tres	**88** ochenta y ocho
13 trece	**39** treinta y nueve	**64** sesenta y cuatro	**89** ochenta y nueve
14 catorce	**40** cuarenta	**65** sesenta y cinco	**90** noventa
15 quince	**41** cuarenta y uno	**66** sesenta y seis	**91** noventa y uno
16 dieciséis	**42** cuarenta y dos	**67** sesenta y siete	**92** noventa y dos
17 diecisiete	**43** cuarenta y tres	**68** sesenta y ocho	**93** noventa y tres
18 dieciocho	**44** cuarenta y cuatro	**69** sesenta y nueve	**94** noventa y cuatro
19 diecinueve	**45** cuarenta y cinco	**70** setenta	**95** noventa y cinco
20 veinte	**46** cuarenta y seis	**71** setenta y uno	**96** noventa y seis
21 veintiuno	**47** cuarenta y siete	**72** setenta y dos	**97** noventa y siete
22 veintidós	**48** cuarenta y ocho	**73** setenta y tres	**98** noventa y ocho
23 veintitrés	**49** cuarenta y nueve	**74** setenta y cuatro	**99** noventa y nueve
24 veinticuatro	**50** cincuenta	**75** setenta y cinco	**100** cien
25 veinticinco			

Hay doscientos alumnos en la escuela.
Hay trescientas sillas en el auditorio.
Hay cuatrocientas cincuenta uvas en la caja.
Hay quinientos pájaros en el parque.
Hay seiscientos libros en mi biblioteca.
Hay setecientas alumnas en la escuela.
Hay ochocientas computadoras en las oficinas.
Hay novecientos veinticinco bolígrafos.
Hay mil quinientas cerezas en la mesa.

Countries and Nationalities

Países donde se habla español	La gente
(la) **Argentina**	el argentino, la argentina
Bolivia	el boliviano, la boliviana
Chile	el chileno, la chilena
Colombia	el colombiano, la colombiana
Costa Rica	el costarricense, la costarricense
Cuba	el cubano, la cubana
(el) **Ecuador**	el ecuatoriano, la ecuatoriana
El Salvador	el salvadoreño, la salvadoreña
España	el español, la española
(los) **Estados Unidos**	el estadounidense, la estadounidense
Guatemala	el guatemalteco, la guatemalteca
(la) **Guinea Ecuatorial**	el guineo, la guinea
Honduras	el hondureño, la hondureña
México	el mexicano, la mexicana
Nicaragua	el nicaragüense, la nicaragüense
Panamá	el panameño, la panameña
(el) **Paraguay**	el paraguayo, la paraguaya
(el) **Perú**	el peruano, la peruana
Puerto Rico (Estado Libre Asociado [Commonwealth] de Estados Unidos)	el puertorriqueño, la puertorriqueña
(la) **República Dominicana**	el dominicano, la dominicana
(el) **Uruguay**	el uruguayo, la uruguaya
Venezuela	el venezolano, la venezolana

Los continentes	La gente
(el) **África**	el africano, la africana
América del Norte	el norteamericano, la norteamericana
América del Sur	el sudamericano, la sudamericana
Antártida	—
Asia	el asiático, la asiática
Australia	el australiano, la australiana
Europa	el europeo, la europea

Otros países	La gente
Alemania	el alemán, la alemana
Belice	el beliceño, la beliceña
(el) **Brasil**	el brasileño, la brasileña
(el) **Canadá**	el canadiense, la canadiense
China	el chino, la china
Egipto	el egipcio, la egipcia
Francia	el francés, la francesa
Grecia	el griego, la griega
Haití	el haitiano, la haitiana
Inglaterra	el inglés, la inglesa
Irlanda	el irlandés, la irlandesa
Italia	el italiano, la italiana
Jamaica	el jamaiquino, la jamaiquina
Japón	el japonés, la japonesa
Marruecos	el marroquí, la marroquí
Nigeria	el nigeriano, la nigeriana
Portugal	el portugués, la portuguesa
Rusia	el ruso, la rusa
Turquía	el turco, la turca

Word List

Spanish-English

The Spanish-English Word List contains the Spanish words you've already learned in *¡Hola!* and *¿Qué tal?* and the words you learn in each unit of *¡Adelante!* A number in parentheses indicates the unit where a word was taught. (Q) indicates that a word comes from *¿Qué tal?* and (H) indicates that a word comes from *¡Hola!*

Here's a sample entry—a word and its English equivalent:

     la **computadora**   computer   (H)

The bold letters in different type tell you that **computadora** is the entry. "La" tells you to use "la," (not "el") with **computadora.** (H) tells you that **computadora** was taught in one of the units of *¡Hola!*

Here's another entry:

     la **agencia de viajes**   travel agency (5)

(5) tells you that **agencia de viajes** is taught in *Unidad 5* of *¡Adelante!*

Here are the complete Word List abbreviations:

Abbreviations

adj.	adjective	*inf.*	infinitive
adv.	adverb	*m.*	masculine
com.	command	*pl.*	plural
f.	feminine	*s.*	singular

A

a to, at (H)
    a la derecha to the right (3)
    a la izquierda to the left (3)
    ¿A qué hora? At what time? (H)
    a tiempo on time (6)
    a veces sometimes (H)
abierto, abierta open (8)
el **abrelatas** (*pl.: los abrelatas*) can opener (Q)
el **abrigo** coat (Q)
abril April (H)
abrir to open (Q)
abrochar to buckle, to fasten (3)
    abrocharse el cinturón to fasten your seatbelt (3)
la **abuela** grandmother (H)
el **abuelo** grandfather (H)
los **abuelos** grandparents (H)
aburrido, aburrida boring (H)
acabar to finish, to just finish (Q)
    acabar de (*+ inf.*) to have just (done something) (Q)
acostarse (**o ➡ ue**) (*reflexive*) to go to bed (Q)
adiós good-bye (H)
¿adónde? (to) where? (H)
el **aeropuerto** airport (4)
la **agencia de viajes** travel agency (5)
el **agente de viajes** (male) travel agent (5)
la **agente de viajes** (female) travel agent (5)
agosto August (H)
el **agua** (*f.*) water (Q)
ahora now (H)
ahorrar to save (8)
el **ajedrez** chess (1)
al (*a + el*) to the (H)
las **albóndigas** meatballs (Q)
la **alcaldía** city hall (9)
la **alfombra** rug, carpet (Q)
alguien somebody, someone (2)
la **almohada** pillow (Q)
almorzar (**o ➡ ue**) to eat (have) lunch (Q)
el **almuerzo** lunch (Q)
alto, alta tall (H)
la **alumna** (female) student (H)
el **alumno** (male) student (H)
amarillo, amarilla yellow (H)
América Central Central America (4)

América del Norte North America (4)
América del Sur South America (4)
la **amiga** (female) friend (H)
el **amigo** (male) friend (H)
los **amigos** (male or male and female) friends (H)
anaranjado, anaranjada orange (color) (H)
el **anillo** ring (11)
el **animal** (*pl.: animales*) animal (H)
antes before (Q)
antiguo, antigua old-fashioned, ancient (objects) (7)
antipático, antipática unpleasant (H)
el **año** year (H)
    ¿Cuántos años tiene? How old is he (she)? (H)
    el año pasado last year (8)
    los meses del año the months of the year (H)
apagar to extinguish (2)
el **apartamento** apartment (Q)
aprender to learn (H)
    aprender a (*+ inf.*) to learn (how to do something) (H)
aquel (*m.*) that (over there) (12)
aquella (*f.*) that (over there) (12)
aquellas (*f.*) those (over there) (12)
aquellos (*m.*) those (over there) (12)
la **arena** sand (12)
los **aretes** earrings (11)
el **arroz** rice (Q)
el **arte** art (H)
el **ascensor** elevator (7)
así so (H)
así, así so-so (H)
el **asiento** seat (6)
la **asistente administrativa** (female) administrative assistant (Q)
el **asistente administrativo** (male) administrative assistant (Q)
el **asistente de vuelo** (male) flight attendant (6)
la **asistente de vuelo** (female) flight attendant (6)
la **aspiradora** vacuum cleaner (Q)
    pasar la aspiradora to vacuum (Q)
aterrizar to land (6)
el **ático** attic (Q)
atlético, atlética athletic (Q)

el **audiocasete** cassette (11)
el **auditorio** auditorium (Q)
el **autobús** bus (3)
la **avena** oatmeal (Q)
la **avenida** avenue (3)
el **avión** (*pl.: aviones*) airplane (4)
ayer yesterday (8)
ayudar to help (2)
el **azúcar** sugar (Q)
azul blue (H)

B

bailar to dance (H)
bajar to go down (Q)
   bajar las escaleras to go down the stairs (Q)
bajo, baja short (H)
el **balcón** (*pl.: balcones*) balcony (Q)
el **baloncesto** basketball (1)
el **banco** bank (8)
la **bandera** flag (H)
bañarse (*reflexive*) to take a bath (Q)
   el traje de baño bathing suit, swimsuit (Q)
la **bañera** bathtub (7)
barato, barata cheap (11)
el **barco** boat, ship (4)
   el barco de vela sailboat (12)
barrer to sweep (Q)
   barrer el piso to sweep the floor (Q)
la **basura** trash (Q)
   sacar la basura to take out the trash (Q)
la **bata** robe, bathrobe (Q)
la **batidora eléctrica** electric mixer (Q)
batir to beat, to whisk (food) (Q)
beber to drink (Q)
el **béisbol** baseball (1)
la **biblioteca** library (H)
la **bibliotecaria** (female) librarian (Q)
el **bibliotecario** (male) librarian (Q)
la **bicicleta** bicycle (1)
   andar en bicicleta to ride a bike (1)
bien well, fine (H)
   Me queda bien. It fits me well. (Q)
   muy bien very well (H)
¡Bienvenidos! Welcome! (H)
el **billete** (plane) ticket (5), (money) bill (8)
la **bisabuela** great-grandmother (H)
el **bisabuelo** great-grandfather (H)
los **bisabuelos** great-grandparents (H)

blanco, blanca white (H)
blando, blanda soft (7)
la **blusa** blouse (Q)
la **boca** mouth (Q)
el **bol** (*pl.: boles*) bowl (Q)
el **bolígrafo** ballpoint pen (H)
la **bolsa** handbag, bag (11)
la **bombera** (female) firefighter (2)
el **bombero** (male) firefighter (2)
la **bombilla** light bulb (Q)
bonito, bonita pretty (Q)
el **borrador** (*pl.: borradores*) chalk eraser (H)
las **botas** boots (Q)
el **brazalete** bracelet (11)
el **brazo** arm (Q)
bronceado, bronceada suntanned (12)
bucear to dive (12)
buen good (*before a s. m. noun*) (H)
   Hace buen tiempo. The weather is good. (H)
bueno, buena good (H)
   ¡Buenas noches! Good evening!, Good night! (H)
   ¡Buenas tardes! Good afternoon! (H)
   ¡Buenos días! Good morning! (H)
buscar to look for (9)
el **buzón** (*pl.: buzones*) mailbox (Q)

C

el **caballo** horse (1)
   montar a caballo to ride a horse (1)
la **cabeza** head (Q)
el **café** coffee (Q)
la **cafetería** cafeteria (Q)
la **caja** box (Q)
la **cajera** (female) cashier (8)
el **cajero** (male) cashier (8)
   el cajero automático cash dispenser (ATM) (8)
el **cajón** (*pl.: cajones*) drawer (Q)
el **calcetín** (*pl.: calcetines*) socks, knee socks (Q)
el **calendario** calendar (H)
caliente hot (7)
la **calle** street (3)
el **calor** heat (H)
   Hace calor. It's hot. (H)
   Tengo calor. I'm hot. (H)
la **cama** bed (Q)

la **camarera** (female) server (8)

el **camarero** (male) server (8)

cambiar to change (8)

caminar to walk (H)

la **camisa** shirt (Q)

la **camiseta** T-shirt, undershirt (Q)

el **canario** canary (H)

la **cancha** court, field (1)

canoso, canosa gray (hair) (Q)

cansado, cansada tired (9)

cantar to sing (H)

la **cara** face (Q)

el **caracol** conch shell (12)

la **carne** meat (Q)

caro, cara expensive (11)

el **cartel** (*pl.: carteles*) poster (Q)

la **casa** house, home (H)

castaño, castaña brown, chestnut (hair) (Q)

la **ceja** eyebrow (Q)

celebrar to celebrate (H)

la **cena** dinner (Q)

cenar to have dinner (Q)

el **centro** downtown (3)

cepillarse (*reflexive*) to brush oneself (Q)

   cepillarse los dientes (*reflexive*)
to brush one's teeth (Q)

la **cerca** fence (Q)

cerca de near, close to (Q)

el **cereal** cereal (Q)

la **cereza** cherry (Q)

cerrado, cerrada closed (8)

cerrar (e ➡ ie) to close, to shut (Q)

la **chaqueta** jacket (Q)

el **cheque** check (8)

la **chica** girl (H)

el **chico** boy (H)

la **chimenea** fireplace, chimney (Q)

el **chocolate** chocolate (Q)

el **chofer** (male) driver (3)

la **chofer** (female) driver (3)

las **ciencias** science (H)

el **cine** movie theater, movies (H)

   ir al cine to go to the movies (H)

la **cintura** waist (Q)

el **cinturón** seat belt (3), belt (11)

el **círculo** circle (H)

la **ciudad** city (3)

claro of course (H)

   ¡Claro que sí! Of course! (H)

la **clase** class (H)

   la clase de computadoras computer
class (H)

   el salón de clase classroom (H)

el **coche** car (3)

la **cocina** kitchen (Q)

cocinar to cook (Q)

la **cocinera** (female) cook (Q)

el **cocinero** (male) cook (Q)

el **codo** elbow (Q)

coleccionar estampillas to collect stamps (1)

colgar (o ➡ ue) to hang up (Q)

   colgar la ropa to hang up clothes (Q)

el **collar** necklace (11)

el **color** (*pl.: colores*) color (H)

   ¿De qué color es? What color is it? (H)

el **comedor** dining room; (school)
cafeteria (Q)

comenzar (e ➡ ie) to begin, to start (Q)

comer to eat (Q)

cómico, cómica funny, amusing (Q)

la **comida** food (Q)

¿Cómo...? How...?, What...? (H)

   ¿Cómo me queda? How does it fit me? (Q)

   ¿Cómo se dice? How do you say it? (H)

cómodo, cómoda comfortable (6)

la **compañía** company (2)

comprar to buy (H)

comprender to understand (H)

la **computadora** computer (H)

   la clase de computadoras
computer class (H)

   usar la computadora
to use the computer (H)

la **comunidad** community (2)

con with (Q)

la **concha** seashell (12)

el **conejo** rabbit (H)

confundido, confundida confused (9)

conocer to know, to meet (2)

el **conserje** (male) custodian (Q)

la **conserje** (female) custodian (Q)

contento, contenta happy (9)

correr to run (Q)

las **cortinas** curtains (Q)

corto, corta short (H)

costar (o ➡ ue) to cost (5)

la **crema** cream (Q)

   la crema de cacahuate peanut butter (Q)

el **cuaderno** notebook (H)

la **cuadra** city block (10)

el **cuadrado** square (H)

el **cuadro** painting (Q)

¿Cuál? (*pl.: ¿Cuáles?*) What?, Which one(s)? (H)

¿Cuál es tu número de teléfono?
What is your telephone number? (H)

¿Cuándo? When? (H)

¿Cuánto? (*m. s.*) **¿Cuánta?** (*f. s.*)
How much? (H)

¿Cuánto es... más...?
How much is... plus... ? (H)

¿Cuántos? (*m. pl.*) **¿Cuántas?**
(*f. pl.*) How many? (H)

¿Cuántos/ Cuántas... hay?
How many... are there? (H)

¿Cuántos años tienes? How old
are you? (H)

el **cuarto** quarter (H); room (Q)

un cuarto de hora a quarter of an hour (H)

una hora y cuarto an hour and a
quarter (H)

el **cuarto de baño** bathroom (Q)

la **cuchara** spoon, tablespoon (Q)

la **cucharita** teaspoon (Q)

el **cuchillo** knife (Q)

el **cuello** neck (Q)

la **cuenta** restaurant check, bill (8)

el **cuerpo** body (Q)

las partes del cuerpo parts of the body (Q)

cultivar plantas to grow plants (1)

el **cumpleaños** birthday (H)

¿Cuándo es tu cumpleaños? When is
your birthday? (H)

D

las **damas** checkers (1)

dar to give (8)

dar la mano to shake hands (8)

dar las gracias to thank (8)

de of, in, from (H)

de acuerdo okay, in agreement (9)

¿De quién? Whose? (H)

de viaje taking a trip (5)

debajo de under, underneath (Q)

débil weak (Q)

el **dedo** finger (Q)

del (de + el) of the, from the (Q)

delante de in front of (Q)

dentro de inside, in (Q)

departamento department (2)

los **deportes** sports (H)

practicar deportes to practice (play)
sports (H)

la **derecha** the right (3)

a la derecha to the right, on the right (3)

derecho (*adv.*) straight ahead (3)

el **desayuno** breakfast (Q)

descansar to rest (5)

el **desierto** desert (5)

el **despacho** study, office (Q)

despacio slow (10)

despegar to take off (6)

despertarse (*reflexive*)
to wake up (Q) **(e ➡ ie)**

detrás de behind, in back of (Q)

el **día** day (H)

el día de la semana weekday (H)

el día de fiesta holiday (H)

dibujar to draw (H)

diciembre December (H)

el **diente** tooth (Q)

difícil (*pl.: difíciles*) difficult (H)

el **dinero** money (8)

el **director** (male) director, school
principal (Q)

la **directora** (female) director, school
principal (Q)

el **disco compacto** compact disc (11)

la **distancia** distance (4)

divertido, divertida amusing, fun (H)

doblar to turn (3)

el **dólar** (*pl.: dólares*) dollar (5)

doler (o ➡ ue) to hurt, to ache (Q)

Me duele la cabeza. My head hurts.
I have a headache. (Q)

Le duele el pie. His/her foot hurts. (Q)

Le duelen los pies. His/her feet
hurt. (Q)

Te duele la cabeza. Your head hurts. (Q)

el **domingo** Sunday (H)

los domingos on Sundays (H)

el **dominó** domino (1)

¿dónde? where? (H)

dormirse to fall asleep (7)

el **dormitorio** bedroom (Q)

la **ducha** shower (7)

ducharse (*reflexive*) to take a shower (Q)

la **dueña** (female) owner (2)
el **dueño** (male) owner (2)
el **durazno** peach (Q)
    duro, dura hard (7)
el **DVD** DVD (disc) (Q)

E

el **ecuador** equator (H)
el **edificio** building (3)
    el edificio de apartamentos apartment building (9)
la **educación física** physical education (H)
    el *(m. s.)* the (H)
    él he (H)
    eléctrico, eléctrica electric, electrical (Q)
    ella she (H)
    ellas *(f.)* they (Q)
    ellos *(m.)* they (Q)
la **empleada** (female) employee (2)
el **empleado** (male) employee (2)
    en in, on (H)
    en autobús by bus (3)
    en avión by plane (4)
    en punto on the dot, sharp (time) (H)
    en tren by train (4)
el **enchufe** plug, electrical socket (Q)
    encontrarse (o ➡ ue) *(reflexive)* to meet, to be found (10)
    enero January (H)
la **enfermera** (female) nurse (Q)
la **enfermería** infirmary, nurse's office (Q)
el **enfermero** (male) nurse (Q)
    enojado, enojada angry, upset (9)
la **ensalada** salad (Q)
la **entrada** entrance (Q)
    entre among, between (H)
    entre amigos among friends (H)
el **equipaje** baggage (6)
el **equipo** team (1)
    Es... It's … (H)
    esa *(f.)* that (12)
    esas *(f.)* those (12)
las **escaleras** stairs (Q)
    bajar las escaleras to go down the stairs (Q)
    subir las escaleras to go up the stairs (Q)
la **escoba** broom (Q)
    escribir to write (H)
el **escritorio** (large) desk (H)

    escuchar to listen (H)
la **escuela** school (H)
la **escultura** sculpture (9)
    ese *(m.)* that (12)
    esos *(m.)* those (12)
los **espaguetis** spaghetti (Q)
    los espaguetis con albóndigas spaghetti with meatballs (Q)
la **espalda** back (Q)
el **español** Spanish (H)
    especial special (11)
    espectacular spectacular (H)
el **espejo** mirror (Q)
el **esquí acuático** water skiing (12)
la **esquina** corner (10)
    esta *(f.)* this (12)
la **estación** season (H)
la **estación de bomberos** fire station (2)
la **estación de policía** police station (2)
la **estación de trenes** train station (4)
el **estacionamiento** parking lot (3)
el **estadio** stadium (1)
el **estante** shelf (Q)
la **estantería** bookcase (Q)
    estar to be (H)
    Está lloviendo. It's raining. (H)
    Está nevando. It's snowing. (H)
    Está nublado. It's cloudy. (H)
    estás you *(familiar)* are (H)
    Estoy muy mal. I don't feel well at all. (H)
    estas *(f.)* these (12)
    este *(m.)* this (12)
el **este** east (10)
el **estéreo** sound system, stereo (Q)
    estos *(m.)* these (12)
    estudiar to study (H)
los **estudios sociales** social studies (H)
la **estufa** stove (Q)
    examinar to examine (2)

F

la **fábrica** factory (2)
    fabuloso, fabulosa fabulous (H)
    fácil *(pl.: fáciles)* easy (H)
la **falda** skirt (Q)
la **familia** family (H)
    fantástico, fantástica fantastic (H)
la **farmacia** pharmacy, drug store (3)
el **farol** street lamp (10)

el **favor** favor (Q)
    por favor please (Q)
favorito, favorita favorite (H)
febrero February (H)
la **fecha** date (H)
    ¿Qué fecha es hoy? What's today's date? (H)
feliz (*pl.: felices*) happy (H)
    ¡Feliz cumpleaños! Happy birthday! (H)
feo, fea ugly (Q)
el **fin** (*pl.: fines*) end (H)
    el fin de semana weekend (H)
flaco, flaca thin (H)
el **flamenco** flamingo (H)
flotar to float (12)
el **fregadero** sink (Q)
la **frente** forehead (Q)
la **fresa** strawberry (Q)
fresco, fresca cool, fresh (H)
    Hace fresco. It's cool (weather). (H)
los **frijoles** beans (Q)
frío, fría cold (H)
    Hace frío. It's cold (weather). (H)
    tener frío to be cold (H)
frito, frita fried (Q)
la **fruta** fruit (Q)
la **fuente** fountain (9)
    la fuente de agua drinking fountain, water fountain (Q)
fuera de out, outside (Q)
fuerte strong (Q)
el **fútbol** soccer (1)
    el fútbol americano football (U.S.) (1)

G

el **gabinete** cabinet (Q)
el **garaje** garage (Q)
la **gasolinera** gas station (3)
gastar to spend (8)
el **gato** cat (H)
generoso, generosa generous (Q)
la **gente** people (2)
el **gimnasio** gymnasium (H)
el **globo** globe (H)
gordo, gorda fat (H)
la **gorra** cap (Q)
gracias thank you (H)
grande big, large (H)
el **grifo** faucet (Q)

la **gripe** flu (H)
    tener la gripe to have the flu (H)
gris gray (H)
guapo, guapa good-looking (H)
el **guisante** pea (Q)
gustar to like, to please (H)
    ¿Qué te gusta hacer...? What do you like to do...? (H)
    Le gusta el verano. He/She likes summer. (H)
    Me gusta la primavera. I like spring. (H)
    ¿Te gusta pintar? Do you like to paint? (H)

H

la **habitación** room (7)
hablar to speak, to talk (H)
hacer to do, to make (H)
    Hace frío. It's cold. (H)
    Hace sol. It's sunny. (H)
    hacer fila to stand in line (6)
    ¿Qué tiempo hace? What's the weather like? (H)
    ¿Qué vas a hacer? What are you going to do? (H)
el **hambre** (*f.*) hunger (H)
    tener hambre to be hungry (H)
la **hamburguesa** hamburger (Q)
hasta until (H)
    ¡Hasta luego! See you later! (H)
    ¡Hasta mañana! See you tomorrow! (H)
    ¡Hasta pronto! See you soon! (H)
hay there is, there are (H)
el **helado** ice cream (Q)
la **hermana** sister (H)
la **hermanastra** stepsister (H)
el **hermanastro** stepbrother (H)
el **hermano** brother (H)
los **hermanos** brothers and sisters, brothers (H)
la **hija** daughter (H)
el **hijo** son (H)
los **hijos** children, sons and daughters (H)
la **hoja de papel** sheet of paper (H)
    ¡Hola! Hello!, Hi! (H)
el **hombre** man (H)
el **hombro** shoulder (Q)
la **hora** hour, time (H)
    ¿A qué hora...? At what time...? (H)
    ¿Qué hora es? What time is it? (H)

el **horario** schedule (6)

el **horno** oven (Q)

el **hospital** hospital (2)

el **hotel** hotel (7)

hoy today (H)

¿Qué día es hoy? What day is
today? (H)

el **huevo** egg (Q)

los huevos fritos fried eggs (Q)

los huevos pasados por agua
hard-boiled eggs (Q)

los huevos revueltos scrambled
eggs (Q)

I

impaciente impatient (Q)

el **impermeable** raincoat (Q)

importante important (H)

el **incendio** fire (2)

incómodo, incómoda uncomfortable (6)

el **inglés** English (H)

el **instrumento** (musical) instrument (1)

inteligente intelligent (Q)

interesante interesting (H)

el **invierno** winter (H)

ir to go (H)

ir a (+ *inf.*) to be going to (do
something) (H)

ir a pie to go on foot (3)

ir de pesca to go fishing (1)

irse (*reflexive*) to leave, to go away (Q)

Me voy a la escuela. I'm leaving for
school. (Q)

la **izquierda** left (3)

a la izquierda to the left, on the left (3)

J

el **jabón** (*pl.: jabones*) soap (7)

el **jamón** (*pl.: jamones*) ham (Q)

el **jardín** (*pl.: jardines*) garden (Q)

joven (*pl.: jóvenes*) young (H)

las **joyas** jewelery (11)

la **joyería** jewelery store (11)

la **joyera** (female) jeweler (11)

el **joyero** (male) jeweler (11)

el **juego electrónico** (electronic) computer
game (1)

el **jueves** Thursday (H)

los jueves on Thursdays (H)

el **jugador** (male) player (1)

la **jugadora** (female) player (1)

jugar (u ➔ ue) to play (a game or
sport) (H)

el **jugo** juice (Q)

julio July (H)

junio June (H)

K

el **kilómetro** kilometer (10)

L

la (*f. s.*) the (H)

el **labio** lip (Q)

lacio, lacia straight (hair) (Q)

el **lago** lake (5)

la **lámpara** lamp (Q)

la **lancha** motor boat (12)

el **lápiz** (*pl.: lápices*) pencil (H)

largo, larga long (H)

las (*f. pl.*) the (H)

la **lata** can (Q)

la **lavadora** washing machine (Q)

el **lavaplatos** (*pl.: los lavaplatos*)
dishwasher (Q)

lavar to wash (Q)

lavar la ropa to wash clothers, to do
laundry (Q)

lavarse (*reflexive*) to wash oneself (Q)

le to him/her/you (*formal*) (H)

la **lección** (*pl.: lecciones*) lesson (H)

la **leche** milk (Q)

la **lechuga** lettuce (Q)

el **lector de DVD** DVD player (4)

la **lectura** reading (H)

leer to read (H)

lejos de far from (Q)

la **lengua** tongue (Q)

levantarse (*reflexive*) to get up (Q)

el **libro** book (H)

la **licuadora** blender (Q)

el **limón** (*pl.: limones*) lemon (Q)

limpiar to clean (H), to wash (Q)

limpiar el piso to clean/wash
the floor (Q)

limpio, limpia clean (Q)

la **línea aérea** airline (6)

llamarse to be called (H)

la **llave** key (7)

el **llavero**   key ring, key chain (11)
la **llegada**   arrival (6)
llegar   to arrive (6)
llevar   to wear (Q), to take (12)
llover (o → ue)   to rain (H)
Llueve.   It's raining. (H)
el **loro**   parrot (H)
los   *(m. pl.)*   the (H)
luego   *(adv.)*   later, then (Q)
¡Hasta luego!   See you later! (H)
el **lugar**   place (10)
el **lunes**   Monday (H)
los lunes   on Mondays (H)
la **luz** *(pl.: luces)*   light (H)

M

la **madrastra**   stepmother (H)
la **madre**   mother (H)
la **maestra**   (female) teacher (H)
el **maestro**   (male) teacher (H)
el **maíz**   corn (Q)
mal *(adj., before a m. s. noun)* bad; *(adv.)*
not well, badly (H)
Hace mal tiempo.   The weather
is bad. (H)
Me queda mal.   It fits me badly. (Q)
la **maleta**   suitcase (6)
malo   bad (H)
la **mamá**   mother, mom (H)
la **mano**   hand (Q)
la **manta**   blanket (7)
el **mantel** *(pl.: manteles)* tablecloth (Q)
la **mantequilla**   butter (Q)
la **manzana**   apple (Q); city block (10)
mañana   *(adv.)*   tomorrow (H)
¡Hasta mañana! See you tomorrow! (H)
la **mañana**   morning (H)
de/por la mañana   in the morning
(a. m.) (H)
el **mapa**   map (H)
el **mar**   sea (12)
maravilloso, maravillosa   wonderful (H)
el **marcador**   marker (H)
la **margarina**   margarine (Q)
la **mariposa**   butterfly (H)
marrón *(pl.: marrones)*   brown (H)
el **martes**   Tuesday (H)
los martes   on Tuesdays (H)
marzo   March (H)

más   plus (H); more (Q)
el más, la más   the most (Q)
más o menos   so-so (H)
más... que   more... than (Q)
las **matemáticas**   mathematics (H)
mayo   May (H)
la **mayonesa**   mayonnaise (Q)
me   (to) me, myself (H)
Me gusta...   I like... (H)
Me llamo...   My name is... (H)
mediano, mediana   medium (Q)
la **medianoche**   midnight (H)
a medianoche   at midnight (H)
las **medias**   pantyhose, stockings (Q)
la **médica**   (female) medical doctor (2)
el **médico**   (male) medical doctor (2)
medio, media   half (H)
media hora   a half-hour (H)
una hora y media   an hour and a half (H)
el **mediodía**   noon, midday (H)
a mediodía   at midday, noon (H)
la **mejilla**   cheek (Q)
menos   to, of (time) (H); less, minus (Q)
menos... que   less... than (Q)
Son las dos menos cuarto.   It's fifteen
to two., It's a quarter to (of) two. (H)
el **menú**   menu (8)
el **mercado**   market (3)
el mercado al aire libre   open-air
market (9)
la **mermelada**   jam, marmalade (Q)
el **mes** *(pl.: meses)*   month (H)
la **mesa**   table (H)
la **mesita de noche**   night table (Q)
el **metro**   subway (9); meter (10)
mi *(pl.: mis)*   my (H)
el **microondas**   microwave (oven) (Q)
el **miedo**   fear (H)
tener miedo   to be afraid, to be
scared (H)
el **miércoles**   Wednesday (H)
los miércoles   on Wednesdays (H)
la **milla**   mile (10)
el **minuto**   minute (H)
mirar   to look (at), to watch (Q)
moderno, moderna   modern (7)
la **moneda**   coin (8)
la **montaña**   mountain (5)

montar a caballo to ride a horse (1)

el **monumento** monument (9)

morado, morada purple (H)

la **mostaza** mustard (Q)

mucho (*adv.*) a lot (H)

mucho, mucha (*adj.*) much (Q)

muchos, muchas (*adj.*) many (Q)

los **muebles** furniture (Q)

la **mujer** (*pl.: mujeres*) woman (H)

el **museo** museum (9)

la **música** music (H)

muy very (H)

Muy bien, gracias. Very well, thank you. (H)

N

nada nothing (Q)

nadar to swim (H)

nadie nobody (2)

la **naranja** orange (fruit) (Q)

la **nariz** (*pl.: narices*) nose (Q)

la **Navidad** Christmas (H)

necesitar to need (Q)

negro, negra black (H)

nervioso, nerviosa nervous (9)

nevar (e → ie) to snow (H)

Nieva. It's snowing. (H)

la **nieta** granddaughter (H)

el **nieto** grandson (H)

los **nietos** grandchildren, grandsons (H)

la **niña** girl (H)

el **niño** boy (H)

no no, not (H)

la **noche** night, evening (H)

¡Buenas noches! Good evening!, Good night! (H)

el **norte** north (10)

nosotras (*f.*) we, us (Q)

nosotros (*m.*) we, us (Q)

noviembre November (H)

nublado, nublada cloudy (H)

Está nublado. It's cloudy. (H)

nuestro, nuestra, nuestros, nuestras our (Q)

nuevo, nueva new (Q)

el **número** number (H)

el número de teléfono telephone number (H)

nunca never (H)

O

la **obrera** (female) factory worker (2)

el **obrero** (male) factory worker (2)

octubre October (H)

el **oeste** west (10)

la **oficina** office (Q)

el **ojo** eye (Q)

la **ola** wave (12)

ondulado, ondulada wavy (hair) (Q)

la **oreja** ear (Q)

el **oso** bear (H)

el **otoño** fall, autumn (H)

P

el **paciente** (male) patient (2)

la **paciente** (female) patient (2)

el **padrastro** stepfather (H)

el **padre** father (H)

los **padres** parents, fathers (H)

pagar to pay (5)

el **país** (*pl.: países*) country (4)

el **pájaro** bird (H)

el **pan** bread (Q)

el pan tostado toast (Q)

los **pantalones** slacks, trousers, pants (Q)

la **papa** potato (Q)

el **papá** father, dad (H)

los **papás** parents, fathers (H)

el **papel** (*pl.: papeles*) paper (H)

la hoja de papel sheet of paper (H)

la **papelera** wastebasket (H)

para for, in order to (11, 12)

la **parada de autobús** bus stop (3)

la **pared** (*pl.: paredes*) wall (H)

el **parque** park (H)

la **parte** part (Q)

participar to participate, to take part in (H)

la **pasajera** (female) passenger (6)

el **pasajero** (male) passenger (6)

pasar to pass (Q)

pasar la aspiradora to vacuum (Q)

pasar por... to go by/past... (3)

el **pasatiempo** hobby (1)

el **pasillo** corridor, hall, hallway (Q)

el **paso de peatones** pedestrian crossing (10)

patinar to skate (H)

el **patio** courtyard, patio (Q)

el **pavo** turkey (Q)

el **peatón** (*pl.: peatones*) pedestrian (10)
pedir (e ➡ i) to ask for, to order (3)
peinarse (*reflexive*) to comb one's hair (Q)
el **peligro** danger (12)
el **pelo** hair (Q)
    el pelo canoso gray hair (Q)
    el pelo castaño brown (chestnut) hair (Q)
    el pelo lacio straight hair (Q)
    el pelo ondulado wavy hair (Q)
    el pelo rizado curly hair (Q)
    el pelo rojizo red hair (Q)
    el pelo rubio blond hair (Q)
la **pelota** ball (1)
pensar (e ➡ ie) (*+ inf.*) to think (of doing), to plan (to do) (Q)
pequeño, pequeña small, little (H)
la **pera** pear (Q)
perderse (e ➡ ie) to get lost, to be lost (10)
pero but (Q)
el **perro** dog (H)
la **persona** person (Q)
el **pescado** (in cooking) fish (Q)
las **pestañas** eyelashes (Q)
el **pez** (*pl.: peces*) (live) fish (H)
el **pie** (*pl.: pies*) foot (Q)
la **pierna** leg (Q)
el **pijama** pajamas (Q)
el **piloto** (male) pilot (6)
la **piloto** (female) pilot (6)
la **pimienta** pepper (Q)
pintar to paint (H)
la **piña** pineapple (Q)
el **piso** floor (Q)
el **pizarrón** chalkboard, blackboard, whiteboard (H)
plancha iron (appliance) (Q)
planchar to iron (Q)
    planchar la ropa to iron clothes (7)
la **planta** plant (Q)
    cultivar plantas to grow plants (1)
    regar las plantas to water the plants (Q)
el **plátano** banana (Q)
el **platillo** saucer (Q)
el **plato** dish, plate (Q)
la **playa** beach (5)
la **plaza** public square (3)
poco little (amount) (Q)
    un poco a little bit (Q)

pocos, pocas few (Q)
poder (o ➡ ue) to be able (Q)
el **policía** (male) police officer (2)
la **policía** (female) police officer (2)
el **pollo** chicken (Q)
el **polvo** dust (Q)
    quitar el polvo to dust (Q)
poner to set, to place (Q)
    poner la mesa to set the table (Q)
ponerse (*reflexive*) to put on, to wear (Q)
    ponerse la ropa to get dressed (Q)
popular popular (Q)
por in (time) (H)
    por la mañana in the morning (H)
    por la tarde in the afternoon (H)
    por la noche in the evening (H)
    ¡Por favor! Please! (Q)
    ¿Por qué? Why? (H)
    ¿Por qué no? Why not? (H)
    ¡Por supuesto! Of course! (Q)
    por último last, finally (Q)
practicar to practice (H)
    practicar deportes to practice (play) sports (H)
preferir (e ➡ ie) to prefer (8)
la **prima** (female) cousin (H)
la **primavera** spring (H)
primero, primera (*adj.*) first (H)
el **primero** the first (of the month) (H)
el **primo** (male) cousin (H)
los **primos** cousins (H)
la **prisa** hurry (H)
    tener prisa to be in a hurry (H)
probar (o ➡ ue) to taste, to try (Q)
prohibir to forbid (12)
    Se prohíbe nadar. No swimming. (12)
pronto soon (H)
    ¡Hasta pronto! See you soon! (H)
la **propina** tip (8)
el **protector solar** sunscreen lotion (12)
próximo, próxima next (H)
    la próxima semana next week (H)
la **puerta** door (H)
    la puerta de embarque (airport) gate (6)
el **puerto** port (4)
la **puesta del sol** sunset (H)
el **pupitre** student's desk (H)

Q

que   than (Q)
  más... que   more... than (Q)
  menos... que   less... than (Q)
¿Qué?   What? (H)
  ¿Qué tal?   How's it going? (H)
  ¿Qué tienes?   What's the matter?, What
    do you have? (H)
  ¿Qué vas a comprar?   What are you going
    to buy? (Q)
quedar   to fit (clothes) (Q)
  Me queda bien/mal.   It fits me
    well/badly. (Q)
quedar más adelante   to be located ahead (10)
quedar más atrás   to be located further
    back (10)
el **quehacer** (*pl.: quehaceres*)   chore (Q)
quemado, quemada   burnt, sunburnt (12)
querer (e ➡ ie)   to want (Q)
el **queso**   cheese (Q)
¿Quién?   Who? (H)
  ¿Quién es...?   Who is...? (H)
quitar   to remove, to take off (Q)
  quitar el polvo   to dust (Q)
quitarse la ropa   undress, to take off one's
    clothes (Q)

R

el **radio**   radio (Q)
rápido   rapidly, quickly (10)
el **rascacielos**   skyscraper (3)
el **ratón** (*pl.: ratones*)   mouse (H)
la **raza**   race (H)
la **razón** (*pl.: razones*)   reason (H)
  tener razón   to be right (H)
recoger   to pick up, to clean up (Q)
  recoger las cosas   to straighten up (Q)
el **rectángulo**   rectangle (H)
el **refrigerador** (*pl.: refrigeradores*)
    refrigerator (Q)
el **regalo**   gift, present (11)
regar (e ➡ ie) las plantas   to water the
    plants (Q)
la **regla**   ruler (H)
el **reloj** (*pl.: relojes*)   clock (H)
el **restaurante**   restaurant (8)
el **retrato**   portrait (Q)
el **río**   river (5)

rizado, rizada   curly (hair) (Q)
la **rodilla**   knee (Q)
rojizo, rojiza   red (hair) (Q)
rojo, roja   red (H)
la **ropa**   clothes, clothing (Q)
el **ropero**   closet, wardrobe (Q)
rosado, rosada   pink (H)
rubio, rubia   blond (hair) (Q)

S

el **sábado**   Saturday (H)
  los sábados   on Saturdays (H)
la **sábana**   sheet (7)
saber (*+ inf.*)   to know how to (do
    something) (Q)
  ¿Sabías que...?   Did you know that...?
sacar   to take out, to get out (Q)
  sacar fotos   to take photographs (1)
  sacar la basura   to take out the trash (Q)
la **sal**   salt (Q)
la **sala de estar**   living room (Q)
la **salida**   exit (Q); departure (6)
la **salida del sol**   sunrise (H)
el **salón de clase**   classroom (H)
la **salsa de tomate**   tomato sauce,
    ketchup (Q)
el **salvavidas**   life preserver (12)
la **salud**   health (H)
la **sandalia**   sandal (11)
la **sandía**   watermelon (Q)
el **sándwich** (*pl.: sándwiches*) sandwich (Q)
la **secadora**   dryer   (Q)
secar   to dry (Q)
  secar la ropa   to dry clothes (7)
secarse (*reflexive*)   to dry oneself (Q)
la **sed**   thirst (H)
  tener sed   to be thirsty (H)
seguir   to continue, to go on (3)
la **selva**   jungle (5)
el **semáforo**   traffic light (3)
la **semana**   week (H)
  el día de la semana   weekday (H)
  el fin de semana   weekend (H)
  esta semana   this week (H)
  la próxima semana   next week (H)
  la semana pasada   last week (11)
sensacional   sensational (H)
señor, Sr.   Mr. (H)
el **señor**   man, gentleman (H)

señora, Sra. Mrs., ma'am (H)

la **señora** woman, lady (H)

señorita, Srta. Miss (H)

la **señorita** young lady (H)

septiembre September (H)

ser to be (H)

    eres you *(familiar)* are (Q)

    es he/she is, you *(formal)* are (Q)

    son they are (Q)

    soy I am (H, Q)

la **servilleta** napkin (Q)

servir (e ➡ i) to serve (3)

sí yes (H)

siempre always (H)

la **silla** chair (H)

el **sillón** *(pl.: sillones)* armchair (Q)

simpático, simpática nice, pleasant (H)

sin without (Q)

sobre on, on top of (Q)

el **sofá** sofa (Q)

el **sol** sun (H)

    Hace sol. It's sunny. (H)

    la puesta del sol sunset (H)

    la salida del sol sunrise (H)

el **sombrero** hat (Q)

la **sombrilla** (sun) umbrella (12)

la **sopa** soup (Q)

el **sótano** basement, cellar (Q)

Sr. (see *señor*)

Sra. (see *señora*)

Srta. (see *señorita*)

su *(pl.: sus)* his, her, your *(formal)*, their (H)

subir to go up (Q)

    subir las escaleras to go up the stairs (Q)

sucio, sucia dirty (Q)

el **sueño** sleep (H)

    tener sueño to be sleepy (H)

la **suerte** luck (H)

    tener suerte to be lucky (H)

el **suéter** *(pl.: suéteres)* sweater (Q)

el **supermercado** supermarket (9)

el **sur** south (10)

T

también also, too (H)

tampoco neither, either (H)

la **tarde** afternoon, evening (H)

    ¡Buenas tardes! Good afternoon!
        Good evening! (H)

de/por la tarde in the afternoon
    (p. m.) (H)

tarde late (6)

la **tarjeta de crédito** credit card (8)

la **tarjeta postal** postcard (7)

el **taxi** taxi (3)

el **taxista** (male) taxi driver (3)

la **taxista** (female) taxi driver (3)

la **taza** cup (Q)

te to you *(familiar)*, yourself (H)

    te duele(n)... your... hurt(s) (Q)

    te queda(n)... (it) fit(s) you, look(s)...
        on you (Q)

el **té** tea (Q)

el **teatro** theater (3)

el **techo** ceiling (Q)

el **teléfono** telephone (H)

la **televisión** television (program) (Q)

el **televisor** television set (Q)

temprano early (6)

el **tenedor** fork (Q)

tener to have (H)

    ¿Qué tienes? What's the matter?,
        What do you have? (H)

    tener que *(+ inf.)* to have to
        (do something) (Q)

el **tenis** tennis (1)

terrible terrible (H)

la **tía** aunt (H)

el **tiempo** weather, time (H)

    a tiempo on time (6)

    Hace buen tiempo. The weather is nice. (H)

    Hace mal tiempo. The weather is bad. (H)

    ¿Qué tiempo hace? What's the weather
        like? (H)

la **tienda** store (H)

    la tienda de discos record store (11)

    la tienda por departamentos
        department store (2)

el **tigre** tiger (H)

tímido, tímida shy (Q)

el **tío** uncle (H)

los **tíos** aunts and uncles, uncles (H)

la **tiza** chalk (H)

la **toalla** towel (7)

el **tobillo** ankle (Q)

el **tocador** *(pl.: tocadores)* dresser (Q)

tocar to touch (Q)

tocar un instrumento to play an instrument (1)

el **tocino** bacon (Q)

todavía still (6)

todos, todas all, every (Q)

tomar to have (meals), to drink (Q)

tomar el desayuno to have breakfast (Q)

tomar el sol to sunbathe (12)

tomar el tren to take the train (4)

el **tomate** tomato (Q)

la salsa de tomate tomato sauce, ketchup (Q)

la **toronja** grapefruit (Q)

tostado, tostada toasted (Q)

el pan tostado toast (bread) (Q)

el **tostador** toaster (Q)

trabajar to work (H)

traer to bring (Q)

el **traje de baño** swimsuit (Q)

el **transporte** transportation (4)

el **trapeador** mop (Q)

el **trapo** rag (Q)

el **tren** (*pl.: trenes*) train (4)

el **triángulo** triangle (H)

triste sad (9)

tu (*pl.: tus*) your (*familiar*) (H)

tú you (*familiar*) (H)

el **turista** (male) tourist (7)

la **turista** (female) tourist (7)

U

último, última last (Q)

Por último, me visto. I get dressed last. (Q)

un, una a, an (H)

unas (*f. pl.*) some, a few (H)

unidad (*pl.: unidades*) unit (H)

unos (*m. pl.*) some, a few (H)

¡Úsalo! Use it! (H)

usar to use (H)

usar la computadora to use the computer (H)

usted (*s. formal; pl.: ustedes*) you (H)

la **uva** grape (Q)

V

el **valle** valley (5)

el **vaso** glass (Q)

veces a sometimes (H)

el **vendedor** (male) salesperson (2)

la **vendedora** (female) salesperson (2)

vender to sell (2)

la **ventana** window (H)

la **ventanilla** bank teller's window (8)

el **ventilador** fan (Q)

ver to see (9)

el **verano** summer (H)

¿verdad? right?, correct (Q)

verde green (H)

la **verdura** vegetable (Q)

el **vestido** dress (Q)

vez time; occasion (H)

a veces sometimes (H)

viajar to travel (5)

el **viaje** trip (5)

la **viajera** (female) traveler (5)

el **viajero** (male) traveler (5)

viejo, vieja old (H)

el **viento** wind (H)

Hace viento. It's windy. (H)

el **viernes** Friday (H)

los viernes on Fridays (H)

visitar to visit (5)

vivir to live (Q)

volar (o ➡ ue) to fly (6)

el **volcán** volcano (5)

el **volibol** volleyball (1)

volver (o ➡ ue) to return (Q)

el **vuelo** flight (6)

Y

y and (H)

¿Y tú? And you? (H)

yo I (H)

Z

la **zanahoria** carrot (Q)

la **zapatería** shoe store (11)

la **zapatera** (female) shoemaker, shoe salesperson (11)

el **zapatero** (male) shoemaker, shoe salesperson (11)

el **zapato** shoe (Q)

el **zoológico** zoo (9)

Word List

English-Spanish

This list gives the English translation of Spanish words that you've learned in *¡Adelante!*
A number in parentheses indicates the unit where a word is taught. (H) indicates that a word was
first presented in *¡Hola!* and (Q) indicates that a word was first presented in *¿Qué tal?*

A

a, an   un *(m.)*, una *(f.)* (H)
a lot   mucho (H)
administrative assistant   el asistente administrativo, la asistente administrativa (Q)
afternoon   la tarde (H)
ahead   adelante (10)
airline   la línea aérea (6)
airplane   el avión *(pl.: aviones)* (4)
airport   el aeropuerto (4)
all   todos, todas (Q)
also   también (H)
always   siempre (H)
among   entre (H)
amusing   divertido, divertida (H)
and   y (H)
angry   enojado, enojada (9)
animal   el animal *(pl.: animales)* (H)
ankle   el tobillo (Q)
antique   antiguo, antigua (7)
apartment   el apartamento (Q)
  apartment building   el edificio de apartamentos (9)
apple   la manzana (Q)
April   abril (H)
arm   el brazo (Q)
armchair   el sillón (Q)
arrival   la llegada (6)
to **arrive**   llegar (6)
art   el arte (H)
to **ask for**   pedir (e ➡ i) (3)
athletic   atlético, atlética (Q)
ATM   el cajero automático (8)
attic   el ático (Q)
auditorium   el auditorio (Q)

August   agosto (H)
aunt   la tía (H)
aunts and uncles   los tíos (H)
autumn   el otoño (H)
avenue   la avenida (3)

B

back   la espalda (Q)
  in back of   detrás de (Q)
bacon   el tocino (Q)
bad   mal *(adj.; before a m. s. noun)*, malo, mala (H)
badly   mal (H)
bag   la bolsa (11)
baggage   el equipaje (6)
balcony   el balcón (Q)
ball   la pelota (1)
ballpoint pen   el bolígrafo (H)
banana   el plátano (Q)
bank   el banco (8)
  bank teller   el cajero (8)
  bank teller window   la ventanilla (8)
baseball   el béisbol (1)
basement   el sótano (Q)
basketball   el baloncesto (1)
bath, to take a   bañarse (Q)
bathing suit   el traje de baño (Q)
bathrobe   la bata (Q)
bathroom   el cuarto de baño (Q)
bathtub   la bañera (7)
to **be**   ser; (in a place, for a time) estar; tener (H)
  to be able to   poder (o ➡ ue) (Q)
  to be called   llamarse (H)
  to be found   encontrarse (o ➡ ue) (10)
  to be going to   ir a *(+inf)* (H)

to **be located** quedar (10)
to **be located ahead** quedar más adelante (10)
to **be located behind** quedar más atrás (10)
beach la playa (5)
beans los frijoles (Q)
bear el oso (H)
to **beat** batir (food) (Q)
bed la cama (Q)
bedroom el dormitorio (Q)
before antes (Q)
to **begin** comenzar (e ➡ ie) (Q)
behind detrás de (Q); atrás (10)
belt el cinturón (11)
beneath debajo de (Q)
bicycle la bicicleta (1)
  to ride a bike andar en bicicleta (1)
big grande (H)
bill (money) el billete (5), (restaurant) la cuenta (8)
bird el pájaro (H)
birthday el cumpleaños (H)
  When is your birthday?
    ¿Cuándo es tu cumpleaños? (H)
  Happy birthday! ¡Feliz cumpleaños! (H)
black negro, negra (H)
blanket la manta (7)
blender la licuadora (Q)
blond rubio, rubia (Q)
blouse la blusa (Q)
blue azul (H)
boat el barco (4)
body el cuerpo (Q)
book el libro (H)
bookcase la estantería (Q)
boots las botas (Q)
boring aburrido, aburrida (H)
bowl el bol (pl.: boles) (Q)
box la caja (Q)
boy el chico, el niño (H)
bracelet el brazalete (11)
bread el pan (Q)
breakfast el desayuno (Q)
to **bring** traer (Q)
broom la escoba (Q)
brother el hermano (H)
brothers and sisters los hermanos (H)
brown marrón (H)
brown (hair, eyes) castaño, castaña (Q)
to **brush** cepillar (Q)

to **brush one's teeth** cepillarse los dientes (Q)
to **buckle** abrocharse (3)
  to buckle your seatbelt abrocharse el cinturón (3)
building el edificio (3)
  apartment building el edificio de apartamentos (9)
burnt (sun) quemado, quemada (12)
bus el autobús (3)
  bus stop la parada de autobús (3)
but pero (Q)
butter la mantequilla (Q)
butterfly la mariposa (H)
to **buy** comprar (H)
by por; en (transportation) (4)
  by bus en autobús (4)
  by plane en avión (4)
  by train en tren (4)

C

cabinet el gabinete (Q)
cafeteria (school) el comedor, la cafetería (Q)
calendar el calendario (H)
can (noun) la lata (Q)
can opener el abrelatas (Q)
canary el canario (H)
cap la gorra (Q)
car el coche (3)
carpet la alfombra (Q)
carrot la zanahoria (Q)
cash dispenser (ATM) el cajero automático (8)
cashier el cajero, la cajera (8)
cassette el audiocasete (11)
cat el gato (H)
Central America América Central (4)
ceiling el techo (Q)
to **celebrate** celebrar (H)
cereal el cereal (Q)
chair la silla (H)
chalk la tiza (H)
chalkboard el pizarrón (H)
chalk eraser el borrador (H)
to **change** cambiar (8)
cheap barato, barata (11)
check el cheque (8)
checkers las damas (1)
cheek la mejilla (Q)
cheese el queso (Q)
cherry la cereza (Q)

chess   el ajedrez (1)
chicken   el pollo (Q)
children   los hijos, los niños (H)
chimney   la chimenea (Q)
chocolate   el chocolate (Q)
chore   el quehacer (*pl.: quehaceres*) (Q)
circle   el círculo (H)
city   la ciudad (3)
city block   la cuadra, la manzana (10)
city hall   la alcaldía (9)
class   la clase (H)
classroom   el salón de clase (H)
clean   limpio, limpia (Q)
to **clean**   limpiar (Q)
to **climb**   subir (Q)
clock   el reloj (H)
to **close**   cerrar (e ➡ ie) (Q)
closed   cerrado, cerrada (8)
closet   el ropero (Q)
clothes   la ropa (Q)
cloudy   nublado, nublada (H)
   It's cloudy.   Está nublado. (H)
coat   el abrigo (Q)
coffee   el café (Q)
coin   la moneda (8)
cold   frío, fría (H)
   I'm cold.   Tengo frío. (H)
   It's cold.   Hace frío. (H)
to **collect stamps**   coleccionar estampillas (1)
color   el color (H)
to **comb one's hair**   peinarse (*reflexive*) (Q)
comfortable   cómodo, cómoda (6)
compact disc   el disco compacto (11)
company   la compañía (2)
community   la comunidad (2)
computer   la computadora (H)
computer game   el juego electrónico (1)
conch shell   el caracol (12)
confused   confundido, confundida (9)
connection   conexión (H)
to **continue**   seguir (e ➡ i) (3)
cook   el cocinero, la cocinera (Q)
to **cook**   cocinar (Q)
cool   fresco, fresca (H)
   It's cool. (weather)   Hace fresco. (H)
corn   el maíz (Q)
corner   la esquina (10)
corridor   el pasillo (Q)
to **cost**   costar (o ➡ ue) (5)
country   el país (*pl.: países*) (4)
court   la cancha (1)

courtyard   el patio (Q)
cousin   el primo, la prima (H)
cousins   los primos (H)
cream   la crema (Q)
credit card   la tarjeta de crédito (8)
cup   la taza (Q)
curly (hair)   rizado, rizada (Q)
curtains   las cortinas (Q)
custodian   el conserje, la conserje (Q)

D

dad   el papá (H)
to **dance**   bailar (H)
danger   el peligro (12)
date   la fecha (H)
   What's today's date?   ¿Qué fecha es hoy? (H)
daughter   la hija (H)
day   el día (H)
December   diciembre (H)
department   el departamento (2)
departure   la salida (6)
desert   el desierto (5)
desk (student's)   el pupitre (H)
desk (teacher's)   el escritorio (H)
difficult   difícil (*pl.: difíciles*) (H)
dining room   el comedor (Q)
dinner   la cena (Q)
director   el director, la directora (Q)
dirty   sucio, sucia (Q)
disc   el disco (11)
dish   el plato (Q)
dishwasher   el lavaplatos (*pl.: los lavaplatos*) (Q)
distance   la distancia (4)
to **dive**   bucear (12)
to **do**   hacer (H)
dog   el perro (H)
dollar   el dólar (5)
domino   el dominó (1)
door   la puerta (H)
down the stairs, to go   bajar las escaleras (Q)
downtown   el centro (3)
drawer   el cajón (*pl.: cajones*) (Q)
dress   el vestido (Q)
dresser   el tocador (Q)
to **drink**   beber (Q)
drinking fountain   la fuente de agua (Q)
driver   el chofer, la chofer (3)
drugstore   la farmacia (3)

to **dry** secar (Q)
    to dry the clothes secar la ropa (Q)
to **dry oneself** secarse *(reflexive)* (Q)
    dryer la secadora (Q)
    dust el polvo (Q)
to **dust** quitar el polvo (Q)
    DVD player el lector de DVD (Q)

E

ear la oreja (Q)
early temprano (6)
earrings los aretes (11)
east el este (10)
easy fácil *(pl: fáciles)* (H)
to **eat** comer (Q)
    to eat breakfast tomar el desayuno (Q)
    to eat lunch almorzar (o ➡ ue) (Q)
egg el huevo (Q)
    fried eggs los huevos fritos (Q)
    hard-boiled eggs los huevos pasados por agua (Q)
    scrambled eggs los huevos revueltos (Q)
either tampoco (H)
elbow el codo (Q)
electric mixer la batidora eléctrica (Q)
electrical socket el enchufe (Q)
elevator el ascensor (7)
employee el empleado, la empleada (2)
end el fin *(pl.: fines)* (H)
English el inglés (H)
entertaining divertido, divertida (H)
entrance la entrada (Q)
equator el ecuador (H)
eraser el borrador (H)
evening la tarde, la noche (H)
to **examine** examinar (2)
exit la salida (Q)
expensive caro, cara (11)
to **extinguish** apagar (2)
eye el ojo (Q)
eyebrow la ceja (Q)
eyelashes las pestañas (Q)

F

face la cara (Q)
factory la fábrica (2)
factory worker el obrero, la obrera (2)
fall el otoño (H)
to **fall asleep** dormirse *(reflexive)* (o ➡ ue) (12)

family la familia (H)
fan el ventilador (Q)
fantastic fantástico, fantástica (H)
far from lejos de (Q)
fast *(adv.)* rápido (10)
to **fasten** abrochar (3)
    to fasten your seatbelt abrocharse el cinturón (3)
fat gordo, gorda (H)
father el padre (H)
faucet el grifo (Q)
favor el favor (Q)
favorite favorito, favorita (H)
fear el miedo (H)
February febrero (H)
fence la cerca (Q)
few pocos, pocas (Q)
few, a unos, unas (H)
field (sports) la cancha (1)
fine bien (H)
finger el dedo (Q)
to **finish** acabar (Q)
fire el incendio (2)
fire station la estación de bomberos (2)
firefighter el bombero, la bombera (2)
first, the el primero (H)
fish (in cooking) el pescado (Q)
fish (live) el pez *(pl.: peces)* (H)
to **fit** (clothes) quedar (Q)
flag la bandera (H)
flamingo el flamenco (H)
flight el vuelo (6)
flight attendant el asistente de vuelo, la asistente de vuelo (6)
to **float** flotar (12)
floor el piso (Q)
flu la gripe (H)
to **fly** volar (o ➡ ue) (6)
food la comida (Q)
foot el pie (Q)
football (American) el fútbol americano (1)
for para (11, 12)
to **forbid** prohibir (12)
forehead la frente (Q)
fork el tenedor (Q)
fountain la fuente (9)
Friday el viernes (H)
    on Fridays los viernes (H)
fried frito, frita (Q)

from   de (H)
fruit   la fruta (Q)
fun   divertido, divertida (H)
funny   cómico, cómica (Q)
furniture   los muebles (Q)

G

garage   el garaje (Q)
garden   el jardín *(pl.: jardines)* (Q)
gas station   la gasolinera (3)
gate (airport)   la puerta de embarque (6)
generous   generoso, generosa (Q)
gentleman   el señor (H)
to **get dressed**   ponerse la ropa *(reflexive)* (Q)
to **get lost**   perderse *(reflexive)* (10)
to **get up**   levantarse *(reflexive)* (Q)
gift   el regalo (11)
girl   la chica, la niña (H)
to **give**   dar (8)
glass   el vaso (Q)
globe   el globo (H)
to **go**   ir (H)
    to go away   irse *(reflexive)* (Q)
    to go down   bajar (Q)
    to go down the stairs   bajar las escaleras (Q)
    to go fishing   ir de pesca (1)
    to go on   seguir (3)
    to go on foot   ir a pie (3)
    to go by/past...   pasar por... (3)
    to go to bed   acostarse *(reflexive)* (o ➡ ue) (Q)
    to go up   subir (Q)
    to go up the stairs   subir las escaleras (Q)
good   buen *(before a m. s. noun),* bueno, buena (H)
good-looking   guapo, guapa (H)
Good afternoon.   Buenas tardes. (H)
Good-bye!   ¡Adiós! (H)
Good evening.   Buenas noches. (H)
Good morning.   Buenos días. (H)
Good night.   Buenas noches. (H)
grandchildren   los nietos (H)
granddaughter   la nieta (H)
grandfather   el abuelo (H)
grandmother   la abuela (H)
grandparents   los abuelos (H)
grandson   el nieto (H)
grape   la uva (Q)
grapefruit   la toronja (Q)

gray   gris (H); canoso (hair) (Q)
great-grandfather   el bisabuelo (H)
great-grandmother   la bisabuela (H)
great-grandparents   los bisabuelos (H)
green   verde (H)
to **grow plants**   cultivar plantas (1)
gymnasium   el gimnasio (H)

H

hair   el pelo (Q)
half   medio, media (H)
    half-hour, a   media hora (H)
hallway   el pasillo (Q)
ham   el jamón (Q)
hamburger   la hamburguesa (Q)
hand   la mano (Q)
handbag   la bolsa (11)
to **hang (up)**   colgar (o ➡ ue) (Q)
    to hang up clothes   colgar la ropa (Q)
happy   feliz *(pl.: felices)* (H); contento, contenta (9)
    Happy birthday!   ¡Feliz cumpleaños! (H)
hard   duro, dura (7)
hat   el sombrero (Q)
to **have**   tener (H); tomar (meals) (Q)
    to have breakfast   tomar el desayuno (Q)
    to have just   acabar de + *inf.* (Q)
    to have to   tener que + *inf.* (Q)
he   él (H)
head   la cabeza (Q)
health   la salud (H)
heat   el calor (H)
Hello!   ¡Hola! (H)
to **help**   ayudar (2)
her   su *(pl.: sus)* (H)
Hi!   ¡Hola! (H)
his   su *(pl.: sus)* (H)
hobby   el pasatiempo (1)
home   la casa (H)
horse   el caballo (1)
    to ride a horse   montar a caballo (1)
hospital   el hospital (2)
hot   caliente (7)
    It's hot.   Hace calor. (H)
    I'm hot.   Tengo calor. (H)
hotel   el hotel (7)
hour   la hora (H)
    hour and a half, an   una hora y media (H)
    hour and a quarter, an   una hora y cuarto (H)

house la casa (H)
How? ¿Cómo? (H)
  How do you say it? ¿Cómo se dice? (H)
  How many? ¿Cuántos...?, ¿Cuántas...? (H)
  How much? ¿Cuánto...?, ¿Cuánta...? (H)
hunger el hambre (*f.*) (H)
hungry, to be tener hambre (H)
hurry la prisa (H)
  hurry, to be in a tener prisa (H)
to **hurt** doler (o ➡ ue) (Q)
  My head hurts. Me duele la cabeza. (Q)

I

I yo (H)
ice cream el helado (H)
impatient impaciente (Q)
important importante (H)
in en (H)
in back of detrás de (Q)
in front of delante de (Q)
in order to para (12)
infirmary la enfermería (Q)
inside dentro de (Q)
intelligent inteligente (Q)
interesting interesante (H)
iron (appliance) la plancha (Q)
to **iron** planchar (Q)
  to iron clothes planchar la ropa (Q)
It's... Es... (H)
  It's cloudy. Está nublado. (H)
  It's cold. Hace frío. (H)
  It's cool. Hace fresco. (H)
  It's hot. Hace calor. (H)
  It's raining. Está lloviendo. Llueve. (H)
  It's snowing. Está nevando. Nieva. (H)
  It's sunny. Hace sol. (H)
  It's windy. Hace viento. (H)

J

jacket la chaqueta (Q)
jam la mermelada (Q)
janitor el conserje, la conserje (Q)
January enero (H)
jeweler el joyero, la joyera (11)
jewelry las joyas (11)
jewelry store la joyería (11)
juice el jugo (Q)
July julio (H)
June junio (H)
jungle la selva (5)

K

ketchup la salsa de tomate (Q)
key la llave (7)
  key chain/ring el llavero (11)
kilometer el kilómetro (10)
kitchen la cocina (Q)
knee la rodilla (Q)
knife el cuchillo (Q)
to **know** conocer (2); (how to do something) saber (+ *inf.*) (Q)
  Did you know that...? ¿Sabías que...? (H)

L

lady la señora (H)
  young lady la señorita (H)
lake el lago (5)
lamp la lámpara (Q)
to **land** aterrizar (6)
large grande (H)
last último, última (Q)
  last week la semana pasada (11)
  last year el año pasado (11)
last (*adv.*) por último (Q)
late tarde (6)
to **learn** aprender (H)
to **leave** irse (*reflexive*) (Q)
left la izquierda (3)
  to/on the left a la izquierda (3)
leg la pierna (Q)
lemon el limón (*pl.: limones*) (Q)
less menos (Q)
  less... than menos... que (Q)
lesson la lección (*pl.: lecciones*) (H)
lettuce la lechuga (Q)
librarian el bibliotecario, la bibliotecaria (Q)
library la biblioteca (H)
to **lie down** acostarse (*reflexive*) (o ➡ ue) (Q)
life preserver el salvavidas (12)
light la luz (*pl.: luces*) (H)
light bulb la bombilla (Q)
to **like** gustar (H)
  What do you like to do? ¿Qué te gusta hacer? (H)
lip el labio (Q)
to **listen** escuchar (H)
little pequeño, pequeña (H); (amount) poco (9)

to **live** vivir (Q)
  living room la sala de estar (Q)
  long largo, larga (H)
to **look (at)** mirar (Q)
to **look for** buscar (9)
  luck la suerte (H)
  lucky, to be tener suerte (H)
  lunch el almuerzo (Q)

M

  mailbox el buzón (*pl.: buzones*) (Q)
to **make** hacer (H)
  man el hombre (H)
  many muchos, muchas (Q)
  map el mapa (H)
  March marzo (H)
  margarine la margarina (Q)
  marker el marcador (H)
  market el mercado (3)
  marmalade la mermelada (Q)
  marvelous maravilloso, maravillosa (H)
  mathematics las matemáticas (H)
  May mayo (H)
  mayonnaise la mayonesa (Q)
  meat la carne (Q)
  meatballs las albóndigas (Q)
  medical doctor el médico, la médica (2)
  medium mediano, mediana (Q)
to **meet** conocer (2); encontrarse (10)
  menu el menú (8)
  meter el metro (10)
  microwave (oven) el microondas (Q)
  midday el mediodía (H)
    at midday a mediodía (H)
  midnight la medianoche (H)
    at midnight a medinoche (H)
  mile la milla (10)
  milk la leche (Q)
  minute el minuto (H)
  mirror el espejo (Q)
  Miss Señorita (Srta.) (H)
  modern moderno, moderna (7)
  mom la mamá (H)
  Monday el lunes (H)
    on Mondays los lunes (H)
  money el dinero (8)
  month el mes (*pl.: meses*) (H)
  monument el monumento (9)
  mop el trapeador (Q)
  more más (H)
    a lot more mucho más (Q)

  more... than más... que (Q)
  morning la mañana (H)
    in the morning de/por la mañana (H)
  most, the el más, la más (Q)
  mother la madre (H)
  motor boat la lancha (12)
  mountain la montaña (5)
  mouse el ratón (*pl.: ratones*) (H)
  mouth la boca (Q)
  movie theater el cine (H)
  Mr. Señor (Sr.) (H)
  Mrs. Señora (Sra.) (H)
  much mucho, mucha (Q)
  museum el museo (9)
  music la música (H)
  musical instrument el instrumento (1)
  mustard la mostaza (Q)
  my mi (*pl.: mis*) (H)

N

  name el nombre (H)
    My name is... Me llamo... (H)
  napkin la servilleta (Q)
  near cerca de (Q)
  neck el cuello (Q)
  necklace el collar (11)
to **need** necesitar (Q)
  neither tampoco (H)
  nervous nervioso, nerviosa (9)
  never nunca (H)
  new nuevo, nueva (5)
  next próximo, próxima (H)
    next week la próxima semana (H)
  nice simpático, simpática (H)
  night la noche (H)
    Good evening! Good night! ¡Buenas noches! (H)
  night table la mesita de noche (Q)
  no no (H)
  nobody nadie (2)
  noon el mediodía (H)
    at noon a mediodía (H)
  north el norte (10)
  North America América del Norte (4)
  nose la nariz (*pl.: narices*) (Q)
  not no (H)
  notebook el cuaderno (H)
  nothing nada (Q)
  November noviembre (H)
  now ahora (H)
  number el número (H)

nurse el enfermero, la enfermera (Q)
 nurse's office la enfermería (Q)

O

oatmeal la avena (Q)
October octubre (H)
of de (H)
 Of course! ¡Claro!, ¡Claro que sí! (H);
  ¡Por supuesto! (Q)
office el despacho, la oficina (Q)
Oh! ¡Ay! (H)
old viejo, vieja (H)
old-fashioned antiguo, antigua (7)
on en (Q)
 on foot a pie (3)
 on time a tiempo (6)
 on top of en sobre (Q)
open abierto, abierta (8)
to **open** abrir (Q)
open-air market mercado al aire libre (9)
orange (color) anaranjado, anaranjada (H)
orange (fruit) la naranja (Q)
to **order** (food) pedir (3)
Ouch! ¡Ay! (H)
our nuestro, nuestra (s.); nuestros,
  nuestras (pl.) (Q)
out fuera (Q)
outside (adv.) fuera de (Q)
oven el horno (Q)
owner el dueño, la dueña (2)

P

to **paint** pintar (H)
painting el cuadro (Q)
pajamas el pijama (Q)
pants los pantalones (Q)
pantyhose las medias (Q)
paper el papel (pl.: papeles) (H)
parents los papás, los padres (H)
park el parque (H)
parking lot el estacionamiento (3)
parrot el loro (H)
part la parte (Q)
to **participate** participar (H)
passenger el pasajero, la pasajera (6)
patient el paciente, la paciente (2)
patio el patio (Q)
to **pay** pagar (5)
pea el guisante (Q)
peach el durazno (Q)

peanut butter la crema de cacahuate (Q)
pear la pera (Q)
pedestrian el peatón (pl.: peatones) (10)
pedestrian crossing el paso de
  peatones (10)
pen (ballpoint) el bolígrafo (H)
pencil el lápiz (pl.: lápices) (H)
people la gente (2)
pepper la pimienta (Q)
person la persona (Q)
pharmacy la farmacia (3)
physical education la educación física (H)
to **pick up** recoger (Q)
pillow la almohada (Q)
pilot el piloto (male), la piloto
  (female) (6)
pineapple la piña (Q)
pink rosado, rosada (H)
place el lugar (pl.: lugares) (10)
to **plan** (to do something) pensar + inf.
  (e ➞ ie) (Q)
plants las plantas (1)
 to **grow plants** cultivar plantas (1)
 to **water the plants** (Q)
plate el plato (Q)
to **play** jugar (u ➞ ue) (1)
 to play an instrument tocar un
  instrumento (1)
 to play sports practicar deportes (H)
player el jugador, la jugadora (1)
pleasant simpático, simpática (Q)
please por favor (Q)
to **please** gustar (H)
plug el enchufe (Q)
plus más (H)
police officer el policía, la policía (2)
police station la estación de policía (2)
popular popular (Q)
port el puerto (4)
portrait el retrato (Q)
postage stamps estampillas (1)
postcard la tarjeta postal (7)
poster el cartel (Q)
potato la papa (Q)
to **practice** practicar (H)
to **prefer** preferir (e ➞ ie) (8)
present el regalo (11)
pretty bonito, bonita (Q)
principal el director, la directora (Q)
public square la plaza (3)

purple   morado, morada (H)

to **put**   poner (Q)

   to put on   ponerse *(reflexive)* (Q)

   to put out   (fires, light)   apagar (2)

Q

quarter   un cuarto (H)

   quarter-hour, a   un cuarto de hora (H)

   an hour and a quarter   una hora y cuarto (H)

quick   rápido (10)

R

rabbit   el conejo (H)

radio   el radio (Q)

rag   el trapo (Q)

to **rain**   llover (o ➡ ue) (H)

   It's raining.   Llueve. (H)

raincoat   el impermeable (Q)

to **read**   leer (H)

reading   *(noun)*   la lectura (H)

reason   la razón (H)

rectangle   el rectángulo (H)

red   rojo, roja (H)

red   (hair)   rojizo, rojiza (Q)

refrigerator   el refrigerador *(pl.: refrigeradores)* (Q)

to **rest**   descansar (5)

restaurant   el restaurante (8)

restaurant check   la cuenta (8)

to **return**   volver (o ➡ ue) (Q)

rice   el arroz (Q)

to **ride a bike**   andar en bicicleta (1)

to **ride a horse**   montar a caballo (1)

right   derecha (3)

   to/on the right   a la derecha (3)

right, to be   tener razón (H)

ring   el anillo (11)

river   el río (5)

robe   la bata (Q)

room   el cuarto (Q); (hotel) la habitación (7)

rug   la alfombra (Q)

ruler   la regla (H)

to **run**   correr (Q)

S

sad   triste (9)

sailboat   el barco de vela (12)

salad   la ensalada (Q)

salesperson   el vendedor, la vendedora (2)

salt   la sal (Q)

sand   la arena (12)

sandals   las sandalias (11)

sandwich   el sándwich *(pl.: sándwiches)* (Q)

Saturday   el sábado (H)

   on Saturdays   los sábados (H)

saucer   el platillo (Q)

to **save**   ahorrar (8)

schedule   el horario (6)

school   la escuela (H)

school principal   el director, la directora (Q)

science   las ciencias (H)

sculpture   la escultura (9)

sea   el mar (12)

seashell   la concha (12)

season   las estación *(pl.: estaciones)* (H)

seat   el asiento (6)

seatbelt   el cinturón (3)

   to fasten your seatbelt   abrocharse el cinturón (3)

to **see**   ver (6)

   See you later.   Hasta luego. (H)

   See you soon.   Hasta pronto. (H)

   See you tomorrow.   Hasta mañana. (H)

to **sell**   vender (2)

sensational   sensacional (H)

September   septiembre (H)

to **serve**   servir (e ➡ i) (3)

server   (male) el camarero, (female) la camarera (8)

to **set the table**   poner la mesa (Q)

to **shake hands**   dar la mano (8)

she   ella (H)

sheet   la sábana (7)

sheet of paper   la hoja de papel (H)

shelf   el estante (Q)

shell   la concha; el caracol (12)

ship   el barco (4)

shirt   la camisa (Q)

shoe   el zapato (Q)

shoe maker   el zapatero, la zapatera (11)

shoe salesperson   (male) el zapatero, (female) la zapatera (11)

shoe store   la zapatería (11)

short   (length)   corto, corta; (height)   bajo, baja (H)

shoulder   el hombro (Q)

shower   la ducha (7)

shower, to take a   ducharse *(reflexive)* (Q)

shut   cerrar (e ➡ ie) (Q)

shy   tímido, tímida (Q)

to **sing**   cantar (H)

sink el fregadero (Q)
sister la hermana (H)
to **skate** patinar (H)
skirt la falda (Q)
skyscraper el rascacielos
  (pl.: los rascacielos) (3)
slacks los pantalones (Q)
sleep el sueño (H)
sleepy, to be tener sueño (H)
slow *(adv.)* despacio (10)
small pequeño, pequeña (H)
to **snow** nevar (e ➡ ie) (H)
  It's snowing. Nieva. (H)
so así (H)
soap el jabón (7)
soccer el fútbol (1)
social studies los estudios sociales (H)
sock el calcetín *(pl.: calcetines)* (Q)
sofa el sofá (Q)
soft blando, blanda (7)
some unos, unas (H)
somebody alguien (2)
sometimes a veces (H)
son el hijo (H)
  sons, sons and daughters los hijos (H)
soon pronto (H)
  See you soon! ¡Hasta pronto! (H)
so-so así, así; más o menos (H)
sound system el estéreo (Q)
soup la sopa (Q)
soupspoon cuchara (Q)
south el sur (10)
South America América del Sur (4)
spaghetti espaguetis (Q)
  spaghetti with meatballs los espaguetis con albóndigas (Q)
Spanish el español (H)
to **speak** hablar (H)
special especial (11)
to **spend** gastar (8)
spoon la cuchara (Q)
sports los deportes (H)
  to play sports practicar deportes (H)
spring la primavera (H)
square el cuadrado (H)
stadium el estadio (1)
stairs las escaleras (Q)
to **stand in line** hacer fila (6)
to **start** comenzar (e ➡ ie) (Q)
stepbrother el hermanastro (H)

stepfather el padrastro (H)
stepmother la madrastra (H)
stepsister la hermanastra (H)
still *(adv.)* todavía (6)
stereo el estéreo (Q)
stockings las medias (Q)
store la tienda (H)
  music store la tienda de discos (11)
stove la estufa (Q)
straight (hair) lacio (Q)
straight (ahead) derecho (3)
strawberry la fresa (Q)
street la calle (3)
street lamp el farol (10)
strong fuerte (Q)
student el alumno, la alumna (H)
study (room) el despacho (Q)
to **study** estudiar (H)
subway el metro (9)
sugar el azúcar (Q)
suitcase la maleta (6)
summer el verano (H)
sun el sol (H)
(sun) umbrella la sombrilla (12)
to **sunbathe** tomar el sol (12)
sunburned quemado, quemada (12)
Sunday el domingo (H)
  on Sundays los domingos (H)
sunrise la salida del sol (H)
sunscreen lotion el protector solar (12)
sunset la puesta del sol (H)
suntanned bronceado, bronceada (12)
supermarket el supermercado (9)
supper la cena (Q)
sweater el suéter (Q)
to **sweep** barrer (Q)
to **swim** nadar (H)
swimsuit el traje de baño (Q)

T

table la mesa (H)
tablecloth el mantel *(pl.: manteles)* (Q)
to **take** tomar (Q)
  to take a shower ducharse *(reflexive)* (Q)
  to take off (plane) despegar (6)
  to take off one's clothes quitarse la ropa *(reflexive)* (Q)
  to take out the trash sacar la basura (Q)
  to take part in participar (H)

to take photographs sacar fotos (1)
to take the train tomar el tren (4)
to be taking a trip estar de viaje (5)
to **talk** hablar (H)
tall alto, alta (H)
to **taste** probar (o ➡ ue) (Q)
taxi el taxi (3)
taxi driver el taxista, la taxista (3)
tea el té (Q)
teacher el maestro, la maestra (H)
team el equipo (1)
teaspoon la cucharita (Q)
telephone el teléfono (H)
telephone number el número
    de teléfono (H)
television (program) la televisión (Q)
television set el televisor (Q)
tennis el tenis (1)
terrible terrible (H)
thank you gracias (H)
thanks gracias (H)
that ese, esa (12)
that (over there) aquel, aquella (12)
the (s. m. f.) el, la; (pl.) los, las (H)
theater el teatro (3)
their su, sus (H)
then luego (Q)
there is, there are hay (H)
thin flaco, flaca (H)
to **think** pensar (e ➡ ie) (Q)
to think of doing pensar (+ inf.) (Q)
thirst la sed (H)
thirsty, to be tener sed (H)
this este, esta (12)
this week esta semana (H)
Thursday el jueves (H)
  on Thursdays los jueves (H)
those este, esta (12)
those (over there) aquellos, aquellas (12)
ticket el billete (5)
tiger el tigre (H)
time el tiempo, la hora (H)
timid tímido, tímida (Q)
tip la propina (8)
tired cansado, cansada (9)
to a (H)
  to the left a la izquierda (3)
  to the right a la derecha (3)
toast el pan tostado (Q)
toasted tostado, tostada (Q)

toaster el tostador (Q)
today hoy (H)
tomato el tomate (Q)
  tomato sauce la salsa de tomate (Q)
tomorrow mañana (H)
  See you tomorrow! ¡Hasta mañana! (H)
tongue la lengua (Q)
too también (H)
tooth el diente (Q)
to **touch** tocar (Q)
tourist el turista, la turista (7)
towel la toalla (7)
town hall la alcaldía (9)
town square la plaza (3)
traffic light el semáforo (3)
train el tren (pl.: trenes) (4)
train station la estación de trenes (4)
transportation el transporte (4)
trash la basura (Q)
to **travel** viajar (5)
travel agency la agencia de viajes (5)
travel agent el agente de viajes,
    la agente de viajes (5)
traveler el viajero, la viajera (5)
triangle el triángulo (H)
trip el viaje (5)
to **try** probar (o ➡ ue) (Q)
T-shirt la camiseta (Q)
Tuesday el martes (H)
  on Tuesdays los martes (H)
turkey el pavo (Q)
to **turn** doblar (3)

U

ugly feo, fea (Q)
umbrella (sun) la sombrilla (12)
uncle el tío (H)
  uncles, uncles and aunts los tíos (H)
uncomfortable incómodo, incómoda (6)
under(neath) debajo de (Q)
undershirt la camiseta (Q)
to **understand** comprender (H)
to **undress** quitarse la ropa (reflexive) (Q)
unit la unidad (pl.: unidades) (H)
unpleasant antipático, antipática (H)
until hasta (H)
upset enojado, enojada (9)
to **use** usar (H)
  to use the computer usar la
    computadora (H)

V

to **vacuum**   pasar la aspiradora (Q)
vacuum cleaner   la aspiradora (Q)
valley   el valle (5)
VCR   la videocasetera (Q)
vegetable   la verdura (Q)
very   muy (H)
   very well   muy bien (H)
to **visit**   visitar (5)
volcano   el volcán (*pl.: volcanes*) (5)
volleyball   el volibol (1)

W

waist   la cintura (Q)
to **wake up**   despertarse (*reflexive*) (Q)
to **walk**   caminar (H)
wall   la pared (H)
to **want**   querer (Q)
to **wash**   lavar (Q)
   to wash clothes   lavar la ropa (Q)
   wash oneself   lavarse (reflexive) (Q)
   to wash the floor   limpiar el piso (Q)
washing machine   la lavadora (Q)
wastebasket   la papelera (H)
water   el agua (*f.*) (Q)
water fountain   la fuente de agua (Q)
water skiing   el esquí acuático (12)
watermelon   la sandía (Q)
to **water the plants**   regar las plantas
   (e ➡ ie) (Q)
wave   la ola (12)
wavy (hair)   ondulado (Q)
we   nosotros, nosotras (Q)
weak   débil (Q)
to **wear**   llevar; ponerse (*reflexive*) (Q)
weather   el tiempo (H)
Wednesday   el miércoles (H)
   on Wednesdays   los miércoles (H)
week   la semana (H)
weekday   el día de la semana (H)
weekend   el fin de semana (H)
Welcome!   ¡Bienvenidos! (H)
well   bien (H)
   It fits me well.   Me queda bien. (12)
west   el oeste (10)
What?   ¿Qué?, ¿Cómo? (H)
   At what time?   ¿A qué hora? (H)

What are you going to do? ¿Qué vas a hacer? (H)
What color is it?   ¿De qué color es? (H)
What do you have?   ¿Qué tienes? (H)
What is it?   ¿Qué es? (H)
What's (the boy's) name?   ¿Cómo se llama (el chico)? (H)
What's the weather like?   ¿Qué tiempo hace? (H)
What's your name?   ¿Cómo te llamas? (H)
What's your phone number?   ¿Cuál es tu número de teléfono? (H)
When?   ¿Cuándo? (H)
Where?   ¿Dónde?, ¿Adónde? (H)
Which? (*s.*)   ¿Cuál?, (*pl.*) ¿Cuáles? (H)
to **whip** (food)   batir (Q)
white   blanco, blanca (H)
Who?   ¿Quién? (H)
   Who is...?   ¿Quién es...? (H)
Whose?   ¿De quién? (H)
Why?   ¿Por qué? (H)
   Why not?   ¿Por qué no? (H)
window   la ventana (H); (bank teller) la ventanilla (8)
winter   el invierno (H)
with   con (Q)
without   sin (Q)
woman   la mujer (H)
wonderful   maravilloso, maravillosa (H)
to **work**   trabajar (Q)
to **write**   escribir (H)

Y

years old, to be...   tener... años (H)
yellow   amarillo, amarilla (H)
yes   sí (H)
yesterday   ayer (11)
you   (*familiar*) tú; (*formal*); usted (*pl.: ustedes*) (H)
young   joven (H)
   young woman/lady   la señorita (H)
your   (*familiar*) tu (*pl.: tus*), (*formal*), su (*pl.: sus*) (H)

Z

zoo   el zoológico (9)

Index

Acknowledgments

Photo Credits: © AFP/Corbis, pp. 27 left, left center, 273 top left; © José Azel/Aurora, p. 147 top left; © Bill Bachmann/Photo Edit Inc., p. 114 inset; © James Baigrie/FoodPix, p. 99 right inset; © Bettmann/Corbis, pp. 147 top right, 151 left; © Martin Barlow/Art Directors, p. 47 right; © Chris Barton/Photographers Direct, p. 115 top right, 129 right inset; © Tom Bean, p. 47 left; © Leslye Borden/Photo Edit Inc., p. 45 right inset; © Gary Braasch/Corbis, p. 3 top inset; © Bruce Clarke/Index Stock Imagery, p. 114 inset; © Corbis, p. 65 top; © Pablo Correl/Corbis, p. 98 inset; © Studio Carlo Dani/Animals Animals, p. 63 bottom left; © Steve Dunwell/Index Stock Imagery, p. 169 top; © Victor Engleberg, pp. 204 bottom, 253 right; © Susan Van Etten/Photo Edit Inc., p. 191 bottom left; © MacDuff Everton/Image Bank/Getty Images, p. 149 bottom right; © Georg Fischer/ Bilderberg/Peter Arnold Inc., pp. 210-211 spread; © Fotos and Photos/Index Stock Imagery, p. 87 top inset; © Owen Franken/Corbis, p. 98 inset; © Franz-Marc-Frei/Corbis, pp. 188-189 spread; © Robert Frerck/Stone/Getty Images, pp. 64-65 spread; © Robert Frerck/Odyssey Productions, p. 189 top left; © Arvind Garg/Corbis, pp. 63, 98 inset; © Lowell Georgia/Corbis, p. 167 top; © Getty Images, pp. 34 center, left, 99 bottom right, top left, 114 left inset; © Russell Gorden/Danita Delimont, p. 99 top right; © David Grey/Corbis, pp. 22-23 spread; © Jeff Greenberg/Photo Edit Inc, pp. 3 bottom inset, 23 top, 191 top left, top right; Hangarter/Index Stock Imagery, p. 167 right inset; © Jon Hicks/Corbis, p. 43 © HIRB/Index Stock Imagery, pp. 98 inset, 211 top right; © Jeremy Horner/Corbis, pp. 2-3 spread; 71 left; © Dan Jenkins/Index Stock Imagery, p. 251; © Lou Jones/Image Bank/Getty Images, pp. 86-87 spread; © Wolfgang Kaehler, p. 84 bottom; © Wolfgang Kaehler/Corbis, p. 99 bottom center; © Bob Krist/Corbis, p. 98 inset; © Danny Lehman/Corbis, pp. 85 bottom, 98 inset; © Erich Lessing/Art Resource, NY, p. 151 right; © Chris Lisle/Corbis, p. 98 inset; © Richard Lord/Photo Edit Inc., pp. 45 top, 232-233 spread; © Larry Luxner, pp. 128–129 spread, 233 top left; © Maps.com/Corbis, p. 211 top left; © Bob Masters/Photographers Direct, p. 107 right; © Buddy Mays/Corbis, p. 51 bottom; © John Mitchell/DDBstock Photo, p. 114 inset; © Juergen Mueller/Taxi/Getty Images, p. 170 bottom; © Nasa, p. 115 inset; © Rueters Newmedia Inc./Corbis, pp. 22-23 spread, 23 right, 27 bottom right, 135 bottom, 209 inset; © John Neubauer/Photo Edit Inc., pp. 44-45 spread, 187 bottom; © North Wind Picture Archives, p. 251; © Frank Nowikowski, pp. 129 top inset, 233 right inset; © Timothy O'Keefe/Index Stock Imagery, p. 114 bottom; © Tim Page/Corbis, 147 bottom; © 2004 Estate of Pablo Picasso/Artists Rights Society (ARS), New York, p. 151 right; © Giraud Philippe/Corbis Sygma, pp. 252–253 spread; © Time Life Pictures/Getty Images, p. 27 right center; © Fotos and Photos/Index Stock Imagery, p. 87 inset; © Vittoriano Rastelli/Corbis, p. 65 right brochure; © Helene Rogers/Art Directors, p. 87 top, 107 top inset ; © Martin Rogers/Corbis, p. 98 inset; © Kevin Schafer/Stone/Getty, p. 104 inset; © Jorgen Schytte/Still Pictures/Peter Arnold Inc., pp. 168-169 spread; © Stephen Simpson/ Taxi/Getty Images, p. 34 top right; © John Slater/Corbis, pp. 106-107 spread; © Hubert Stadler/Corbis, p. 127 bottom; © Ricardo Carrasco Stuparich, pp. 34 right, 149 top left; © Torleif Svensson/Corbis, pp. 148–149 spread; © Rugero Vanni/Corbis, p. 43; © Patrick Ward/Corbis, p. 167 bottom; © Nik Wheeler/Corbis, p. 126 bottom; © Art Wolfe/Image Bank/Getty Images, p. 253 top; © David Young-Wolff/Photo Edit Inc., p. 191 bottom right inset.